# Forensic Psychology of Spousal Violence

# Forensic Psychology of Spousal Violence

Mauro Paulino

ELSEVIER

AMSTERDAM • BOSTON • HEIDELBERG • LONDON
NEW YORK • OXFORD • PARIS • SAN DIEGO
SAN FRANCISCO • SINGAPORE • SYDNEY • TOKYO

Academic Press is an imprint of Elsevier

Academic Press is an imprint of Elsevier
125 London Wall, London EC2Y 5AS, UK
525 B Street, Suite 1800, San Diego, CA 92101-4495, USA
50 Hampshire Street, 5th Floor, Cambridge, MA 02139, USA
The Boulevard, Langford Lane, Kidlington, Oxford OX5 1GB, UK

**British Library Cataloguing-in-Publication Data**
A catalogue record for this book is available from the British Library

**Library of Congress Cataloging-in-Publication Data**
A catalog record for this book is available from the Library of Congress

ISBN: 978-0-12-803533-7

For information on all Academic Press publications
visit our website at https://www.elsevier.com/

Working together
to grow libraries in
developing countries

www.elsevier.com • www.bookaid.org

*Publisher:* Sara Tenney
*Acquisition Editor:* Elizabeth Brown
*Editorial Project Manager:* Joslyn Chaiprasert-Paguio
*Production Project Manager:* Lisa Jones
*Designer:* Victoria Pearson
*Translator:* João F. Lino

Typeset by TNQ Books and Journals
www.tnq.co.in

# Contents

## 6.     Spousal Homicide

## 7.     Explanatory Models of Spousal Violence

## 8.     Considerations Regarding Spousal Violence Intervention

## 9.     Tips on Investigating in the Domain on Domestic Violence

## 10.    Reality

# Foreword

Domestic violence occurs when one family member, household member, or intimate harms another. The harm inflicted can be physical, emotional, psychological, or even economic. A single occurrence of domestic violence is not the norm; rather, the realization of one instance suggests that related behavior is longstanding and ongoing. As an existing framework within a relationship dynamic, it is both simple and horrific.

Each case of domestic violence is different, but historical and psychological similarities, even patterns, are hard to miss. It is most often the result of accumulated as opposed to situational rage, and it is often the result of a power imbalance. Things become uneven when one or both parties want complete control over the other or where one or both feel powerless over the other. There are of course many exceptions, but power and control are the most common themes—rendering an abusive dynamic from tools and experiences forged in relationships past and present.

Domestic violence is commonly associated with social isolation, chronic arguing, jealousy, and the fear of inadequacy made real through betrayal or abandonment. It also frequently occurs in association with drug and alcohol abuse. It arrives as a mechanism for control, punishment, and emotional expression—when the abuser feels angry, weak, or frightened.

Sometimes the victims will receive medical attention, and sometimes they will suffer injuries left untreated. All of this will occur over a period of years, while they are trapped inside of a relationship with bars made of fear, money, and shame. If they are fortunate, they will eventually find a means of escape; if they are not, then they may die miserable and alone, perhaps as the result of a violent altercation that is most likely to occur in the kitchen or bedroom.

Domestic violence, it must be understood, involves some of the more violent and aberrant behaviors that behavioral analysts will need to examine—often more—than one sees in relation to serial murderers. Indeed, this examiner has analyzed his share of such cases in 20 years of research and forensic practice—from an abusive husband who cut off his wife's head during an argument, in front of their 5-year-old daughter; to an abusive husband who beat his wife nearly to death with a hammer, leaving her brain damaged, during a bitter custody dispute; to yet another abusive husband who bit and choked his wife to death during one of their usual rough sex encounters, while both were high on meth. All of this and more have featured prominently in this examiner's domestic homicide casework.

It is well known that domestic violence, including spousal abuse, is a regular occurrence in the United States, to say nothing of the rest of the world. We need more professional awareness about domestic violence to help us recognize when the evidence is before us demanding a response. But we also need tools that help us understand it more clearly, so that our response is informed and indeed helpful. Otherwise we will be incompetent when we respond, if we don't miss the indicators entirely. This work is a step in that direction and, as such, is a valuable reference for the forensic behavioral analyst.

**Brent E. Turvey**
Forensic Solutions LLC, Sitka, Alaska, United States

# Acknowledgments

Mariza, Portuguese fado singer and one of the most acclaimed stars of "world music," sings in a unique way the fado song "Rain," in which one of the lyrics is "There are people who remain a part of us, and become part of our own story, while there are others whose names we hardly remember." So this is the time to thank those who are part of my story because, after all, we are not isolated islands.

Let's start at the beginning with my sincere thanks to Elsevier Academic Press for embracing this project, which in addition to the scientific sharing also has a social mission. It is unthinkable not to stress and emphasize the professionalism, diligence, and quality of the entire team, from the conception and planning of the book to its birth. A very special thank you to Dr. Elizabeth Brown, Dr. Joslyn Paguio, and Dr. Lisa Jones.

To Professor Brent Turvey, an unavoidable worldwide name in the field of forensic science and a great traveling companion, my thanks for giving me the honor of writing the preface of this work. The clairvoyance and scientific rigor of his contribution is again commendable.

Thank you, Professor Vicente Garrido, for the precious willingness to close this book in the best possible way. His extensive experience is manifested in his relevant considerations.

Thank you João F. Lino for the brilliant work of translation, who always sought to maintain the logic and meaning of the text when looking for the best language match, never losing track of the deadlines. Thank you very much!

The research done and shared in this book has the important contribution of a teacher who accompanied me for many years in academic and investigative roads and who has a remarkable "manliness" that some people don't have—my friend, lecturer, and mentor Silva Pinto, for once again giving me the privilege of teaming up with you. He is a person of immeasurable value. His attention to detail, zeal, and always relevant and enriching criticism are essential and promote growth for those he is in contact with, as well as for projects where he is involved. Words are few to express my gratitude and appreciation for the many hours that you have worked with me.

To all the organizations (CIG, thanks to Dr. Marta Silva; APAV, thanks to Dr. João Lázaro, Dr. José Félix, and Dr. Daniel Cotrim; Associação de Mulheres contra a violência, thanks to Dr. Maria Macedo; Casa Sant'Ana, thanks to Dr. Susana Simões; Centro de Saúde de Setúbal, thanks to Dr. Helena

Salazar; Espaço Vida, thanks to Dr. Sónia Paixão, Dr. Mónica Gomes, Dr. Rita Tibério, Dr. Fernanda Pereira, Dr. Isabel Pereira, and Dr. Helena Oliveira; GNR, thanks to Dr. Carla Pereira, Comandante Albano Pereira, Tenente-coronel João Nortadas, and Sargento Luís Pereira; Rede Integrada da Intervenção na Violência na Amadora, thanks to Dr. Ana Costa and Dr. Rute Gonçalves; SEIES, thanks to Dr. Joana Silva and Dr. Isabel do Carmo; UMAR, thanks to Dr. Elisabete Brasil and Dr. Sónia Soares; Pelo Sonho – Cooperativa de Solidariedade Social, thanks to Dr. Margarida Saramago, Dr. Ana Rufino, and Dr. Hugo Santos) that opened doors and accepted in serving as a link between the participants and the investigation. These people have all my deepest and most genuine thanks in unveiling part of their life story. Without their availability, partnership, and flexibility it would have been impossible to finish the investigation. Thank you so much!

Thanks to everyone with whom I have the chance to learn, grow, and develop excellent professional and/or personal relationships and whom I hope I will never disappoint or offend: Dr. Carlos Anjos, Dr. Carlos Calado, Dr. Carlos Casimiro Nunes, Dr. Carlos Farinha, Dr. Fernando Viegas, Dr. Fernando Vieira, Dr. Ferreira dos Santos, Dr. Horácio Lopes, Dr. Mário João, Dr. Pedro Alves, Dr. Ramiro Sousa, Dr. Rui do Carmo, Dr. Alexandra André, Dr. Dobrila Nikolíc, Dr. Fátima Almeida, Dr. Joana Teixeira, Dr. Manuela Martins, Dr. Maria João Reis, Dr. Matilde Fernandes, Dr. Matilde Sirgado, Dr. Olindina Graça, Dr. Raíssa Santos, Dr. Rita Annes, Dr. Sandra Correia, Dr. Sofia Gouveia, Dr. Tâmara Rodrigues, Dr. Vanda Abreu, *Engenheira* Manuela Annes, *Engenheiro* Frederico Annes, Major Frederico Galvão, Professor Carlos Fernandes, Professor Duarte Nuno Vieira, Professor João Pinheiro, Professor Leandro Almeida, Professor Mário Simões, Professor Ana Sani, Professor Cristiana Palmela Pereira, Professor Cristina Soeiro, Professor Dália Costa, Professor Filomena Ponte, Professor Sónia Quintão, Professor Teresa Magalhães and Sr. Rui Gonçalves.

To the students and trainers that I had the opportunity and delight to talk to and train as a public speaker and thinker regarding the familiar violence theme.

In other books I've written, I would always write "even if words are not enough to describe how grateful I am for everything they've done for me, I leave here a deep and heartfelt thank you to my grandparents who are all alive." During the making of this book, the misfortune of life robbed me one of the pillars of my existence, but this is also an opportunity to materialize the love and longing that remains. A very special thanks to my maternal grandmother, Maria Rosa, whose name deserves to be recorded here. It was such a privilege to have you in my life. To my other grandparents (which is still a privilege to have you with three alive), my mother, my father, and brother, I thank all of you. Each of you knows to what extent you've contributed and it was important to end this and other steps.

To my stability and my other half, Andreia Baptista, a kind thank you for completing and unconditionally pushing me forward to do more and better, fighting beside me. Together, united, firm and persistent…forever!

To all my friends who built strong bonds of love and brotherhood, which are the family I chose and adopted me also in your lives. Thank you to the Sousa family (on both sides of the Atlantic), Rocha family, and Silva family. Without underestimating the rest, Andreia Catarino and Nelson Garcez deserve, for all the reasons and a few more that your name be a part of these thanks, for all that is now possible is because you fully and genuinely fomented my growth. Words are not enough!

To this range of more restricted people who know me beyond the suit and tie, my apologies for the time and attention that I did not give you at some point so that these pages were written and other projects were implemented; my apologies for the quick telephone conversations or short SMS; my apology for several weekend plans that were unfulfilled. I am sure you share my joy in this publication and support me in the upcoming challenges. These pages are scarce to cover the gratitude and love I have for you. To all of you my thanks for making real what my friends Nelson and Sérgio (to you also my thanks) intone: Life is good for me!

**Mauro Paulino**
Mind I Institute of Clinical and Forensic Psychology, Lisbon (Portugal)
February 22, 2016

# Introduction

Claude Bernard, in his book *An Introduction to the Study of Experimental Medicine* states that "every man has, at first glance, ideas about what surrounds them and is driven to interpret in advance the nature of the issues before meeting them by experience. This trend is spontaneous (…) [of which] it has always been, and always will be the first move of a researcher spirit" (1978, p. 41).

In this sense, this book is a corollary of the need for evolving from the first instances resulting from reflections shared between colleagues and practice of either clinical or forensic sciences to the scientific understanding of the problems of women victims of conjugal violence.

Thus, although we recognize that domestic violence is also perpetrated against men by women, as well as in homosexual relationships, at the heart of our work is a focus on spousal violence perpetrated by men over women.

We will talk about a secret and muted violence that escapes public scrutiny and is rarely discussed. Meloy (2003) considers that one of the great paradoxes of human existence is the fact that the majority of interpersonal violence occurs between people who are related to each other. Within the family, many homes are marked by violence, with the idea of "home" being "(...) one of the most dangerous places in modern societies. In statistical terms, regardless of sex and age, a person will be more subject to violence at home than in the street at night" (Giddens, 2001, p. 196).

The chapter "The Phenomenon of Spousal Violence," is devoted to the phenomenon of domestic violence. It begins with a historical summary on marriage, followed by a conceptual review of the key terms, from violence in the broad sense to, more specifically, the phenomenon we seek to discuss—domestic violence.

The chapter "Statistical Data Regarding Spousal Violence," refers to statistics on domestic violence, highlighting two studies performed by the author. It is a matter of sensitive study because of the difficulty in determining the exact prevalence, since the precise knowledge of this problem is hindered by several aspects, such as silence, the feeling of inability of the victims to act, the lack of their rights, the proximity between the aggressor and the victim (eg, emotional ambiguity, fear of new attacks), as well as disparate terminology used in investigations (Matos, 2003). It is considered that the increased visibility of violence in the couple hardly is due to a real increase in occurrences because spousal violence is not a new phenomenon, but is of late better known due to the fact that women are denouncing more cases of violence (Esplugues, 2008).

Chapter "The Different Forms of Spousal Violence," focuses on the different forms of domestic violence taken into account, regarding understanding and pedagogical issues, organized through a presentation on physical, psychological, or emotional violence and sexual violence. It should be noted that in reality these categories are often mixed, not arising as a single case and/or isolated. There are also a few remarks on scenario simulation and dissimulation of violence, which deserve the most attention in the forensic setting.

The consequences of the abuse(s) are discussed in the chapter "The Consequences of Spousal Violence," which focuses mainly on the psychological impact. We have decided to also explore a widely mentioned topic in the literature, specifically the battered woman syndrome (Duros et al., 2009; Kaser-Boyd, 2004), which has been the target of criticism due to methodological flaws and conceptual inaccuracies. Controversy also occurs with respect to the theory of cycles of violence, despite its usefulness for understanding domestic violence (Follingstad, 2003; McGrath, 2009; Walker, 2009a).

Chapter "Characterization of Spousal Violence Victims," constitutes the core of our analysis on the topic. Using the contributions of forensic victimology as a starting point, it focuses on personality characteristics, the molds for understanding the victim relative to the violence, and the importance of accountability in the process of change. There are also a few dedicated lines to the issue of Stockholm syndrome as well as the main characteristics of the offender.

Chapter "Spousal Homicide," turns to the extreme manifestation of violence in the context of a relationship with two adults who share, or no longer share, their lives and bodies, through marriage or consensual union. We are talking about spousal homicide.

Due to the importance that it assumes, there have been several theoretical and explanatory approaches to domestic violence, which are briefly explored in chapter "Explanatory Models of Spousal Violence." It is worth reminding that despite the various existing theoretical approaches, domestic violence is recognized by the World Health Organization as a public health problem and therefore requires scientific approaches and not merely ideological ones. The phenomenon of domestic violence does not need a fencing of unfounded arguments but a combined effort for the sake of those who suffer.

Thus arises a paradigm shift regarding intervention in domestic violence, and therefore we present in the chapter "Considerations Referring to Spousal Violence Intervention," a number of considerations on the subject of intervention that include costs, family and school contributions, the importance of specialized training, the role of shelters, and the need for psychological intervention, in addition to the social aspects.

In chapter "Tips on Investigating in the Domain on Domestic Violence," we can find topics of methodological tips of scientific research, in order to obtain consistent results that enable a better understanding of this phenomenon and a consequent effective intervention, adjusted to the real needs of each specific biography.

Speaking of biography, in the chapter "Reality," the reader will find several real stories told in the first person, including minors exposed to interparental violence. The stories collected for this book drive us to seek to do more and better in the intervention of this social scourge.

Throughout this book, we want the rigor of scientific writing to not impede the enjoyment of reading it. This may as well contribute to another step in the increase of knowledge in the field of domestic violence, one of the most serious problems of contemporary society.

Chapter 1

# The Phenomenon of Spousal Violence

## HISTORICAL PRECEDENT: FROM THE MARRIAGE OF CONVENIENCE TO THE MARRIAGE OF LOVE MATERIALIZED ON SEXUAL INTERCOURSE

In a topic where the union of two adults is used as a background, it is important that we reflect on love and marriage, even if we approach it in a synoptic form.

It is important to start by highlighting that marriage is constructed as a cultural product. It is an invention created at a certain moment in time (Aires, 2009a), which has been differently understood throughout the ages.

In 3000 BCE in Mesopotamia, marriage was arranged by the fathers of future spouses, and, in case the woman could not get pregnant, she could be expelled from society (Magalhães, 2010).

Marriage first appears as a solemn moment in Ancient Rome and Greece. The Romans also created the Marriage Law and instituted the practice of monogamy (Aires, 2009a).

Engels (2002) wrote that individual sexual love is not related to the creation of marriage. The genesis of marriage is marked by issues regarding the management of material goods, which is a very different notion than passion and love (Aires, 2009a).

In the Middle Ages, women did not have the right to choose their husband. The family's attention was focused only on the task of choosing who would receive the dowry, as well as the sharing of seeds for agriculture, since some families had more seeds and of better quality than others (Aires, 2009a).

Throughout the Middle Ages, women did not have the status of being a "real person," since they were seen as objects. Primarily, the father and the husband (after marriage) were their owners, claiming that women were physically and mentally weak. Consequently, these men could be violent toward their women, either by enslaving, selling or killing them after a case of adultery or infertility. In the aforementioned time period, men always had a woman that they fully controlled (Magalhães, 2010).

Engels (2002) states that marriages started as convenience marriages and not the result of individual sexual love. This means that the main issue resided on the male sovereignty of the family and on the procreation of descendants that could only be theirs, which carried the role of inheriting the family's wealth.

Forensic Psychology of Spousal Violence. http://dx.doi.org/10.1016/B978-0-12-803533-7.00001-6

1

We can see the importance of the woman's fidelity, resulting in the paternity of the descendants. In Pais' (2010) understanding, the lack of love in marriage translates itself as some kind of freakish phenomenon.

Engels (2002, p. 90) hits a weak spot by stating that "it is quite frequently … [that] marriages of convenience … (become) the most crass prostitution— sometimes by the action of both partners, but more usually by the woman who is only distinguished from the usual courtesan for not renting her body as a piecework like a salaried worker but for selling it once and for all into slavery."

The history of marriage is marked by the effort in saving family names and goods, stopping them from disappearing. This way, one of the reasons that marriage existed was the negotiation between families that would arrange their sons' and daughters' marriages at a young age. Everybody knew in advance whom they were going to marry, when the boy reached 10 and the girl 12 or 13 (Aires, 2009a).

The strong implementation of marriage was merely for economic reasons, since nobody would convey much importance to it.

Engels (2002) defends that complete liberty in marriage would only be possible when the suppression of capitalist production and its consequent property relations would have extinguished all economic factors that would strongly influence the choosing of the husband's choices.

In the 12th century, courtier love is strongly present, that is, a love that is not dedicated to the partner but to adulterous relationships. Pais (2010) points out that marriage that distant from love created a double standard when talking about spousal fidelity, tolerating the man's infidelity and forcing it on the woman. Today, spousal infidelity is taken by law as one of the foundations of divorce requests, where the offended requests the dissolution of the union, while the violator supports the inherent economic expenses.

Engels (2002) reflects that until the 19th century, it was not possible to talk about a family history, nor about individual sexual love before the Middle Ages.

The first reference in history to a marriage bound by love appears in the 19th century, with the marriage of Queen Victoria of the United Kingdom (Aires, 2009a). Costa (2003) states that at the beginning of the 20th century, the acceptable basis relative to choosing a partner for the rest of your life was loving attraction.

With more than 400,000 years of humanity's history, only two or three hundred years ago did the emotional function of love assume an important role in marriage, with love being an integral part of a human being's concerns. These outlines help to understand the difficulty of thinking about marriage bound to love, as well as the resistance to end a marriage where passion does not evolve into love. The former socioeconomic marriage forbade the cessation of the marriage through society's control, particularly the extended family's control (grandparents, parents, uncles), who were the main people interested in the already invested negotiations (Aires, 2009a).

The notion of inseparability in marriage is related to the control exercised by society as one of the results of the Spanish Inquisition, a repressive and dogmatic movement that emerged after the reform in the 15th century (Costa, 2003). Only at the end of the 20th century do we see the possibility of divorce without the stigma of something socially negative or pathological (Aires, 2009a), even though Engels (2002) stated decades ago that marriage without love is amoral. However, the current understanding of psychological science points to marriage as a space of personal achievement, "a space for psychological development and sharing …, in which, through an intimate and affective relationship, each human being develops into the most evolved state our society allows. It is not a place to suffer and destroy our close ones" (Aires, 2009a, p. 57).

Aires (2007) describes love as a basic need for humans, similar to breathing and eating, being the most important discovery someone can make during their life. Love is contemplated as a learning experience, like a construction that allows happiness and the feeling of accomplishment when achieved and not suffering, in other words, the opposite of spousal violence.

However, Western culture's understanding of love is somewhat related to suffering. Pain is seen as proof of the intensity of a person's loving feelings for someone else: a cultural production (eg, soap operas, poetry, music) that is surrounded by love passion or tragic love. In this perspective, a happy love will never become true as a reflection of human experience (Sánchez, 2008).

Aires (2007) states that love as an ingredient of marriage is the guarantee of mental health, with sex being the means of construction of the love bond between two loving adults. As we shall see, sex constitutes a target category of misrepresentations due to its primitive idea that the sexual act represents an obligation for women, being often overwhelmed by the aggressor. Hirigoyen (2006) states that in many cases of couples where spousal violence prevails, the sexual act often resembles a mutual masturbation without any affective exchange. Mintz (2004) underlines the role of sex as a promoter of the construction and reinforcement of bonds. Complementing the issue, Cassidy wrote in 2001 that the physical proximity and comfort ensured by sexual behaviors provide a basis for the development of emotional intimacy (Faria et al., 2009)

In 1997, Fuertes and López stated that the physical and emotional search for intimacy with the partner manifests in the capital form through a sexual context, with sexuality presenting itself as a way of expressing fondness and affection, and as an intimate communication with the partner (Faria et al., 2009). Sexuality represents one of the most universally gratifying experiences, being its motivational power comparable to the needs of survival and nourishment (Csikszentmihalyi, 2002).

According to Aires (2009a), married people present better physical and mental statistics. Marriage allows intimacy and sharing that is materialized through sex. It develops the human personality throughout the years that go beyond what is genetically programmed. However, this only occurs when you are truly happy in your marriage.

Samson (2010) defines that a sane, loving relationship is one that allows the development of the couple. He also adds that a stimulating loving relationship allows the couple to mature and develop themselves. The sexual contact will appear naturally when both partners show interest in the relationship. Sánchez (2008) contemplates in his article four parameters that allow us to define and differentiate the couple's bond from other dyadic bonds (friends), namely daily life, shared life projects, sex, and monogamous tendencies (as a definer of a united loving object).

In short and to paraphrase Garrido (2002, p. 239), "love is incompatible with violence," a love that is materialized through sex with a focus on building a marriage that promotes psychological growth, hopefully with no traces of a marriage by convenience, which was common in the past. However, according to the same author (Garrido, 2002), the core of this dissertation focuses on the matrimonial unions where love is absent and is marked by spousal violence, a definition that we shall discuss later.

## CONCEPTIONAL DIFFICULTIES

Similarly to what happens in other domains (eg, sexual abuse of children), the concept of spousal violence also goes through large difficulties in the unification of integrating criteria for a unique operational definition (Paulino, 2009). However, the big names of Russian psychology (Leontiev, 1978; Luria, 1976; Vygotsky, 2001) underlined the importance of communication as a mediator of thought. This means that it is important to take into account the words used to define a certain phenomenon to the extent that they will orient and guide our thoughts and, consequently, reach understanding regarding situations of spousal violence.

We are witnessing an indiscriminate use of concepts that are wrongly and frequently used as synonyms toward the phenomenon that it is trying to project through speech (eg, domestic violence, family violence, gender violence, spousal violence, violence in intimate relationships). Anglo-Saxon literature also clarifies very little due to its indistinct use of certain notions (eg, domestic violence, spousal violence, intimate partner violence) and so does Spanish literature (eg, *violencia de pareja, violencia doméstica, violencia familiar, violencia contra la mujer*).

Facing this issue, the need of a focused revision is of extreme importance, with the goal of integrating and facilitating definitions for a better understanding of the "spousal violence" category and its respective variables. In addition, this clarification will serve as a compass for the empirical study presented in the second part of this dissertation, being an aid in terms of the inclusion and exclusion criteria of the participants.

However, no matter what concept is used, the researched bibliography is unanimous in highlighting that spousal violence is a phenomenon that is present in all cultural, economic, sexual, or religious groups and that it occurs in developed and developing countries (Garcia, 2010; Hadley, 2009; Markowitz and Prulhiere, 2006; Matos, 2003; Rojas et al., 2002; Turvey, 2009a; Verde, 2005), that constitutes a serious public health issue (Antunes, 2003; Hirigoyen, 2006; Machado et al., 2008b, 2006; Polsky et al., 2006), violating fundamental human rights (Antunes; 2003; Esplugues, 2008; Falcón, 2004; Garcia, 2010; Samson, 2010). However, although there are cases of mistreatment in all social classes, there is a proportionally inverse relation between economical level and mistreatment. This means that the risk of occurring violence is bigger in social groups with fewer economic resources (González, 2010; Garrido, 2002).

## Violence in a Broad Sense

Pais (2010) considers that there is no universal definition of violence due to the temporal and spatial variation of its meaning. Etymologically, *violentia* comes from Latin, meaning violence, violent character or wild, strength, referencing *violare* as treating with violence, disrespecting and transgressing.

In 2002 the World Health Organization defined violence as an intentional use of force or physical power, in the past or present, against oneself (self-inflicted), against others (interpersonal) or against a group or community (collective), where it can result or create a high probability of death, injury, psychological damage, bad development or deprivation (Redondo, 2010). Examples of intentional violence are: homicide, domestic violence, sexual violence and self-inflicted violence. However, there are cases such as traffic, work, domestic or sport accidents where we should refer to the term *nonintentional violence*.

Magalhães (2010) points out that violence, which covers the notion of abuse, represents a rather serious and complex social dilemma, leading to physical and psychological damage, as well as socioeconomic repercussions.

## The Notion of Aggression

The concept of aggression refers to interactive situations where there is a type of behavior whereby an individual attacks and/or offends another person to hurt them. The term *aggression* should be contemplated in its diverse areas (interindividual aspect and social context), answering the norms that approve it or not, the valued social categories and tolerated acts.

Focusing now on the motivation for aggression, there is such a thing as an aggression that aims to hurt another person directly (hostile aggression), an aggression that is a means to reach a certain end (instrumental aggression) and an aggression that is expressed through an aggressive behavior (expressive behavior) (Magalhães, 2010).

In 1998, Geen established a distinction between angry aggression and instrumental aggression. The former relates to an emotionally negative state of anger as a reaction to some previous provocation and leads to producing damage. The latter is deprived of emotion, where the action is merely calculated and its purpose is not to cause damage. In other words, aggression represents a mean to reach a purpose (González, 2010).

Rodriguez considered in 1995 that aggression is not the aggressor's goal but instead the instrument for domination. It is part of a series of domination strategies (González, 2010).

## Domestic Violence

As an introduction, the notion of domestic violence comes from the notion *domus,* meaning "house" (Magalhães, 2010).

Antunes (2003) alerts us to the fact that the victims of domestic violence do not mean they are only women. We can also mention children, elderly people and the disabled. Thus, it is categorized by an enormous complexity. There is no existing homogeneity in terms of the legal, police and judicial focus, as well as other institutions that face this phenomenon.

Plana (1999) states that it is possible to face domestic violence as a pathology that affects society from a biomedical and social perspective. In addition, the perspective of domestic violence as a pathology allows us to focus on its knowledge, starting from a basic structure that includes its definition as an illness, to its treatment, causes, history, prevalence, severity levels, and others. This means that it allows us to apply control standards similar to the ones in clinical epidemiology.

Santos (2008) refers to domestic violence as not limited to physical aggression, ranging to any type of behavior that aims to control and subjugate another person that shares or has shared the same domestic space through fear, humiliation and physical or verbal aggression. As the abusive conducts tend to happen repetitively, the aggressor despoils the victim of their rights and liberties, damaging their integrity concretely or potentially in the short or medium term (psychological, physical and/or sexual), as well as quality of life and dignity (Magalhães, 2010).

Matos (2006) moves away from the term *domestic violence* by acknowledging an implicit concept of a problem that is managed by themselves or internally, preferring the term *family violence.* However, Davis (2008) states that there is little consensus on what is family or not.

In 1997, Gelles mentioned that investigators have been addressing other phenomenon of family violence, such as violence amongst brothers and aggressions of children toward parents (Matos, 2006). Zawitz et al. (1993) wrote that family violence is difficult to assess, since there is no existing consensus on what constitutes family violence. On the other hand, it is a phenomenon that occurs in the private domain. The victims are frequently reluctant to report the incidents of family violence because of shame and fear of consequences (Poirier, 1999).

Arroyo (2004) defines family violence as a situation of mistreatments amongst people who are linked by consanguinity and/or present or past spousal bonds. Violence in the family has three major victims, namely women, children and the elderly.

Fálcon (2004) clarifies that when talking about intrafamilial violence or family violence, it is not clear who attacks whom. We also add that the same happens when we use the term *domestic violence*, which is part of the category "family violence."

## The Legal Perspective Toward Domestic Violence in Portugal

The classification of crime depends on historical and cultural factors. Even so, it is a complex social and political process. This way, crime is a dynamic concept and new developments produce new forms of crime (Pakes and Pakes, 2009). Therefore, what represents a crime in one country could possibly not be considered in another. What was a crime in the past may not constitute a crime today, and what is not a crime today could become one in the future (Pais, 2010).

With the recent changes to the criminal code, the terms *domestic violence* and *mistreatments* are now considered two legal types of crimes, in which the protected legal interest is the person's well-being in the physical, psychic and mental domains, which are part of human dignity. They are different in terms of the contexts in which they occur. When talking about domestic violence, the behaviors that are associated or treated as a familial relationship are contemplated. Mistreatments, on the other hand, focus on behaviors that are exercised in an institutional environment or in the domain of a caring relationship (Magalhães, 2010).

With the intent of avoiding any misunderstandings between these two legal types of crimes (domestic violence and mistreatments), Magalhães (2010) recommends the use of the broad notion of abuse when talking about any type of behavior used by an individual to dominate and control another person in a relationship.

Schifrin and Waldron reinforced in 2002 the need to distinguish the concepts of domestic violence and mistreatments against women that, when used as synonyms, lead to misunderstandings (Matos, 2003).

According to Portuguese law (Código Penal Português, 2008), we can consider domestic violence as "any form of physical and/or emotional behaviour that is not accidental and inadequate, which results from dysfunctions and/or unfulfilled needs in an interpersonal relationship, present in a context of dependency for the victim (physical, emotional and/or psychological) and a context of trust and power (arbitrarily exercised) by the aggressor that could be a spouse or ex-spouse, partner or ex-partner, son, daughter, father, mother, grandfather, grandmother or another relative. This means that violence is generally used at the core of a family relationship, disregarding the gender and age of the victim or aggressor" (Magalhães, 2010, p. 23).

In Portugal, when referring to its law system, domestic violence is seen as a public crime. This way, news of an aggression is enough for the Public Ministry to take necessary action, regardless of any manifestation of will on the part of the victim regarding that intervention (Garcia, 2010; Magalhães, 2010).

## Violence Against Women

In terms of the victimization of women, there are a few types of violence that require more specific terminology (Magalhães, 2010).

The idea of violence against women is characterized for being generic and referent to violence situations inside and outside of family frames that can originate physical and/or psychological suffering and physical/sexual damage. It can cover acts and/or threats of physical violence, coercion and deprivation of freedom. Beyond the violence committed in the context of intimate relationships, this category includes female genital mutilation, female infanticide, trafficking of women and forced prostitution (Magalhães, 2010).

As a supplement, violence committed against women is expressed in distinct domains of life, namely family, work (eg, sexual harassment) and in contexts of migration (eg, immigrant women, refugees), exclusion (eg, working in the sex industry) and globalization of commerce (eg, trafficking of women) (Cousineau et al., 2008).

The first official definition of violence against women emerged in 1993 in the Declaration on the Elimination of Violence Against Women of the United Nations' General Assembly. According to this, violence against women is all the violent behavior that is focused toward the female gender that resulted or could result in physical, psychological or sexual damage/suffering, as well as threats of said acts, coercion or arbitrary deprivation of freedom, either at a public life level or at an intimate level (Pérez and Martínez, 2009).

The term *gender violence* is related to "to the violence perpetrated against women as a result of gender issues that derive from historical asymmetry of power relations between men and women, which is a source of significant social inequalities where men exert their power through violence, often considered socially legitimized."

In this way, the focus is on the violence perpetrated by men against the opposite sex, being a universal phenomenon and across all social classes and age groups, particularly in the intrafamilial context, which is part of domestic violence.

In 2003, Velázquez defined gender violence as all acts that discriminate, ignore, subject and subordinate women in the various aspects of their existence. The victim's freedom, dignity, safety, privacy and integrity (moral and/or physical) is attacked in a material or symbolic manner (Carbó, 2006).

## Spousal Violence

Regarding domestic violence committed against women by their partners, Magalhães (2010) highlights a number of commonly used expressions such as violence in intimate relationships, domestic violence, intimate violence, spousal violence or violence in loving relationships. They are reported as a commonly repeated behavior with general domestic violence characteristics, but that occur in an intimate relationship that involves sensual and/or sexual contacts. Today, domestic violence is being paid attention to, regardless of the couple's sexual orientation (heterosexual or homosexual) and their bond (marriage, consensual union or flirtation, divorced or separated).

Close to the notion of spousal violence is violence against intimate partners. In the eyes of Renner (2009), violence against intimate partners is related to violent acts between current and former couples, cohabiting partners or people in a loving relationship. This means that it is violence that occurs between two adults in a current or former significant relationship. The intimate partners are the ones who have or had a loving relationship with the victim, which include spouse, ex-spouse, boyfriend, ex-boyfriend, girlfriend or ex-girlfriend. Violence against intimate partners refers to romantic relationships that were marked by physical abuse, including couples, consensual unions or legal divorces, regardless of affective-sexual orientation (Karmen, 2010).

Baccino's (2006) perspective toward spousal violence is that it relates to a process where the individual has an aggressive and destabilizing behavior against his partner in a private and privileged relationship. As intentional and interpersonal violence, domestic violence is established at various levels, such as faith, freedom or physical integrity. It represents an attack on the exercise of a right that is considered fundamental or a conception of fulfilling human development at any given time. This means that it always involves a violation (Magalhães, 2010).

Machado et al. (2008a) adopted the term *spousal violence* with a focus on defining formal and informal intimate relationships, such as current or former marriages and consensual unions (eg, violence perpetrated by ex-spouse or ex-partner).

Matos (2005) states that investigation highlights two qualitatively distinct forms of spousal violence, namely the violence that covers mutual conflict between spouses and violence based on male power over women. The former reveals a dynamic of reciprocal violence—an unstable interpersonal response facing a particular conflict where the exercise of control is confined to a specific situation. These cases are less prevalent, with fewer possibilities of the violence scaling with time and causing severe damage to the victims. The latter covers the illegitimate exercise of control of a male partner over the female. This typology is characterized by a more grievous and frequent violence with fewer possibilities of the victim's self-defense, containing more serious consequences (eg, posttraumatic stress disorder) and an expressive number of separation attempts by the victim from the aggressor.

Pistole expressed his understanding on the matter in 1994, stating that violence arises in any close relationship as a means to regulate the proximity and distance between the partners of a relationship (Doumas et al., 2008). Matos (2005) defines spousal violence as a set of behaviors with an abusive nature that are committed intentionally against the spouse. It can include violent and nonviolent actions (eg, verbalizations, omissions). Its purpose lies on the victim by deliberately inflicting damage, causing fear and inducing feelings of incompetence, submission and insignificance.

In our opinion, the conceptual confusion evidenced in the bibliographic research resides in the somewhat reckless use of the terms *intimate partner/intimacy* and *spousal/marital*. The former are extendible to flirtation and spousal relationships, while the latter are exclusive to spousal relationships (consensual union, civil marriage and religious marriage) and are not extendible to flirtation (eg, teenager flirtation, where we can see a gradual increase in violence). Even if it consists of an intimate relationship, it does not involve a conjugal/spousal bond.

We aim to include in this book women who exclusively were at one time victims of abuses by their current or former husbands and partners (eg, consensual union). After an exhaustive conceptual exploration, it is clear why the title of the book integrates this notion specifically (spousal violence) over the remaining addressed notions.

In other words, we focus our attention on formal and informal intimate relationships, such as marriage (civil or religious) and current or former consensual unions (eg, violence by ex-husband or ex-partner). This way, we exclude the intimate relations of flirtation for its nonexisting matrimonial bond.

It is important to add that due to the variety of definitions and their commonly careless uses, it was necessary to adopt a greater wariness in the writing of the remaining chapters. This will ensure that they integrate concepts that are in line with the adopted concept. Take for example, when referring the possible violence types, we do not slide into fields applicable to mistreatment of the elderly that are under the category of domestic violence but not under intimate partner violence.

González (2010) states that the greater the social awareness and legal protection, the more strategic the violence becomes and, therefore, less visible the injuries. This is the importance of dedicating a chapter to the typology of integrating behaviors of spousal violence.

Chapter 2

# Statistical Data Regarding Spousal Violence

Around the world, the rates of violence perpetrated against women by their partner are significant (Archer, 2000, cited in Houry et al., 2008; Garcia, 2010).

Every 9 s, somewhere in the United States, a woman is assaulted by her intimate partner or ex-companion. This is more than 8.7 million women who are assaulted every year (Roberts, 2002, cited in Roberts and Roberts, 2005). Johnson pointed out in 1993 that Swedish statistical data revealed that a woman is assaulted every 20 min. Annually, about 30 women are assaulted to death by their partners (Antunes, 2003). Introducing the European context on violence against women, the latest barometer produced in 2014 estimated that about 13 million women between the ages of 18 and 74 suffered physical violence by their male companions, that 3.7 million have experienced sexual violence, and 24–39 million were victims of sexual harassment (European Union Agency for Fundamental Rights, 2014).

According to the Council of Europe in 2002, violence inside the family structure was the main cause of death and incapacitation toward women between 16 and 44 years old. These statistics are greater than cancer and traffic accidents (Gracia, 2009).

The prevalence of this phenomenon ranges between 18% and 30% in countries like Canada, the United States, and the United Kingdom (Sev'er, Dawson, and Johnson, 2004, cited in Matos, 2006). In Holland, 20.8% of women between 20 and 60 years old were victims of physical violence perpetrated by their partners (Romkens, 1989, cited in Hirigoyen, 2006). Esplugues (2008) states that during 2007 in Spain, nearly 400,000 women were victims of spousal violence. In 1993, Mooney reported that in England, one in every four women has declared having experienced spousal violence (Hirigoyen, 2006).

The information collected from 38 countries points to the prevalence of spousal violence throughout life to be between 10% and 67% (World Health Organization, 2002, cited in Machado and Dias, 2010). In a factual review regarding its prevalence, the World Health Organization (2014) indicates that on average, 30% of women that were in a relationship report that they suffered some sort of physical or sexual violence by their partner. Globally, 30% of homicides toward women are perpetrated by an intimate partner.

Forensic Psychology of Spousal Violence. http://dx.doi.org/10.1016/B978-0-12-803533-7.00002-8

Other studies done by Matos (2006) have determined that the prevalence rates in developing countries are significant. About 70% of women in Ghana have mentioned some sort of victimization, and it is calculated that in Nicaragua there is a 52% victimization rate throughout life. A study developed and published in 2005 by WHO, based on interviews with 24,000 women residing in urban and rural areas in 10 countries (eg, Brazil, Ethiopia, Japan, Peru, Serbia, Thailand), reported that women have a greater risk of violence in their own homes rather than outside of the home (Regehr and Roberts, 2010).

Repeated victimization, especially in spousal violence, is unfortunately common (Pakes and Pakes, 2009), being that former reports of domestic violence form a strong indicator that it could occur again (Saavedra and Fonseca, 2013). Regarding North American women, 22% are victims, 7% are aggressors, and 12% have both roles (Houry et al., 2008). Despite spousal violence affecting both genders, most of them are women (Markowitz et al., 2006b) and more than 25% of women have experienced one or more episodes of domestic violence (Hirigoyen, 2006). Baccino (2006) has reported that repeated violence occurs in at least 50% of cases. About 20% of women who were victims of violence recorded 10 or more incidents. The average number of assaults by the same partner is around seven (Burke, 2007, cited in Turvey, 2009a). According to the 1999 Eurobarometer poll, one in every five European women were victims of violence by their partner at least once in their lifetime, and 25% of crimes correspond to a man that assaulted his partner (Hirigoyen, 2006).

Only 16% of aggression cases motivated a complaint after the first assault, while 28% corresponded to isolated events (no more than five times), 40% to a few times (6–20 times), 12% to more than 20 times and less than 100, and lastly, one case recorded continuous aggression (more than 100 times). We highlight that complaints or denunciations of physical violence, either consummated or attempted, in the context of present or former relationships are risk factors for the perpetration of new violent acts (Saavedra and Fonseca, 2013).

Based on the Spanish statistics, in 20% of cases women subject themselves to aggression during a period shorter than a year and 80% over a year. The average number is about 5.92 years, with a minimum of a year and a maximum of 30 years. The period of relationship with the aggressor that is less than a year occurs in about 12% of cases and more than a year in about 80% of cases. This corresponds to an average of 13.8 years, with extreme cases being one year and another 35 years (Arroyo, 2004).

About 63% of cases of violence end with separation (Statistics Canada, 2005, cited in Regehr and Roberts, 2010). Baccino (2006) found that 59% of women who contacted *Violences Conjugales Femmes Info Service* were married and 20% lived in concubinage.

In 68% of cases, the aggressor was the husband and the aggression occurred during the period of matrimony (Arroyo, 2004). However, violence does not occur within matrimonial relationships. It occurs during the dating period, sometimes during its initial phase. It is estimated that one in every 11 teenagers was physically assaulted during their dating years. One in every five teenagers reported verbal, physical, sexual, or emotional violence, and one in every five high school girls was the victim of physical or sexual abuse during their relationships (US Centers for Disease Control and Prevention, 2006, cited in Regehr and Roberts, 2010). As Garrido (2002) alerts, if there is already violence when dating, it will persist with the evolving relationship.

The assaults occur more frequently during the weekends, possibly due to the time spent at home. Nighttime is the most frequent period for aggressions, again reflecting the time couples spend together with each other (Duros et al., 2009).

As was mentioned earlier, the aggressive incidents are more likely to happen at home. They normally start in the living room, kitchen, or bedroom and end in the same house division they started in. If the aggression didn't start at home, the most likely place would be a public location or someone else's house. In the description of these aggressions, women point to their man's jealously as the main cause of violence. They also state that they prefer aggression in front of others in order to minimize damage resulting from their partner's explosive rage (Duros et al., 2009).

According to samples from Spain, most women (73.5%) who are affected are between 30 and 45 years old. The average age is 35.7 years and with a standard deviation of 9.29 (Arroyo, 2004). In a study by Luna and Osuna in 1994, the ages 21–40 are the most with reports of violence.

It is estimated that about 95% of aggressions that are not reported do not leave relevant physical injuries from the victim's perspective (Sánchez and Sierra, 2006). Women that are victims of spousal violence attempt suicide five to eight times more than the general population (Hirigoyen, 2006).

Regarding pregnant women, according to Canadian research one in every four women suffered violence perpetrated by their former or current partner. In 20% of cases, this violence started during pregnancy (Hirigoyen, 2006). Campbell and his colleagues found in 1992 that during pregnancy, mistreatments ranged between 1% and 17% (Hirigoyen, 2006). Gazmarian and his colleagues found in 1996 that 20% of pregnant women were assaulted by their partner during pregnancy (Roberts and Roberts, 2005).

In 2002, Campbell mentioned that between 3% and 13% of pregnant women were targets of spousal violence. In most integrated countries in this investigation, it was found that 4–12% of pregnant women that were interviewed reported that they were assaulted by the child's father during their pregnancy by getting punched or kicked in the abdomen (World Health Organization, 2005, cited in Regehr and Roberts, 2010).

Thus, we can conclude that violence can start or worsen during pregnancy. The aggressors are considered more dangerous during their partner's pregnancy. The acts of violence can represent an intentional act of double violence that incorporates violence toward women and child abuse (Campbell, 2001, cited in Saavedra and Fonseca, 2013).

The aggressions extend to their children at a very high rate (reaching 88%) and with similar characteristics (Álvarez, 2007). In 18% of cases, children supported and encouraged their mothers to report the case and 27.2% of children stated that both parents were to blame. Family members were the main support in 44% of cases and psychiatric or psychological treatment in 36% of cases (Arroyo, 2004).

In a study done in 2000 by Waul, 62% of women that reported a history of spousal violence alluded to children's mistreatment (Ely and Flaherty, 2009).

Catalano wrote in 2007 that alcohol or drug consumption was reported in 42% of total cases of nonfatal spousal violence (Regehr and Roberts, 2010). Foran and O'Leary (2008, cited in Saavedra and Fonseca, 2013) underlined that individuals who consume alcohol excessively and/or use illegal drugs have a significantly larger probability of perpetrating violence against their intimate partners compared to when there is no consumption whatsoever.

Relative to Portuguese statistics originating in the author's country, Matos (2006, p. 34) says that "… any discussion about the detection and prevalence of intimate violence against women in Portugal has a lot of obstacles from the start." Take as an example the nonexistence of official registry systems (eg, hospitals, safe houses).

A study by Lourenço et al. (1997), with a sample of 1000 women, allowed them to determine the predominance of psychological violence (37%), as well as the fact that homes are the most common place for the occurrence of physical and psychological violence. Husbands are the main perpetrators of mistreatment, and younger women in urban areas with a higher level of education are the best at perceiving themselves as victims in situations of violence, especially sexual and discriminatory violence (Matos, 2006).

Lisboa, Barroso, and Marteleira published in 2003 a study with 2160 trials about the social context of violence against women, from the *Instituto Nacional de Medicina Legal* (Portuguese National Institute of Legal Medicine), specifically the Center and North Delegations, and found that regarding civil status, married women were the most prevalent (59.1%) (Matos, 2006).

In 67.2% of cases, assaults happened inside households, especially at night and with children watching the assault (95.3%) or being victims themselves (83.3% in Coimbra and 66.7% in Oporto). Most of the interviewees revealed a history of continuous violence, with the number of cases that were prolonged for more than 10 years being significant (36.7% of total samples), delaying the report (Matos, 2006).

The same author refers to a study by Lisboa and colleagues from 2002 with the title *Os custos sociais e económicos da violência contra as mulheres* (The Social and Economic Costs of Violence Towards Women) where the main focus was the analysis of social domains, physical and psychological health, and the victim's education. The sample consisted of 1500 women of 18 or older. In 39% of cases, violence lasted for more than 10 years. The most frequent location of physical and psychological violence was their household (46%), and the main perpetrator of aggression was the husband or ex-husband/partner (40%).

A study by Machado in 2002 and 2003 allowed us to determine the existence of distinct forms of violence in a relationship. This is something that has assumed a bigger proportion in cases of low-income levels, although we can't deny its prevalence in higher levels of income. Of the 477 identified victims, 393 (82.4%) were equally spousal offenders, highlighting a relation between aggression and spousal victimization.

In line with what happens in other countries, Portuguese women who are victims of intimate violence are assaulted in most cases at home by their partners in former or current spousal or nonspousal relationships (Matos, 2006).

In a sample of 205 elementary school children, Lourenço and Lisboa found in 1992 that 61% had seen their father assaulting their mother (Matos, 2003).

In 2008, according to statistics of the Ministry of Internal Affairs, domestic violence was responsible for 22% of the criminal reports' total growth in national territory, with a total of 27,733 reports (Matos, 2011). In 2009, also according to the Ministry of Internal Affairs, 30,543 domestic violence reports were made with a daily average of 84 reports, registering an increase of 10% in comparison with the former year. Most reports were made by women (82.6%) who were 25 or older. Spousal relationships were the greatest number of cases, either current relationships (63.9%) or former (13.5%) (Matos, 2011).

In 91% of cases that were reported, there was information of previous events of domestic violence (Directorate General of Internal Affairs, 2009, cited in Matos, 2011).

By analyzing the national statistics relative to the year 2010, we can affirm that the family relations between the author of the crime and victim are the most common situations. Just between spouse/partner highlighted about 48.5% of the total number of recorded events (6932 direct crime victims identified by the Portuguese Association for Victim Support, APAV, in 2010).

The male gender perpetrates the preponderance of crimes – 81% of total cases. Continuous victimization is a characteristic in 70% of cases. Most cases lasted more than two years. The most used location for violence was common residence (APAV, 2011).

In 16,972 cases presented by APAV in 2010, the crime of domestic violence was spotted in 82% of situations (13,866). In the domain of domestic violence, the cases that were recorded the most in 2010 were psychological mistreatment (36.8%) and physical mistreatment (30%) (APAV, 2011).

In 2014 the *Associação Portuguesa de Apoio à Vítima* (APAV, 2015) followed 8889 direct victims that were the target of 21,541 crimes and/or other violent acts. We highlight that crimes against people, particularly domestic violence, correspond to 16,881 cases (78.4%). They are followed by psychological mistreatments (6637), physical mistreatments (4506), and threats/coactions (3279).

Phone lines are increasingly becoming a preferential way of contacting for help, with 57.6% phoning for help in 2014 (0.6% increase compared with 2013). However, it is important to report the physical contact (32.2%) and the use of electronic communications (email, etc.) that increased 0.9% compared to 2013. It is the own user that makes these contacts (59%) or close members of their family (18.2%) (APAV, 2015).

Of all the people that reported crimes in 2014, 82.3% were mainly female between 25 and 54 years old (37.1%), married (39.4%) and with children (39.4%), employed (29.6%) and in a relationship with the author of the crime (28.4%). In terms of the aggressors, more than 80% were male, aged between 25 and 54 years old (30%) (APAV, 2015).

In the 2014 Homeland Security Annual Report, which is an official document of the government of Portugal, we noted that relative to 2013, there was a 31 criminal record case increase in domestic violence "against a partner or similar," being the third most reported crime with 22,959 cases, only being surpassed by motor vehicle theft (27,749 cases) and simple voluntary offense to physical integrity (24,255 cases). About 81% of victims were female and 85% of cases were reported against males. In 38% of situations, the occurrence was witnessed by minors (Ministry of Internal Affairs, 2015).

## AUTHOR'S OWN INVESTIGATIONS: THE VICTIM, THE AGGRESSOR, AND THE CONTEXT

Following the approach of statistical data related to spousal violence, I will present the most highlighted results of two qualitative investigations, specifically a data survey of spousal violence cases that were recorded during the first semester of 2011 in the *Delegação do Sul do Instituto Nacional de Medicina Legal e Ciências Forenses* (South Delegation of the National Institute of Legal Medicine and Forensic Sciences, IP) and three associated councils, as well as the application of an investigation protocol in a nonrandomized accidental sample.

The first investigation was based on all the incoming cases involving aggression between partners, ex-partners, husbands, and ex-husbands, perpetrated by males during the first half of 2011, in the South delegation and three associated Legal Medicine cabinets belonging to the region of Lisbon and Vale do Tejo. It is important to clarify that no matter the nature of an offensive crime against physical integrity (public, semi-public, or particular), the investigation requires a production of evidence, specifically expert assessment. It is in this domain that resides the execution of assessments or forensic exams. This makes it necessary for evidentiary purposes that the surviving victims be examined by doctors and/ or other experts as a way to ensure the assessment of injuries and/or sequelae as a result of suffered violence, either physical, sexual, or psychological.

A total of 458 adult female victims were recorded with ages ranging between 18 and 82 years old, with an average of 39.54 years (SD = 12.03), median of 38 years, and mode of 33 years. Most aggressors were the victims' husbands (51.7%; $n = 237$) (Table 2.1).

We have verified that most victims were not assaulted publicly but rather at their homes (56.2%, $n = 205$). The most frequent days for aggression were the weekend days, preferably Sunday (20.2%; $n = 92$) (Table 2.2).

The most common time was between 7 pm and midnight (49.6%; $n = 223$) (Table 2.3). These results are part of international statistics, being a reflection of the time couples spend with each other (Duros et al., 2009; Matos, 2006).

**TABLE 2.1** Relationship With the Aggressor

|  | n | % |
|---|---|---|
| Relationship With the Aggressor |  |  |
| Partner | 138 | 30.1 |
| Husband | 237 | 51.7 |
| Ex-partner | 56 | 12.2 |
| Ex-husband | 27 | 5.9 |

**TABLE 2.2** Day of Violent Event

|  | n | % |
|---|---|---|
| Day of Violent Event |  |  |
| Monday | 52 | 11.4 |
| Tuesday | 65 | 14.3 |
| Wednesday | 48 | 10.5 |
| Thursday | 56 | 12.3 |
| Friday | 67 | 14.7 |
| Saturday | 75 | 16.5 |
| Sunday | 92 | 20.2 |

**TABLE 2.3** Hour of Event

|  | n | % |
|---|---|---|
| Hour of Event |  |  |
| 8 am to 6:59 pm | 176 | 39.1 |
| 7 pm to 0:59 am | 223 | 49.6 |
| 1 am to 7:59 am | 51 | 11.1 |

Almost all victims pointed to physical violence (98.3%; $n=450$) as being the main cause for their report, with the most common items being *punching* (43.9%; $n=201$) and *causing injuries that needed medical assistance* (42.6%; $n=195$). Most cases registered repeated assaults (81.9%; $n=280$), which was a very common phenomenon when studying this type of phenomenon. (Arroyo,

2004). We've verified that most victims resorted to a hospital emergency department (94%, $n=188$), which demonstrates the importance of having health experts (eg, doctors, nurses) ready to act against domestic violence.

There were more victims without a pathological background (81.2%; $n=372$) than with one (15.5%; $n=71$) and, between the ones that had a background, most of these pathologies were not identified (63.4%; $n=45$). In 23.9% ($n=17$) of cases, there was a reference to diagnosed mental disorders. It is specifically important to reflect on etiopathogenesis in order to determine a possible causal link with violence or, on the other hand, the contribution of pathology to violent relational dynamics.

Fig. 2.1 refers to the percentage of children who witnessed any kind of violence. In the cases where it was possible to verify the existence of children through the registry (34 cases), only in 12% ($n=4$) of the reports was it found that the children did not witness the perpetrated violence.

A psychological evaluation of the 458 victims was not requested. This fact deserves a special comment, in which the bibliographic research is aware on one hand that psychological violence is a type of violence of great relevancy and in some cases there was only this type of violence. On the other hand, it emphasizes the impact of spousal violence in the psychological domain, regardless of the type of violence perpetrated. Additionally, the expert evaluation is done first by a doctor (biomedical science) without the necessary skills for a correct psychological assessment (psychological science). As was already mentioned, the majority of victims present claims of physical aggression, concentrating the essence of their narrative on this type of violence that, in a way, conditions the doctor's attitude.

The theoretical reflections of the different types of violence and the psychological impacts from the aggressions show us the importance of a complementary psychological evaluation for a complete medical-legal assessment. On the other hand, the psychological assessment can be an important element of evidence in situations where the report and/or the request for help occurs within a lengthy stretch of time that does not allow the assessment of physical bruises and all that is left is the psychological evidence. Despite this, it appears that a significant number of judges still underestimate the psychological issues and have limited their probative value. For a proper appreciation of the

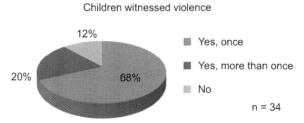

FIGURE 2.1  Percentage of children who witnessed any kind of violence.

psychological findings a paradigm shift seems necessary, which we do not see happening in the short-to-medium-term time horizon.

Separated or divorced women were more the victims of psychological violence than the remaining group and present the biggest number of spotted behaviors in the Spousal Violence Inventory (average of 2.37). This way, the intensity of psychological violence that is allied to a bigger scale of aggressive behaviors can facilitate the decision-making of the victim toward the end of the violent relationship. Older victims are more frequently victims of physical and psychological violence. Results show that victims that need clinical assistance were more frequently victims of physical violence. The more repeated the aggressions are toward the woman, the greater the number of days these women are incapable of performing professional activities. In other words, the greater the number of repeated aggressions, the greater the number of days of incapability for performing professional activities.

Regarding the results of the Investigation Protocols of the Nonrandomized Accidental Sampling, we collected data from a sample group of 76 women victims of spousal violence. Statistically, however, in order to identify continuous variables that discriminate between two or more groups of a categorical variable, we used a discriminative analysis. In this analysis, we used 59 cases because the remaining 17 participants did not answer all items (missing values).

Sociodemographically, there is a major prevalence of Portuguese women (85.5%; $n=65$) with schooling levels up to high school (35.5%; $n=27$) and married/in a de facto union (40.8%; $n=31$), in terms of marital status). They are mostly women without a semiqualified/qualified profession (43.4%; $n=33$) or are unemployed (32.9%; $n=25$). In terms of age, a major number of participants are between 35 and 39 years old (17.1%; $n=13$), with the youngest victim being 19 years old and the oldest being 72.

Table 2.4 refers to a minimum and maximum number of children between the mothers that were victims.

We note that the presence of children, including stepchildren, can increase the risk of domestic abuse toward the mother. They may equally be involved in the violence and suffer from it directly or indirectly (Abransky et al. 2011, cited in Saavedra and Fonseca, 2013). The presence of children increases the risk of domestic violence toward women due to a very strong association between risk and the number of children in a household. The greater the number of children,

**TABLE 2.4** Number of Victims' Children

|  | Min | Max | M |
|---|---|---|---|
| Number of children (between the ones that have children) | 1 | 6 | 2.01 |

the greater the risk (Barnish, 2004, cited in Saavedra and Fonseca, 2013). The situations of violence against children and the violence against the partner can appear associated. This means that the presence of one could increase the probability of the presence of the other (Saavedra and Fonseca, 2013).

Based on their experiences as victims, the majority of participants does not consider existing laws' punishments toward the aggressor as adequate (72.4%; $n = 55$). This is an aspect that can initiate situations of secondary victimization (Matud et al., 2009).

About half the participants (48%; $n = 36$) did not see violence as such after being assaulted for the first time. This shows the importance and the need for early preventive actions together with schools and families (Saavedra and Machado, 2010; Hirigoyen, 2006).

Table 2.5 shows the religion of each participant at the time of the first assault and at the time of completing the protocol.

**TABLE 2.5** Religion

| | n | % |
| --- | --- | --- |
| **Religion at the First Time of Aggression** | | |
| Nonpracticing Catholic | 45 | 59.2 |
| Practicing Catholic | 13 | 17.1 |
| Muslim | 1 | 1.3 |
| Orthodox | 2 | 2.6 |
| Protestant | 3 | 3.9 |
| Other Christian | 4 | 5.3 |
| No Religion | 8 | 10.5 |
| **Current Religion** | | |
| Nonpracticing Catholic | 40 | 52.6 |
| Practicing Catholic | 8 | 10.5 |
| Muslim | 1 | 1.3 |
| Orthodox | 2 | 2.6 |
| Protestant | 7 | 9.2 |
| Other Christian | 6 | 7.9 |
| No Religion | 10 | 13.2 |
| Did not answer | 2 | 2.6 |

Most participants said they were nonpracticing Catholics in both instances they were questioned. There is, however, in Portugal a decrease in Catholics and an increase in Protestants and alternative Christian branches relative to the moment of the first aggression and the current moment.

We assessed if there was a common religious shift after the spousal violence experience. There were some religious shifts between Catholic women, but they were insignificant. Of the 45 nonpracticing Catholic women, merely two changed to become practicing Catholics, two to Protestants, three to alternative Christian branches, and three declared having abandoned religion. Of the 13 practicing Catholics, five shifted to become nonpracticing Catholics and two became Protestants. There was not any other change.

Although 16% ($n = 12$) of participants matched the diagnostic criteria for dependent personality disorder, we registered an average of 2.74 regarding the traits (Fig. 2.2). We highlight their difficulty in decision-making without excessive counseling and being tranquilized by others (57.9%; $n = 44$). They also show difficulty in initiating projects or doing things on their own due to their lack of confidence in their abilities (50%; $n = 38$), as well as feelings of discomfort and helplessness when they are alone (48.7%; $n = 37$) (Table 2.6). Therefore, we ponder that despite the participants not meeting the minimum five diagnostic criteria for the disorder, the marked traits may in some way influence the increased time in the relationship with the offender.

Therefore, we ponder that despite the participants not meeting the minimum five diagnostic criteria for the disorder, the marked traits may, in some way, influence the increased time in the relationship with the offender.

Fig. 2.3 represents after the occurrence of the first assault (physical, psychological, or sexual) when the participants felt they were victims of violence.

About half the participants (48%, $n = 36$) did not view violence as such after being assaulted.

Most participants were assaulted by their husband (64.5%; $n = 49$) and stated in their life history that they had only one aggressive intimate partner. We only detected a maximum of two aggressive partners.

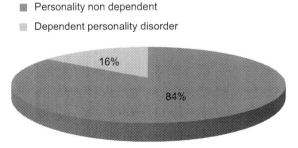

**FIGURE 2.2**   Existence of dependent personality.

**TABLE 2.6** What the Participants Think of Themselves

|  | n | % |
|---|---|---|
| Has Difficulty Making Everyday Decisions Without an Excessive Amount of Advice and Reassurance From Others | | |
| Yes | 44 | 57.9 |
| No | 32 | 42.1 |
| Needs Others to Assume Responsibility for Most Major Areas of His or Her Life | | |
| Yes | 11 | 14.5 |
| No | 65 | 85.5 |
| Has Difficulty Expressing Disagreement With Others Because of Fear of Loss of Support or Approval | | |
| Yes | 34 | 44.7 |
| No | 42 | 55.3 |
| Difficulty in Starting Projects or Taking Care of Things by Themselves due to Lack of Trust in Their Own Abilities | | |
| Yes | 38 | 50.0 |
| No | 38 | 50.0 |
| Goes to Excessive Lengths to Obtain Nurturance and Support From Others, to the Point of Volunteering to Do Things That Are Unpleasant | | |
| Yes | 12 | 15.8 |
| No | 64 | 84.2 |
| Feels Uncomfortable or Helpless When Alone Because of Exaggerated Fears of Being Unable to Care for Himself or Herself | | |
| Yes | 37 | 48.7 |
| No | 39 | 51.3 |
| Urgently Seeks Another Relationship as a Source of Care and Support When a Close Relationship Ends | | |
| Yes | 6 | 7.9 |
| No | 70 | 92.1 |
| Unjustified Fear of Being on Their Own | | |
| Yes | 26 | 34.2 |
| No | 50 | 65.8 |

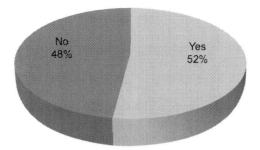

**FIGURE 2.3**    Feeling of victimization after first aggression.

Less than a quarter of participants (21.1%; $n = 16$) were victimized during their dating period with the man of the relationship, influencing them into participating in the investigation. In these cases, we could unveil a situation of psychological violence. However, we can confirm Garrido's (2002) statement: if there is already violence during the period of dating, the same will persist with the progression of the relationship. This seems to escape the understanding of the women in the sample.

Although most assaulted women were not from a family where spousal violence persisted, a significant number of participants (41%; $n = 31$) came from households where this was a problem. As to the perpetrators, it was possible to deny their origin of homes marked by violence in 20 cases (26%). On this topic, it should be noted that we must not become hostages of what happened or did not happen with our parents (Kohlrieser, 2006), as research reveals that "… the greatest contribution for the mental health of an adult is offered the emotional relationships established in adulthood" (Canavarro, 1999, p. 320, cited in Canavarro et al., 2006, p. 173).

About a quarter of participants (24%, $n = 18$) remain in a spousal relationship with a history of violence. The aggressors end their relationship by their own will in 8% of cases ($n = 6$). Most of the participants (68%; $n = 52$) remained in the violent marital relationship for more than six months, with most reasons being the children (34.2%; $n = 26$) still having feelings for the aggressor (18.4%; $n = 14$) and economic dependency (13.2%; $n = 10$) (Table 2.7). However, as mentioned in the chapter "Characterization of Victims of Conjugal Violence," the financial and children issues are excuses. These are arguments people believe but are not the real causes for two adults to decide not to divorce (Aires and Bulha, 2012; Aires, 2012). Most of the participants reported giving birth to children after the aggression had begun (61.8%; $n = 47$). Additionally, the fact that a woman gets pregnant and accepts having children with a man that mistreats her becomes a very interesting element to reflect upon from a psychological point of view.

Most participants were not violent (59%, $n = 45$) and those who reported having been were almost entirely doing it in self-defense (40%, $n = 30$).

**TABLE 2.7** Most Important Reasons Given for Staying in a Marriage for More Than Six Months

|  | n | % |
|---|---|---|
| Still likes the aggressor | 14 | 18.4 |
| Economic dependency | 10 | 13.2 |
| Lack of family support | 8 | 10.5 |
| Fear of being alone | 5 | 6.6 |
| Fear of the aggressor becoming more violent | 6 | 7.9 |
| Because of religion | 1 | 1.3 |
| Because of their children | 26 | 34.2 |
| Hoping for change | 1 | 1.3 |
| Idea that "marriage is forever" | 1 | 1.3 |
| Did not answer | 4 | 5.3 |

Most participants were assaulted by their husband (64.5%, $n=49$) and reported the experienced situation of spousal violence after the end of the relationship (60.5%, $n=46$). About a quarter of the sample (23.6%, $n=18$) did not report the spousal violence targeted toward them.

More than one-third of participants (78.9%; $n=60$) reported or sought support from an institution or psychologist during the first relationship in which they were assaulted. However, as we have seen the average time calculated for the participant to move forward and report or ask for help is about 13 years. We state that 12 participants have reported spousal violence but remain in the relationship. Of the 25 participants who were assaulted after separation, most reported or stated having suffered postseparation assaults in an institution or psychologist (84%; $n=21$).

Most participants did not seek help before reporting or requesting for support from an institution or psychologist (53.9%, $n=41$). Among those who sought help, the majority neither sought legal advice nor help from friends, religious support, psychological support, or support from a specialized institution, but only help from family (25%, $n=19$). However, "the family can be ... both a source of support as well as pressure towards beaten women" (Machado and Dias, 2010, p. 36).

Given this information, there is a letter courtesy of the daughter of a woman who was a victim of domestic violence, written in 1976 to her mother-in-law, serving as an example of frequently resorting to any family member. The author of the letter was married for about 28 years and the violence started in the first week of marriage.

October 1976

Dearest mother (referring to the mother-in-law),

I hope that you are well by the time you receive this letter, as well as father. Everything is well here.

José can already walk and Maria is still playful as ever (referring to her children's fake names).

You asked on your other letter if we hadn't gone to Lisbon or to my godmother's house. We didn't, I don't speak of it anymore either. You know how António is (fake name). He's living with his kids and he doesn't care if they have clothes to wear or food to eat. He cares even less for the ones who are away.

You know how he is, he only cares about spending his money going out and having fun while I have to work day and night to provide for my house. He doesn't care about anything.

At first I didn't tell anyone what he did or said to me, but now that I see he won't change and is getting worse, I don't have a choice except say everything he did.

Last month he spent all the money he had at home. At the end of the month he didn't even have 20 escudos to feed his kids.

As you can see there are many times I want to buy for my kids but I don't have the money. I don't ask for money out of shame.

This is the sad truth that I live. I don't ask him for money or advise him in any way because I know I'm going to get beaten. Last time he hit me my face got completely swollen. My parents were saddened when they know about the beating. My father never came over to my house and my mother would rarely come.

As you can see it's not worth saying anything else, mother is away and they might think that he does this things to me because I'm mean or I do things I shouldn't.

(Note: This is the original version of the letter, unedited.)

---

Most women (64.5%; $n=49$) were assaulted again after the complaint or request for support to an institution or psychologist, which makes the moment of decision a moment of risk (Baccino, 2006; Hirigoyen, 2006). The victim should, if appropriate, prepare their departure under protection (Pais, 2010). Most women reported or referred to an institution or psychologist these or other recent aggressions (52.6%, $n=40$).

In all cases (76 cases) it is possible to affirm the existence of repeated assault in 71 cases (93.4%), with a higher percentage of repeated assaults on the psychological aspects. The maximum number of aggressions was 14,000, namely physical and psychological. This value was obtained by multiplying the number of days the relationship lasted (approximately 40 years), in which the victim stated that aggressions "were almost every day" (sic). These physical and sexual assaults were registered in six and two cases, respectively, in one reported occurrence. This aspect was not verified in psychological violence, which occurs more than once. This means that in some cases, a single occurrence of physical violence (eg, a slap) or sexual violence (eg, force determinate sexual practices) was enough to end the relationship. The same does not happen with psychological violence, which has to happen repeatedly. However, it is marked as being the biggest cause of suffering. In this reality, the value of physical damage over psychological violence is notorious. There is a sort of collective fantasy where physical injuries are the only things considered serious and violent in a relationship.

In terms of suffered damage, we highlight: insulting, defaming, or making serious claims to humiliate or "hurt" (93.4%), yelling or threatening to scare the other person (93.4%), pushing away violently (84.3%), slapping (80.3%), and preventing contact with others (76.3%). On the other hand, the most frequent acts by the victim, particularly regarding self-defense, are: insulting, defaming, or making serious claims to humiliate or "hurt" someone (42.1%) and throwing objects at the other person (19.7%). These actions follow Arroyo's (2004) statement where he affirms that mixed aggressions are more frequent, together with physical mistreatment and verbal violence. However, we are faced with psychological control strategies that were less common. These enable us to conjecture a possible change in aggression patterns in order not to leave visible physical marks on the victim, thus avoiding any social censure or legal implication. This is the result of a bigger social and legal understanding of the topic, turning violence more strategic.

Of the 68 women (89.5%) who reported having children, 34 (44.7%) reported having been physically assaulted, 48 (63.2%) psychologically, and 13 (17.1%) sexually assaulted while they were pregnant. Five participants (6.6%) reported having lost their baby due to assaults, 61.8% ($n = 47$) of women claimed to have had children with some of the attackers after the assaults had begun, and 81.6% ($n = 62$) confirmed that some of their children watched them getting beaten. The most common behaviors of children were crying (72%), supporting and upholding the victim (48%), encouraging divorce/separation (37%), trying to calm the victim (25%), and lastly, trying to separate the aggressor and the victim (23%).

Investigation has shown us that this reality results in a series of consequences in cognitive, behavioral, and emotional terms for the descendants (Black et al., 2008; Coutinho and Sani, 2008; Matos, 2006; Sani, 2006), with the appearance of silenced victims (Holt et al., 2008). Although it digresses from this work's aim, we think it's important to note that despite the exposure to interparental violence being classified by norm as vicarious victimization, we think that it makes more sense given the foregoing that it should also be considered as direct victimization.

It is important to speak of children exposed to interparental violence because there is a range of situations to which the child is subjected, such as directly witnessing the abuse, being in a corner listening, being in their room trying to sleep and hearing the sounds of bodies in conflict, seeing marks of violence the next day, and experiencing a strange environment in the relationship with their parents. Therefore, exposure to interparental violence constitutes a form of bad psychological treatment as it terrorizes the child. For example, when you create a climate of fear, it oppresses and forces the child to live in a hostile and dangerous environment and exposes them to negative and limited models that encourage violent behavior.

We must mention that the exposure to interparental violence must be taken into account when regulating the parental responsibilities, which sometimes results in grounded refusals toward the assaulting parent. To understand the child refusing visits and to allow stability and safety in their life, it would be convenient for the experts who make social reports and tests to have specific formation regarding domestic violence. This way we don't run the risk of misinterpreting a dangerous situation for a child as a mere conflict to be solved through coercive measures or moralistic advice to the parents (Sottomayor, 2014).

Domestic violence has remained mostly outside the regulatory processes of parental responsibilities, marked with typified agreements that women lack the power to negotiate using formally equal reasoning that focuses on the combined exercise of parental responsibilities and the right to visit the offending parent (usually the father), at the expense of the security of the adult victim (usually the mother) and children. Thus remains the myth (thing or person who does not exist, but is supposed real) according to which a man can be aggressive with the woman but good for the children.

Experience has clearly shown that violence continues after separation or divorce, and that children are directly affected when they seek to protect the mother or indirectly attend the violence. A legislative framework exists that focuses on the combined exercise of parental responsibilities, women are subject to having to contact the aggressor, to make decisions regarding their children and to comply with coercive regulated visits, even at the refusal of the child, under penalty of being prosecuted criminally for kidnapping of minors which punishes the breach of coexistence arrangements with the other parent.

To avoid unjustified criminal threats against women and to protect children, the male parent visitation rights, in cases of evidence or suspicion of domestic violence, should be suspended, or at least there should be adequate supervision as a protective measure.

Judicial decisions should reflect the fears and security needs of women and children victims of violence. Visits should not be imposed in cases of evidence or suspicion of domestic violence. The visit should not cause a danger to the health, safety, education, or moral formation of the child. In other words, decisions should be aimed at child protection and not for maintaining this relationship with both parents, because frequently the relationship with the parent is dysfunctional or nonexistent.

According to the Council of Europe Convention on preventing and combating violence against women and domestic violence (Istanbul, May 11, 2011), specifically Article 31:

"1. Parties shall take the necessary legislative or other measures to ensure that in the determination of custody and visitation rights of children, incidents of violence covered by the scope of this Convention are taken into account.

2. Parties shall take the necessary legislative or other measures to ensure that the exercise of any visitation or custody rights does not jeopardise the rights and safety of the victim or children."

We now refer to a case of a teenager who watched her father assault her mother for many years. One of her favorite activities was writing song lyrics. One day when she was at the safe house and anxiously waited for the tribunal's response regarding the responsibility regulations, she wrote a song for her father.

*You are nothing to me*
*You are nothing more*
*You are something less*
*You are a trash*

*You fuck my mom, you fuck my sister*
*And fuck my whole fucking life*
*You motherfucker you don't know how sick*
*You make me' cause*
*Every time I think of you I puke*

In another song's lyrics that she wrote titled "Put a bullet in my head" she tried to show the impact of the violence she was exposed to, writing:

*It's been a while*
*Since I realized*
*I am not so cool*
*And I'll never be*

*Now, I am on this one way road*
*And I aint got no way back*
*I am too fucked up for life*
*And my world became black*

It was found that, on average, violence in relationships starts about two years into the relationship and the victim takes approximately 13 years to report it or ask for support. It is a rather long period of time since the first aggression until the complaint or request for support, confirmed by other studies (cf., Arroyo, 2004; Matos, 2006). We believe this reality highlights the shared perspective of the chapter regarding the importance of the victim's accountability in order to shift from a submissive stance to an active one.

The most frequent reporting place was the *Polícia de Segurança Pública* (Portuguese Public Security Police, PSP) (34.2%; $n = 26$) and the *Guarda Nacional Republicana* (Portuguese National Republican Guard, GNR) (32.9%; $n = 25$). It is important to emphasize here the relevance of the criminal police bodies having a specific highly trained and competent response to the phenomenon under study. This is a situation that involves beneficial effects in preventing secondary victimization, as mentioned previously. We found a significant contribution in the work of Almeida and Soeiro (2010) relative to the development of a specific tool to assist the police specifically in domestic violence risk assessment (Spousal Violence Risk Assessment: Police version; SARA:PV).

About 35% ($n = 26$) of the participants have stated that reporting their cases was ineffective. The reasons given are firstly due to the fact that the legal system failed to deal with the complaint and the victim withdrawing said complaint, not collaborating with the progress of the proceedings. Combining this fact with the average time calculated for the participant to motivate herself to report or ask for support, as well as with a number of representations (eg, depreciation of psychological damage) either from the judge or society itself, we admit the possibility of the victim's credibility being distorted, influencing the processes to become void. Another possible explanation would be the frequent lack of physical or biological evidence with enough probative value, opening a way for the operation of the principle of in dubio pro reo (Santos, 1997).

Table 2.8 shows us the victims' perception of suffering caused by spousal violence.

With 10 being the lowest number, the data showed that psychological violence causes extreme suffering, being much higher than physical or sexual violence. Thus, psychological violence was marked by most participants (94.7%; $n = 72$) as the biggest cause of suffering, contributing, according to Plana (1999), to very pronounced scars.

Statistically, the comparisons between groups and the performed correlations brought produced relevant information for reflection and comprehension of the spousal violence phenomenon.

**TABLE 2.8** Level of Suffering

|  | Physical Violence | | Psychological Violence | | Sexual Violence | |
|---|---|---|---|---|---|---|
|  | n | % | n | % | n | % |
| 1 | 7 | 9.2 | 1 | 1.3 | 42 | 55.3 |
| 2 | 3 | 3.9 | 1 | 1.3 | 2 | 2.6 |
| 3 | 1 | 1.3 | 1 | 1.3 | 0 | 0 |
| 4 | 2 | 2.6 | 0 | 0 | 1 | 1.3 |
| 5 | 5 | 6.6 | 0 | 0 | 3 | 3.9 |
| 6 | 2 | 2.6 | 0 | 0 | 0 | 0 |
| 7 | 7 | 9.2 | 0 | 0 | 0 | 0 |
| 8 | 6 | 7.9 | 7 | 9.2 | 3 | 3.9 |
| 9 | 10 | 13.2 | 5 | 6.6 | 2 | 2.6 |
| 10 | 31 | 40.8 | 60 | 78.9 | 21 | 27.6 |
| Did not answer | 2 | 2.6 | 1 | 1.3 | 2 | 2.6 |

The participants that did not search for help registered slightly higher psychopathological symptoms compared to the participants that searched for help. This data allows us to question if stronger symptomology numbs the ability to ask for help or if the result of getting help assists in reducing the psychopathological symptoms. As result of our bibliographic research, the second option requires more evidence.

No statistically important differences were found between the participants that were and weren't living in safe houses to associate spousal violence with psychopathological symptoms. This raises the necessity, in our view, to equate the type of approach that is done with the victims in these types of houses. These victims, being in a supporting psychoeducational context, even with anxiogenic burdens, make us believe that they would have fewer legitimizing beliefs for violence and fewer psychopathological symptoms.

The Catholic participants are the ones that legitimize women as the aggressor, while non-Catholic women are the ones that legitimize it the least. With this, it is important to mention *marianismo* as an important element of Latin culture that praises submissiveness and feminine sacrifice. The second case that we present in chapter "Reality" allows us to state that the participant accepted the aggressive situation as a sacrifice in the illusion of saving his aggressor (Edelson et al., 2007, cited in Machado and Dias, 2010). Another relevant aspect in terms of some religious groups is that they propose forgiveness as a mechanism of recovery (Walker, 2004), which can influence the idea that victims have regarding the violence they suffer, with more or less violence.

The participants that stated there was no spousal violence in their parents' or caretakers' relationship tend to justify violence for the need to maintain the family's privacy untouched. Results show that the participants that stated the existence of spousal violence in their parents' or caretakers' relationship present a higher level of symptoms in terms of interpersonal sensitivity, hostility, paranoid ideation, and psychoticism.

Women who don't report cases of aggression but remain in the relationship tend to legitimize and trivialize small acts of violence. Women who have not reported it but end their relationship reveal less legitimization and trivialization of small acts of violence. However, results show that women who are not currently separated believe more in the legitimization and trivialization of small acts of violence, the legitimization of violence perpetrated by women, and the legitimization of violence for the preservation of family privacy. These results show the role of beliefs in the management or conclusion of spousal violence relationships, as well as the pertinence of investigations by Machado and colleagues regarding the topic (2001, 2008a,b).

The better the person's education, the less prevalent are the values of legitimization and trivialization of any violence, legitimization of violence perpetrated by women, legitimization of violence through external causes, and legitimization of violence for the preservation of family privacy. In terms of educational level, Luria (1974, cited in Cubero and Mata, 2005) found that literate subjects, in contrast with illiterate ones, amplified their capability of reason and managed to create new types of abstract relationships. School's demands, distinct from those in everyday life, are responsible for the usage of new psychological operations or new ways of classifying the world, making way for a generalization of problem-solving rules. Scribner and Cole (1981, cited in Cubero and Mata, 2005) found that illiterate subjects argued through their knowledge of beliefs of the world. In addition, Cala (2005) concluded that as the educational level increased, the use of more abstract speech, unrelated to concrete situations, also increased. The importance of such data is easily understood taking into account that choice is a mental process for judging the advantages of multiple choices and selecting the action (Kohlrieser, 2006). This is a process that requires a certain level of abstraction.

Women that concluded their relationships present less legitimization and trivialization of any violence, legitimization of violence perpetrated by women, but higher anxiety and higher index of positive symptoms. Once again we highlight that, as a privileged crib for the formation of beliefs, culture and society are intrinsically related to the subject's psychological structure, mediating all human development (Leontiev, 2005), as well as the decision to end a relationship or not. In our perspective, the rising of anxiety matches with situational, temporary factors. These are inherent to a lifestyle change.

In conclusion, the results show that the greater the number of aggressive behaviors by the aggressor, the greater the somatization and psychoticism and the fewer the beliefs on the legitimization of violence for the preservation of family privacy.

# Chapter 3

# The Different Forms of Spousal Violence

Spousal violence can assume many forms that affect the partner, spouse, ex-partner and ex-spouse. Additionally, the theoretical divergence also occurs regarding the involved behavioral forms. Some authors (Albornoz, 2009; Álvarez-Buylla and Herrando, 2007; Antunes, 2003; Baccino, 2006; Cousineau et al., 2008; Samson, 2010) add new categories beyond the most well-known, namely physical violence, sexual violence and psychological or emotional violence (Hadley, 2009; Magalhães, 2010; Markowitz, Polsky and Effron, 2006a; Markowitz et al., 2006b; Matos, 2003, 2005; Mota et al., 2007; Sierra and Buela-Casal, 2009; Verde, 2005). We shall adopt the classification system used by most of them (physical abuse, psychological or emotional abuse) since it makes more sense in our view to do so, which makes it an enabler for better comprehension and builds an effective bridge with the practical reality.

Under the state of Minnesota's Domestic Abuse Intervention Programs, members of the so-called Duluth Model (a small community in northern Minnesota) developed the Power and Control Wheel, among others (see Fig. 3.1). After listening to countless stories of violence, terror and survival, they document the most common abusive behaviors and the most universally experienced tactics against the battered woman.

There are many authors who unanimously affirm that with the passage of time and nonexisting intervention, the mistreatments tend to rise in intensity and frequency (Antunes, 2003; Baccino, 2006; Falcón, 2004; Magalhães, 2010; Matos, 2003; Mota et al., 2007; Hirigoyen, 2006; Walker, 1986; Woffordt et al., 1994, cited in Matos, 2005).

On the other hand, Baccino (2006) is aware that domestic violence (in which spousal violence is inserted in that group) is divided into five types of violence, namely physical aggression, sexual aggression, insults, verbal threats and emotional blackmailing and psychological pressure.

In Samson's view (2010), in addition to emotional, physical and sexual abuse, there is the spiritual background. By spiritual violence, Samson (2010) states that it is disrespectful toward the beliefs, interests and tastes of the victim, canceling their individuality. Religious life is just one component of this type of violence. The author points out three reasons for this type of behavior, namely

Forensic Psychology of Spousal Violence. http://dx.doi.org/10.1016/B978-0-12-803533-7.00003-X
**33**

**FIGURE 3.1** Power and control wheel. *Source:* http://www.theduluthmodel.org/pdf/Power andControl.pdf.

the urge to have the victim available at all times, to isolate her and fear the success the victim might achieve.

González (2010) alludes to environmental violence, which corresponds to any type of violence directed at furniture or household objects. Commonly, environmental violence is confined to the victim's belongings, such as objects of sentimental value, clothing, cosmetics and even pets.

As we shall see later, the last two situations of violence mentioned are part of the domain of psychological or emotional abuse.

In 1994, Walker argued that the acts of violence inflicted on women may be varied in nature, allowing us to speak of a multiple victimization. This mainly includes physical abuse, social isolation, intimidation, emotional mistreatments, verbal and psychological abuse, use of male privileges, threats, sexual violence and economic control (Matos, 2003).

Esplugues (2008) establishes the idea of family violence (which is part of spousal violence) with a distinction between active violence and passive violence. In the former, the aggressor acts in any way and can take different action patterns. The latter is in regard to inactions or intentional omissions.

Similar to what we found in our bibliography, we will use the notions of violence (abuse and aggression) as synonyms in order to make the text more fluid and less repetitive.

## PHYSICAL VIOLENCE

For Samson (2010), physical violence has three objectives, specifically, to restrict the victim's movements, control her and make her feel fear. Its severity can vary depending on the victim's resistance level, her health before the assault and the force exerted to the point where even seemingly less severe movements can cause deep or even fatal wounds (Magalhães, 2010).

Physical violence is the most common manifestation of violence. It can be limited to the use of material and intentional force against a person, voluntarily causing them one or two wounds of variable seriousness. This form of violence refers to any intentional act (not accidental) that causes or may cause physical damage to the victim. Such damage can take the form of physical injuries, asphyxiation or intoxication. It may represent a single or repeated occurrence. It may also leave (or not) evident marks to the extent that often the injuries are located in less visible areas. Sometimes injuries are just internal and may not even be manifested (eg, submersion in cold water). The most typical forms of physical violence are pushing, punching, slapping, pulling hair, pulling ears, kicking, biting, pinching, squeezing, head-butting, hitting the victim's head against a hard surface or wall, violent shaking, suffocation, choking, strangulation, immersion, burning and intoxication (Magalhães, 2010). It also includes throwing objects violently toward the victim (Walker, 1994, cited in Matos, 2003).

Certain practices cause the victim-specific injuries such as those resulting from choking attempts with small reddish, dotted spots, arranged linearly on the neck and sometimes with fingernail marks as a result from finger pressure. It is difficult to present a generic list of these markers that are seen as injuries (Magalhães, 2010).

Common patterns of injury in episodes of domestic violence are the marks caused by blows, showing the outlines of the fingers, bruising (hematoma due to bleeding, which occurs in the soft tissues as a result of a rupture of blood vessels as a result of the trauma's strength) in a sinuous or linear shape due to the use of belts or ropes, bruises due to the pressure exerted by the fingers, scratches caused by fingernails, parallel bruises due to contact with an object, bruises caused by shoe soles and heels, and semicircular injuries due to bites (Markowitz et al., 2006a).

According to the study by Machado et al. (2001), the most common actions are slaps in the face, violent pushing and throwing objects. Perpetrators can use sticks, cutting or firing weapons, ropes or similar objects to tie up or tighten, and corrosive materials, among others (Magalhães, 2010).

This type of violence commonly drives the victim to the emergency room and be the subject of further police or judicial intervention (Plana, 1999). However, according to Arroyo (2004), these physical injuries do not require much medical treatment in most cases, with the average recovery time being about six days. The greatest exception is the more serious injuries caused by weapons. In these cases the injuries can be very serious or even lethal.

When physical abuses are not frequent, women rarely feel victimized (Hirigoyen, 2006). This idea is particularly important when studying the victim's understanding of herself and of the relationship that she remains in, which are central aspects in this investigation.

In the context of physical injuries, what is important is the description of injury/injuries, the mechanism that caused suffering stated by the victim, compatibility in terms of causation, the need for medical assistance and treatment (surgery, temporary and permanent consequences, the effect on generic and occupational activities) (Álvarez, 2007). It is advisable to follow the description with diagrams or even photographs to facilitate observation by other professionals (eg, magistrates), the location of injuries and their presented appearance (Albornoz, 2009). This way, physicians should be encouraged to note the cause of injuries in the medical record when spousal violence is involved and, if possible, take color photographs, which should also be included in the medical record (American Medical Association, 2002).

Hirigoyen (2006) states that physical abuses are not daily occurrences. They arise when there is an inability to talk about a problem and a person cannot think and express uneasiness with words. Garrido (2002) points out that the beatings always carry a psychological burden that causes suffering to the victim. The most common pattern is the existence of physical violence as well as both physical and sexual violence (World Health Organization, 2005 cited in Pérez and Martínez, 2009).

For Hirigoyen (2006), physical aggression is the visible part of the iceberg and does not occur without psychological violence having previously existed, which is seen as a form of abuse that is more difficult to bear. Sometimes physical violence arises only when the woman resists psychological violence. In Hirigoyen's view (2006), physical violence and psychological violence are related, even though impossible to distinguish. When a man assaults a woman, his intentions are not to give her a black eye but to show her who has the authority and the only alternative is to behave well. Thus, what is at stake when violence occurs is always a matter of dominance.

For Pais (2010), physical violence is more common in lower income households and psychological violence is more common in medium–high income households, which does not coincide with the opinion of Hirigoyen (2006) stated above.

## PSYCHOLOGICAL OR EMOTIONAL VIOLENCE

In the past, psychological abuse was considered only as a result of other forms of abuse, particularly physical or sexual abuse. Now, it is recognized as a way of frequent interpersonal violence, with effects that are both short and long term (Public Health Agency of Canada, 2008, cited in Redondo, 2010).

The emotional nature of abuse must exist in conjunction with all other forms of abuse. It should only be considered in isolation when it is represented as the only form of abuse (Magalhães, 2010).

Garrido (2002) states that most studies in recent years focused on physical abuse, giving less attention to psychological abuse.

The World Health Organization in 2005 pointed out specific behaviors as psychological abuse: insulting a woman or fostering a sense of uneasiness, public humiliation, being intimidated or scared, and being threatened with physical harm (Pérez and Martínez, 2009).

Emotional or psychological abuse refers to intentional acts, characterized by the absence or failure, recurrent or significant, active or passive affective base and recognition of the emotional needs of the victim, causing adverse consequences on the balance of their emotional and social skills (decreased self-esteem). It can materialize through injury, humiliation, censure, ridicule, depreciation, threats, induced fear or anxiety, harassment, emotional blackmail, affection denial, indifference, rejection, discrimination, deprivation of decision making, sporadic abandonment, withdrawal, marginalization and blame (Magalhães, 2010).

The previously mentioned behaviors can occur in public or in private through words. We can use as an example verbal threats, frightening screams and accusations. These accusations can have a threatening or intimidating conduct, such as the destruction of objects with high sentimental value, mistreatment of pets and stalking (Magalhães, 2010).

The anticipation of an assault resulting from a threat also causes psychological harm just as an act that exists in reality. Ultimately, the emotional overload can contribute to suicidal ideation (Hirigoyen, 2006).

Zayas and Shoda (2007) considered psychological abuse as any behavior that denigrates and hurts a person's self-esteem, as well as withdrawal of emotional support, taking on a threatening behavior, limiting personal freedom and territory, and extreme jealousy. Pérez and Martínez (2009) point out that the *Instituto de la Mujer* inserts the violation of cultural or religious beliefs of the woman in the form of violence we are analyzing.

Women experience psychological abuse, specifically coercion, isolation, deprivation, threats, humiliation and emotional coldness, as being worse than physical abuse (Markowitz et al., 2006b), stating that certain words injure more that physical violence (Magalhães, 2010).

Physical abuse can occur in isolation and episodically, but the psychological pressure tends to be progressive and lasts much longer than the bruises (Markowitz et al., 2006b). Samson (2010) confirms this, claiming that psychological violence is intensely insidious for causing consequences silently. We shall explore this idea in detail in Chapter 4. Plana's statements (1999) followed the same lines of thought, considering verbal abuse a weapon that sometimes hurts more than physical pain. Devaluation insults or personal cancellation are devastating. Here are a few examples: "you're only good for washing the floor," "all you do is cling on other people," "you're only worth something in bed and you're not even that good at it," "you like to dress like a slut just to tease" and "you don't know how to take care of your kids." The goal of the aggressor by exercising this kind of violence is dominating and controlling the victim, making her submissive and unable to react or disclose the abuse. These essentially intimidating behaviors incite fear towards the abuser, vulnerability and subjugation of the victim, and feeling inability to react (Magalhães, 2010).

Perpetrators often devalue their victims through their physical aspects (eg, "fat shit," "whale," "ironing board with no tits") or compare them with other women (eg, "other women are better in bed than you," "you have less of a body than her") (González, 2010). Take into account the expressions mentioned as the combination of psychological violence with sexual violence content.

Gelles said in 1997 that emotional or psychological violence may reveal more profound consequences than physical victimization (Matos, 2003), but since it is a low visibility abuse and is difficult to diagnose, it is difficult to prove. Therefore, a large number of victims and professionals are faced with the difficulty of moving forward with effective measures (Magalhães, 2010). In 2000, Allister even considered that psychological abuse is the most difficult form to identify and evaluate (Pérez and Martínez, 2009). The opinion of González (2006) goes in the same direction, stating that the psychological sequelae are more difficult to find relative to physical consequences, which may contribute to psychological violence being more common than physical aggression, since findings and evaluation present a greater difficulty (Albornoz, 2009).

Arce (2014) recognizes that in court cases involving domestic violence, the burden of proof by the very private nature of the offense is difficult to obtain. He sought to resolve this difficulty by creating and validating a procedure for distinguishing between real and fake witnesses and the forensic evaluation of psychic damage (Global Evaluation System). Thus, the evaluation of the testimony's credibility is the cornerstone of judicial decisions in cases, especially for crimes committed in private like abuses and sexual assaults or domestic violence. The evaluation of the psychic damage is obtained by measuring the effects of a criminal act on mental health. Forensic psychology can play a key role in the value of mental injury or emotional distress associated with mistreatment.

In 1998, Weihe said that psychological abuse of men against women was identified as the most common abusive practice (Zayas and Shoda, 2007). The most common forms of emotional abuse are shouting or threats with deliberate intent to scare, insult, humiliate or turn the victim into a target of serious accusations with the intent of injuring them as well as making them watch the aggressor throw objects or food on the floor with the intention of scaring the victim (Machado et al., 2001).

To fully understand the main goal of the mental injury assessment, we require more information on its individual points. As such, we must go through the assessment of the psychological state, the need for assistance and medical/surgical treatment, the temporary and permanent consequences, the possible permanent psychological damage and differential diagnosis with other causes of psychological symptoms as a consequence of the very rupture of a long-lasting sentimental relationship (Alvarez, 2007).

Flat (1999) states that we talk about psychological violence when its effects can be categorized by the Diagnostic and Statistical Manual of Mental Disorders (DSM-IV) and the International Classification of Diseases (ICD 10). The psychological expert evidence may assume greater importance when it has a longitudinal character; that is, the repeated observations of the same variables at different times to allow the study of the evolution of symptoms.

In 1995, Picó-Alfonso drew attention to the danger of psychological violence functioning as a good predictor of posttraumatic stress disorder (Perez and Martínez, 2009).

The imprecise limits of psychological violence hinder its detection. Its subjective burden allows for a single act to have different meanings depending on the context in which it happens; the same behavior can be abusive to some people, while at the same time not to others (Hirigoyen, 2006). Magalhães (2010) considers stalking, economic abuse and social isolation as subtypes of such violence.

## STALKING

Regarding harassment (stalking), it should be noted that this is a frequent type of violence in intimate relationships characterized by a form of control by the abuser and/or a way of damaging the victim's reputation through invasion tactics in their private domain. It can occur through physical persecution, for example, repeatedly waiting for the victim outside of her workplace, calling her on the phone and electronic messaging, or even constantly sending gifts (Grangeia and Matos, 2010; Magalhães, 2010).

Persistently trying to contact the victim—on the phone, on the street, at work, sending letters, messages—may be a behavior associated with acts of extreme violence, acts of murder or homicide attempts.

Stalking has been correlated with violence against women and, when combined with physical aggression, it is significantly associated with suicide attempts and murder of the victim toward the stalker. Most women stalked by their partners or former partners had also been assaulted by them (Saavedra and Fonseca, 2013).

## ECONOMIC ABUSE

Economic abuse occurs especially in situations of violence in intimate relationships and against the elderly. The abuser looks for a way to deprive the victim of the use and control over their own money, exploiting them financially through the misuse of their property and/or exerting economic blackmail. Beyond controlling the victim's access to money, the offender may still limit access to basic goods such as food or clothing.

The sudden change of bank accounts for no apparent reason, unauthorized withdrawals, the sudden change of a person's will and the falsification of signatures for financial purposes can also belong in this domain (Magalhães, 2010). In 2006 the *Instituto de la Mujer* also described the aggressor stopping the victim from accessing a job or education as an economic violence indicator (Pérez and Martínez, 2009). Economic deprivation is another strategy used by the abuser using "money as a weapon, a form of threat" (Garrido, 2002, p. 126).

## SOCIAL ISOLATION

Often associated with economic abuse, social isolation covers various strategies in order to divert the victim of their direct social and family network. For this to work in the aggressor's favor, he prevents the victim from communicating with others, emphasizing her vulnerability and therefore assuming greater control and manipulation. This abuse can be accomplished explicitly by objectively prohibiting the victim from acting (eg, use the phone, go outside alone or meet up with others), or through manipulation in a more covert manner. Extreme social isolation is the deprivation of liberty (Magalhães, 2010).

Isolation involves progressively distancing the woman from/of her family and friends and stopping her from having any social or even occupational life. To achieve this, the attacker can suppress phones or computers. Over time, the woman might want to isolate herself to keep the peace and avoid pressure from the husband when she feels like leaving or meeting up with someone. By insinuations or lies, an aggressor can also pit the woman against people close to her (Hirigoyen, 2006).

Another way for someone to exercise control is to call the household phone or her mobile phone and force her to pass it to their children to make sure she is at home, in addition to making surprise home visits or questioning neighbors (Gonzalez, 2010).

By isolating the victim, the offender can control the victim even more, preventing those who are close to them to wonder about the meaning of their relationship (Samson, 2010).

So we see the oppression of the victim's personal annulment through methods of controlling her. These mainly focus on controlling her money, leaving the house alone, schedules, friends or family visits, work, telephone calls and communications in general, and social/professional relations (Gonzalez, 2010).

## SEXUAL VIOLENCE

This type of violence constitutes a misrepresentation of a healthy sexual context that, as mentioned in the first chapter, is immensely important for establishing and maintaining bonds between two adults sharing their lives and bodies in a union founded on love.

There is a common belief regarding sexual abuse where, in the context of an intimate relationship such as marriage, sex is a right for the husband and an obligation for the woman (Datner et al., 2003; Falcon, 2004; Hirigoyen, 2006). For cultural reasons, a significant number of women consider it their duty to submit to this kind of behavior, not considering themselves victims, which means that they do not expose the abuse (Magalhães, 2010). Some of the reasons why women indulge in unwanted sexual intercourse in their marriage is that they think it is their duty, knowing what will happen if they try to resist (eg, become a victim of another form of violence); initially they don't want to have sexual intercourse, but eventually they agree to it after a few minutes (Datner et al., 2003).

Before 1980, no state of the United States recognized spousal rape as a crime (Datner et al., 2003).

Sexual abuse involves subjecting the victim to maintain sexual activity or specific sexual behaviors, as opposed to them being allowed to have their own will and consent. The abuser may resort to physical or emotional violence, which includes threats and coercion. It may occur either outside the family context or in an intrafamily context. This means that even in a spousal relationship, a person cannot be compelled to have sex with her/his partner (Magalhães, 2010).

The victim's exposure to sexual practices or pornography, forcing her to partake in sexual acts with other people and cause injuries to her genitals like burns, genital mutilation and forced anal or vaginal penetration with objects are also part of this type of violence (Magalhães, 2010).

In 2001, Torres further mentioned possible allegations of a sexual nature like nicknaming the victim as "frigid" or "nymphomaniac" (Pérez and Martínez, 2009).

In 2005 the World Health Organization defined sexual violence as any sexual act, attempt to obtain a sexual act, unwanted sexual comments or advances, or acts to traffic or otherwise directed against a person's sexuality using coercion, by any person regardless of their relationship to the victim, in any setting, including but not limited to home and work (Pérez and Martínez, 2009).

There are many acts described by the victim during the violation committed by an intimate partner. Some examples are penetration against their will, forcing to role-play scenarios from films or pornographic magazines, forcing oral and anal sex practices, aggression during penetration, threats with weapons, forcing sex with another person and forcing the insertion of foreign objects into the vagina or anus (Datner et al., 2003). In 1989, Campbell and Alford also focused on other acts like forcing the partner to partake in a homosexual practice, sexual acts with animals or children, as well as forcing prostitution (Datner et al., 2003). Another example of sexual violence is forcing the victim to become pregnant (Hirigoyen, 2006).

In terms of sexual assault, indicators show that recovery is difficult. In most cases, there are no biological remains or injuries and even if there were, they are not always specific to the aggression in question. Sexual violence is often tolerated by the woman as she still believes it was her role, and it does not usually injure her. However, if the interval between the abuse and the forensic examination is longer than 72 h, this makes it difficult or even impossible to obtain positive results in laboratory tests for sperm research and identification of DNA profiles (Magalhães, 2010).

In 1998, Yegidis found that most spousal rape is associated with other types of violence, particularly emotional and physical violence (Datner et al., 2003), and in 2003, Krug and his colleagues stated that a significant number of women who are victims of physical violence are also targets of sexual violence (Perez and Martínez, 2009).

The numbers remain even more difficult to assess since many women only consider their experience as rape when it involves an assault (Datner et al., 2003).

We can argue that after all that we have discussed in this chapter, the different forms of violence are a key aspect worth looking out for. As we have seen, most of the time aggressions are mixed or have multiple components combining physical, psychological (and its subtypes) and also sexual violence.

Baccino (2006) states that the diagnosis is complicated, since it is the physician's role to assess whether the injuries to the victim are compatible with the testimony, which gives way for two aspects worthy of attention, including simulation and concealment.

## SIMULATION AND DISSIMULATION IN SPOUSAL VIOLENCE

In the domain of domestic violence it is possible, for example, in a case of divorce or separation, for there to be simulation of violence with self-inflicted wounds, as well as an attempt to conceal the victim's injuries, giving them an accidental reason. Recently, false allegations of domestic violence have cropped up during the regulation of parental responsibility processes. This happens in an attempt to prevent the other parent, appointed as the aggressor, from having access to the children. The seriousness of this scenario resides in the fact that it contributes (even in real cases of domestic violence) to raising doubt regarding the veracity of the information transmitted by the victim. This makes it difficult for the victim and her defense to inhibit the offender from gaining parental authority, which is seen as fundamental and indispensable in many cases regarding protection issues, whether toward the mother or the child.

In a simulation framework, the victim tends to intentionally produce marks and symptoms or overrate the violent context, revealing a noticeable tendency for exaggeration in the criminal report. However, she can attempt to conceal the situation. This is a very common isolated setting in which she attempts to conceal her injuries or aggressive behaviors, where the victim does not feel like an actual victim on multiple occasions (Albornoz, 2009).

Concealment emerges as a clear alternative in cases where the victim formulates the first complaint when she only seeks to send a warning to the offender or a simple official statement of the facts and not a determinate punitive criminal charge. In these situations, the victim omits certain situations of the event, evokes fake stories about accidental injuries, decreases the real value of the damage suffered or simply fails to appear for trial or attempts to withdraw the complaint. Later, after overcoming her adaptive capacities toward the violence and failing her attempt of forgiving the aggressor, the victim tries desperately to terminate the relationship through simulations (Albornoz, 2009).

An example of what was previously mentioned: Lisboa and his colleagues found out that in 2003, 30% of women did not state that violence was the main reason for consultation, although they went to a hospital (Matos, 2006).

Arce (2014) warns that from a psychological perspective, once psychic damage is identified, you must figure out if the violence is or is not the product of a simulation. The American Psychiatric Association considers that it should be properly analyzed in a forensic context. It should be noted that the absence of posttraumatic stress disorder does not mean that aggression is not real.

Chapter 4

# The Consequences of Spousal Violence

The theme of the consequences of domestic violence is quite complex and not particularly linear. There are elements that mediate its impact and are especially relevant during the victim's recovery. These may include the form and characteristics of violence, victim and offender characteristics, the level of relationship between them and social support networks that the victim can resort to (Magalhães, 2010; Matos, 2005).

It should be noted how important the family and social networks are. In the case of absence of these resources, the consequences will be even more strenuous for the victim, feeling completely abandoned and often in poverty and precarious scenarios (Magalhães, 2010).

It is clear that not all assaulted women experience the same effects of abuse and not all react the same way to the abuse they experience (Albornoz, 2009; Dutton, 1992, cited in Follingstad, 2003; McGrath, 2009). Therefore, when reflecting on the consequences of the abuses on the victim, it is important to consider the victim's overall functioning (eg, family, emotional, social, professional) before being assaulted, as well as their functioning and current adjustment methods after suffering the traumatic event and subsequent rehabilitation (Garrido and Sobral, 2008).

Garrido and Sobral (2008) point out that one cannot formulate general laws, ie, with a certain universality claim regarding intimate consequences of the crime. There are so many different idiosyncrasies that victims can respond with distinct patterns to similar attacks. The authors consider this as a matter of coping styles (coping strategies), cognitive adaptability resources, mechanisms of causal explanation (which are somewhat self-blaming), the previous levels of emotional stability, the existence (or not) of proper support networks and the development of expectations regarding the future.

Garrido and Sobral's (2008) stance is echoed in the 1986 writings by Lazarus and Folkman, who are authors mentioned by Green (2005). According to them the victim should not be considered as a passive agent of the event but as an active one in their adjustment process.

Despite the fluctuations between the consequences of psychological, physical and socioeconomic nature, Magalhães (2010) considers that the consequences will always be relevant. Garrido and Sobral (2008) go in the same

Forensic Psychology of Spousal Violence. http://dx.doi.org/10.1016/B978-0-12-803533-7.00004-1

direction, according to which the sequelae of the assault are extremely important. Together with the victim's reactions, they are in some cases the only record that can lead to understanding what happened in cases where they are the only evidence that can condemn the aggressor.

Markowitz et al. (2006b) claim that the assaults affect more than just the body. They target the spirit, which we understand as the psychological domain. Physical and sexual abuse originates in addition to the physical injuries, psychological consequences.

Domestic violence has devastating consequences on both the physical and mental health of victimized women and their children. Despite the fact that the physical consequences of violence are most visible, the most serious are undoubtedly the psychological ones (Hirigoyen, 2006; Kaser-Boyd, 2008).

Regarding children, Matos (2006) mentions that literature has shown the negative impact on children who experience spousal conflicts, particularly in cognitive, behavioral and emotional domains. Basically these children are more depressed and insecure with introversion problems and low social skills. It is generally agreed that children's exposure to domestic violence is a social, emotional and cognitive risk (Black et al., 2008).

Matos (2006) states that the literature is vast in terms of pointing out that the level of damage and consequences are more pronounced for abused women than for men who were victimized, whether physically or psychologically.

The consequences can manifest themselves immediately, in short or medium terms. As an example of the first consequences, we have injuries, which can be fatal.

As examples of the latter, we have psychological disturbances or changes in work performance, and even suicide (Magalhães, 2010). In extreme situations, the mood for suicide can affect the children (Albornoz, 2009).

In the short term, assaulted women commonly reveal body injuries. The most common ones are on the body surface, with special emphasis on the bruises, abrasions, hematomas, choking injuries, various wounds, traumatic alopecia (type of hair loss that occurs with some type of mechanical action on the scalp, ie, in situations of pressure or traction on the hair) and burns. In more serious situations there are bone fractures (typically in the nose), oral and dental injuries, eye injuries, neurological injuries and injuries in the thoracic and/or abdominal viscera (Magalhães, 2010).

In the medium term, we highlight "changes in sleep cycles and appetite, feelings of fear, shame and/or guilt, low self-esteem and negative self-concept (worthlessness), vulnerability (weakness or emotional dependency and lack of trust in others), passivity, social isolation … and suicidal ideation" (Magalhães, 2010, p. 100). It is also possible for alterations of body image and sexual dysfunction. There are also cognitive disorders in terms of memory (eg, intrusive thoughts about the repeated abuse), attention and concentration, including cognitive distortions (distorted readings of the events of lived situations), anxiety disorders, hypervigilance, phobias, panic attacks, posttraumatic stress disorder and a depressive emotional domain that can culminate in suicide, which may be related to pregnancy and postpartum.

Women abused physically, psychologically and sexually by their husbands, compared to women who are not abused, have more somatic symptoms such as headaches, back pain, vaginal infections and bleeding, pelvic pain, painful intercourse, urinary tract infections, poor appetite, abdominal pain, digestive problems, difficulty walking, trouble doing everyday tasks, memory loss, vertigo and chronic pain (Bermúdez et al., 2009). Albornoz (2009) adds that sexual disorders may appear as injuries or as sequelae of violent conduct in general and sexual violence in particular. The most common disorders are sexual dysfunctions such as hypoactive sexual desire, aversion to sex, orgasmic disorders, dyspareunia or vaginismus.

The severity of all the above effects varies depending on the type and duration of the abuse, as well as the level of violence and inflicted threats (Bermúdez et al., 2009; Magalhães, 2010).

Thus, the time that the victim remains in a stressful event is also known as a major factor in the appearance of psychological disorders (Lazarus and Folkman, 1986, cited in Green, 2005). Additionally, we have registered a greater severity of symptoms when the latest episode of violence suffered was recent and when the woman was sexually forced (Love et al., 2002, mentioned in Bermúdez et al., 2009).

Magalhães (2010) states that the long duration of these events, high frequency, high degree of violence (with increasing severity), events of sexual assaults, stalking, events of multiple assaults by various aggressors, degree of prevailing secrecy in the relationship, threats with weapons and death threats are factors that worsen the consequences of the assault. During the bigger stages of conflict, like during pregnancy or separation, its severity can become extreme.

According to Abbott and Williamson (1999, cited in Matos, 2011) and Schraiber (2010), women who experience violent intimate relationships have, in general, overall more precarious health indicators than women without intimate violence experiences. Heise et al. showed in 2003 that women who were abused by their husbands go through more surgical operations, physician visits, hospital entries, visits to pharmacies and mental health consultations during their lifespan (Bermúdez et al., 2009).

In the case of pregnant women who were victims of domestic violence, we have found that they are more likely to develop a miscarriage as well as have induced abortions. They are as a rule subjected to insufficient prenatal care and develop weight increase problems during pregnancy, trauma and postpartum depression. In addition, the unborn child has a higher chance of having low birth weight or less weight compared to children whose mothers were not assaulted (Markowitz et al., 2006b). According to Baccino (2006), female victims of domestic violence present twice the normal abortion rates.

In 2007, Wallace wrote that the victim's response to a crime usually occurs in three stages: the impact stage, the gathering stage and the reorganization stage

(McGrath, 2009). The first comprises the initial response toward the assault. Its intensity and duration will vary according to the intensity of the assault, the degree of injury and the perception of threat to life. During the gathering phase, the victim tries to deal with the effects of the crime in their lives. Emotions are varied and may include sadness, anger, fear or even guilt. Finally, the third stage involves reorganization in an attempt to return to daily activities. Some people may go through the three stages quickly, while others cannot complete the process.

Curiously, domestic violence is the most common cause of injuries toward women. Even more than car accidents, theft or rape (Starck and Flitcraft, n.d., cited in Álvarez, 2007). In extremis, we must remember that death comes as a more serious consequence (Magalhães, 2010).

With this introductory comprehensive approach to the consequences of domestic violence, we will now focus on the psychological impact since it is the core of this dissertation.

## PSYCHOLOGICAL IMPACT

For Matos (2005, 2011), the impact areas to consider are the cognitive and memory disorders, depressive indicators, indicators of anxiety and a wider area devoted to other aspects (eg, eating and sleeping disorders, constant headaches, addictive behaviors and sexual disorders).

In the area of cognitive disorders and memory, the elements worth evaluating are the cognitive disorganization and intrusive thoughts, recurrent memories of the traumatic event, concentration difficulties, limiting beliefs of the victim toward themselves and compromises in decision-making.

Regarding the depressive indicators, we point out the feelings of shame, social isolation, avoidance in relationships, guilty ruminations, hopelessness, apathy, obtained discouragement (eg, a belief that abuses cannot be surpassed), low self-esteem and low confidence levels, feelings of inferiority and of great vulnerability, changes in perception of self, distrust of others and suicide attempts.

Regarding the anxiety indicators, it is important to consider hypervigilance, multiple fears, perception of lack of control, self-mutilation, phobias, panic attacks, tachycardia and physiological activation. We can see in a wider perspective that there are also eating and sleeping disorders, psychosomatic disorders; that is, physical aching in response to psychological distress (eg, frequent headaches, generalized physical aching), addictive behaviors, changes in body image and dysfunctions in the sexual domain (Matos, 2005).

Echeburúa stated in 2004 that one should speak of psychological sequelae when the psychic damage has been stabilized, resulting in a permanent disability that does not disappear with time or with a specific treatment (González, 2006).

In the field of psychological sequelae, it is possible to distinguish between those derived from organic damage, psychological disorders and psychological harm. The first group occur as a result of the damage of brain structures (traumatic brain injury), such as dysarthrias, dementia or epilepsy. The second group include posttraumatic depression, posttraumatic psychosis and posttraumatic stress disorder. The third group result from chronic personal cancellation and the effect on different areas of behavior and relationships of the victim, as well as their enormous difficulty for adaptation, decision-making and emotional stabilization (González, 2010).

Therefore, to assess the level and pattern of maladjustment, the expert must attend to postvictimization consequences (eg, physical, psychological), conditions that contribute toward the intensification of the impact (eg, contextual, situational aspects) as well as skills and resources (eg, skills of cognitive and behavioral coping, support network) (Matos, 2005).

There is an empirical base that supports the high likelihood of developing posttraumatic stress disorder in women that suffer abuses repeatedly in their home (Bermúdez et al., 2009; Howitt, 2006). McGrath (2009) is more cautious by stating that one should not consider posttraumatic stress disorder as a condition *sine qua non* of victimization. This means that not all victims develop the aforementioned disturbance. Women who were more severely assaulted have a higher risk for developing posttraumatic stress disorders (Herman, 1992a, cited in Follingstad, 2003). Garrido and Sobral (2008) refer to posttraumatic stress disorder as the star of the victimizing diagnoses.

While the development of symptoms triggered by a particular psychologically painful event that is much different from the usual pattern of human experience, posttraumatic stress disorder is one of the most cited psychopathological problems in the field of domestic violence (Matos, 2005). The diagnoses require that the detected changes extend over a month, as we can see in Diagnostic and Statistical Manual of Mental Disorders (DSM-V).

---

**Diagnostic Criteria for 309.81 Posttraumatic Stress Disorder [F.48.1]**

**A.** Exposure to actual or threatened death, serious injury, or sexual violence in one (or more) of the following ways:

**1.** Directly experiencing the traumatic event(s).

**2.** Witnessing, in person, the event(s) as it occurred to others.

**3.** Learning that the traumatic event(s) occurred to a close family member or close friend. In cases of actual or threatened death of a family member or friend, the event(s) must have been violent or accidental.

**4.** Experiencing repeated or extreme exposure to aversive details of the traumatic event(s) (eg, first responders collecting human remains: police officers repeatedly exposed to details of child abuse).

Note: Criterion A4 does not apply to exposure through electronic media, television, movies, or pictures, unless this exposure is work related.

**B.** Presence of one (or more) of the following intrusion symptoms associated with the traumatic event(s), beginning after the traumatic event(s) occurred:

   **1.** Recurrent, involuntary, and intrusive distressing memories of the traumatic event(s).

   Note: In children older than 6 years, repetitive play may occur in which themes or aspects of the traumatic event(s) are expressed.

   **2.** Recurrent distressing dreams in which the content and/or affect of the dream are related to the traumatic event(s).

   Note: In children, there may be frightening dreams without recognizable content.

   **3.** Dissociative reactions (eg, flashbacks) in which the individual feels or acts as if the traumatic event(s) were recurring (Such reactions may occur on a continuum, with the most extreme expression being a complete loss of awareness of present surroundings.)

   Note: In children, trauma-specific reenactment may occur in play.

   **4.** Intense or prolonged psychological distress at exposure to internal or external cues that symbolize or resemble an aspect of the traumatic event(s).

   **5.** Marked physiological reactions to internal or external cues that symbolize or resemble an aspect of the traumatic event(s).

**C.** Persistent avoidance of stimuli associated with the traumatic event(s), beginning after the traumatic event(s) occurred, as evidenced by one or both of the following:

   **1.** Avoidance of or efforts to avoid distressing memories, thoughts, or feelings about or closely associated with the traumatic event(s).

   **2.** Avoidance of or efforts to avoid external reminders (people, places, conversations, activities, objects, situations) that arouse distressing memories, thoughts, or feelings about or closely associated with the traumatic event(s).

**D.** Negative alterations in cognitions and mood associated with the traumatic event(s), beginning or worsening after the traumatic event(s) occurred, as evidenced by two (or more) of the following:

   **1.** Inability to remember an important aspect of the traumatic event(s) (typically due to dissociative amnesia and not to other factors such as head injury, alcohol, or drugs).

   **2.** Persistent and exaggerated negative beliefs or expectations about oneself, others, or the world (eg, "I am bad," "No one can be trusted," "The world is completely dangerous," My whole nervous system is permanently ruined").

   **3.** Persistent, distorted cognitions about the cause or consequences of the traumatic event(s) that lead the individual to blame himself/herself or others.

   **4.** Persistent negative emotional state (eg, fear, horror, anger, guilt, or shame).

   **5.** Markedly diminished interest or participation in significant activities.

   **6.** Feelings of detachment or estrangement from others.

   **7.** Persistent inability to experience positive emotions (eg, inability to experience happiness, satisfaction, or loving feelings).

**E.** Marked alterations in arousal and reactivity associated with the traumatic event(s), beginning or worsening after the traumatic event(s) occurred, as evidenced by two (or more) of the following:

   **1.** Irritable behavior and angry outbursts (with little or no provocation) typically expressed as verbal or physical aggression toward people or objects.

    **2.** Reckless or self-destructive behavior.

    **3.** Hypervigilance.

    **4.** Exaggerated startle response.

    **5.** Problems with concentration.

    **6.** Sleep disturbance (eg, difficulty falling or staying asleep or restless sleep).

**F.** Duration of the disturbance (Criteria B, C, D, and E) is more than 1 month.

**G.** The disturbance causes clinically significant distress or impairment in social, occupational, or other important areas of functioning.

**H.** The disturbance is not attributable to the physiological effects of a substance (eg, medication, alcohol) or another medical condition.

Specify whether:

With dissociative symptoms: The individual's symptoms meet the criteria for posttraumatic stress disorder, and in addition, in response to the stressor, the individual experiences persistent or recurrent symptoms of either of the following:

    **1.** Depersonalization: Persistent or recurrent experiences of feeling detached from, and as if one were an outside observer of, one's mental processes or body (eg, feeling as though one were in a dream; feeling a sense of unreality of self or body or of time moving slowly).

    **2.** Derealization: Persistent or recurrent experiences of unreality of surroundings (eg, the world around the individual is experienced as unreal, dreamlike, distant, or distorted).

    Note: To use this subtype, the dissociative symptoms must not be attributable to the physiological effects of a substance (eg, blackouts, behavior during alcohol intoxication) or another medical condition (eg, complex partial seizures).

Specify if:

With delayed expression: If the full diagnostic criteria are not met until at least 6 months after the event (although the onset and expression of some symptoms may be immediate).

---

    We can also mention acute posttraumatic stress disorder (American Psychiatric Association, DSM-V).

---

**Diagnostic Criteria for 308.3 Acute Posttraumatic Stress Disorder [F43.0]**

**A.** Exposure to actual or threatened death, serious injury, or sexual violation in one (or more) of the following ways:

    **1.** Directly experiencing the traumatic event(s).

    **2.** Witnessing, in person, the event(s) as it occurred to others.

    **3.** Learning that the event(s) occurred to a close family member or close friend.

    Note: In cases of actual or threatened death of a family member or friend, the event(s) must have been violent or accidental.

    **4.** Experiencing repeated or extreme exposure to aversive details of the traumatic event(s) (eg, first responders collecting human remains, police officers repeatedly exposed to details of child abuse).

    Note: This does not apply to exposure through electronic media, television, movies, or pictures, unless this exposure is work related.

**B.** Presence of nine (or more) of the following symptoms from any of the five categories of intrusion, negative mood, dissociation, avoidance, and arousal, beginning or worsening after the traumatic event(s) occurred:

**Intrusion Symptoms**

1. Recurrent, involuntary, and intrusive distressing memories of the traumatic event(s).
   Note: In children, repetitive play may occur in which themes or aspects of the traumatic event(s) are expressed.
2. Recurrent distressing dreams in which the content and/or affect of the dream are related to the event(s).
   Note: In children, there may be frightening dreams without recognizable content.
3. Dissociative reactions (eg, flashbacks) in which the individual feels or acts as if the traumatic event(s) were recurring (Such reactions may occur on a continuum, with the most extreme expression being a complete loss of awareness of present surroundings.)
   Note: In children, trauma-specific reenactment may occur in play.
4. Intense or prolonged psychological distress or marked physiological reactions in response to internal or external cues that symbolize or resemble an aspect of the traumatic event(s).

**Negative Mood**

5. Persistent inability to experience positive emotions (eg, inability to experience happiness, satisfaction, or loving feelings).

**Dissociative Symptoms**

6. An altered sense of the reality of one's surroundings or oneself (eg, seeing oneself from another's perspective, being in a daze, time slowing).
7. Inability to remember an important aspect of the traumatic event(s) (typically due to dissociative amnesia and not to other factors such as head injury, alcohol, or drugs).

**Avoidance Symptoms**

8. Efforts to avoid distressing memories, thoughts, or feelings about or closely associated with the traumatic event(s).
9. Efforts to avoid external reminders (people, places, conversations, activities, objects, situations) that arouse distressing memories, thoughts, or feelings about or closely associated with the traumatic event(s).

**Arousal Symptoms**

10. Sleep disturbance (eg, difficulty falling or staying asleep, restless sleep).
11. Irritable behavior and angry outbursts (with little or no provocation), typically expressed as verbal or physical aggression toward people or objects.
12. Hypervigilance.
13. Problems with concentration.
14. Exaggerated startle response.

**C.** Duration of the disturbance (symptoms in Criterion B) is 3 days to 1 month after trauma exposure.
Note: Symptoms typically begin immediately after the trauma, but persistence for at least 3 days and up to a month is needed to meet disorder criteria.

**D.** The disturbance causes clinically significant distress or impairment in social, occupational, or other important areas of functioning.

**E.** The disturbance is not attributable to the physiological effects of a substance (eg, medication or alcohol) or another medical condition (eg, mild traumatic brain injury) and is not better explained by brief psychotic disorder.

In an opposite pole, some have excluded themselves from using the diagnostic category of posttraumatic stress disorder on assaulted women. They feel that this diagnosis pathologizes the normal reaction facing extreme fear (Dutton, 1996, cited in Kaser-Boyd, 2008).

According to the writings of Gleason (1993), depression is one of the main consequences for the mental health of women who were raped during their spousal relationship (Bermúdez et al., 2009), representing a major reason that pushes the victim to search for help (Matos, 2005). The severity and depressive symptoms experienced by victims are also closely associated with the severity and frequency of the abuses that they suffer (Bermúdez et al., 2009).

Roberts and Roberts (2005) allude to a strong correlation between women who suffered chronic aggression and the beginning of a bipolar disorder, anxiety disorder, posttraumatic stress disorder, panic disorder and/or depression with suicidal ideation.

According to Bermúdez et al. (2009), several studies point to the decrease of self-esteem as a major negative consequence suffered by women victims of physical, psychological or sexual violence from their husbands. Insecurity and the perception of little social support are related to low self-esteem.

A noteworthy detail is the fact that we are witnessing an improvement in self-esteem of women who reorganized their lives and are not abused today (Matud, 2004, cited in Bermúdez et al., 2009).

Some authors (Albornoz, 2009; Markowitz et al., 2006b) further state that it is common for battered women to express dissociative responses. Dissociation is related to a psychological defense mechanism in which the identity, memory, ideas, feelings and perceptions themselves are separated from conscious awareness and cannot be recovered or experienced voluntarily (Gironella, 2008).

Burgess et al. (2010) emphasize that the importance of psychological trauma lies in how the brain is affected, especially in the major regulatory processes that control memory, aggression, sexuality, bonding, emotion, sleep and appetite.

Given the above, it is understandable that the working capacity of women victims of domestic violence work is affected (World Health Organization, 2002, cited in Redondo, 2010). Another important detail is that assaulted women have a higher probability of self-medicating to alleviate the psychological effects of the abuse (Walker et al., 2009c).

As a reflection on the psychosocial effects of victimization, Carbo (2006) mentions the idea of critical perspective. This is obtained through the knowledge of the sociohistorical conditions that allowed the emergence of ideologies and victim-producing dominant speeches. Thus, the critical perspective claims that the psychosocial effects on victims result from sociohistorically produced aspects about the violence. This means that the wound that affects people is socially produced.

In short, victims of continued abuse tend to have a number of psychological characteristics. These would include an intense feeling that the victim's life is constantly threatened, generating a major personal insecurity; a tendency for isolation and hiding the incident (especially through feelings of shame associated with social opinion that culminates in a greater dependency on the perpetrator); feelings of guilt through the actions of hiding the violence (such as lying to her family and friends), concealing her attacker, sexual intercourse without consent, not adequately protecting the children; and finally, depression and low self-esteem (González, 2006).

## THE BATTERED WOMAN SYNDROME

Because of the importance and controversy that is recognized in the literature regarding these topics that we have discussed, we decided to devote some attention to the term *battered woman syndrome* that Lenore Walker first used in 1977 from a survey of over 400 women (Hard et al., 2009).

The concept refers to the set of consequential psychological effects of domestic violence on women. The explanation lies partly in the fact that some women are not aware of other alternatives that are useful for their protection when they experience the abusive situation (González, 2010). This means that according to its original design, this syndrome shows patterns of signs and symptoms that can be found after a woman has been physically, sexually or psychologically abused in an intimate relationship when the partner (almost always men) exercised power and control over her to coerce her to do what he wants without respecting her rights or feelings (Hard et al., 2009).

In 1979, Walker saw a "battered woman" as a woman who was repeatedly subjected to any physical or psychological aggressive behavior by a man with the intent to coerce her to do anything he wanted without respecting the woman's rights (Follingstad, 2003).

Walker wrote in 2000 that assaulted women come from all domains of life. There is no particular characteristic that leads the victim toward the abuse. Battered women's syndrome is present in all socioeconomic groups (McGrath, 2009). According to Matos (2006), it is considered abusive to isolate a homogeneous profile according to the concept in question. However, in a contrary view of what was stated above, Kaser-Boyd (2004) says that most battered women were abused during their childhood. In a study by Walker (1979), 44% of battered women saw their mothers being physically abused (Kaser-Boyd, 2004).

Similarly to a survival tactic, a battered woman becomes hypersensitive to the moods of her attacker, recognizing and learning details that help shape the behavior of the aggressor. These women also tend to develop psychological means to face high levels of anxiety and emotional excitement (Kaser-Boyd, 2004).

In the developed investigations aimed at "battered woman syndrome" and focused victims who killed their husband, Kaser-Boyd (2004) states that most cases included unwanted, forced and painful sexual activities, leaving the woman with a sense of lack of control over her own body. The fatal action of a woman against her man may have been precipitated by physical aggression at the time of the incident or even by a previous injury or the expectation of serious injuries at the time she killed or wounded him (Follingstad, 2003).

Battered women syndrome has been used in psychological literature as a subcategory of posttraumatic stress disorder (Hard et al., 2009; Kaser-Boyd, 2008). However, it has never been empirically shown to have the same or similar criteria (Hard et al., 2009). In 2002, Bosch et al. stated that those who defend battered woman syndrome describe it as being more complex than posttraumatic stress disorder. In addition to include the symptoms of such disorder (including rage, depression, guilt, low self-esteem and anger), they also mention somatic problems, such as sexual dysfunctions, addictive behaviors and difficulties in establishing relationships due to overdependence or absolute avoidance of intimacy (González, 2010).

The investigation revealed that battered woman syndrome has six sets of criteria that have been scientifically tested and can be taken into account to identify the syndrome. The first three groups of symptoms are the same as for posttraumatic stress disorder, while the remaining three groups of additional criteria are present in victims of violence in close relationships (Hard et al., 2009). The six sets of criteria are (1) intrusive recollection(s) of traumatic event(s), (2) hypervigilance and high levels of anxiety, (3) avoidance behaviors and emotional numbing (eg, depression, dissociation, minimization, repression and denial), (4) disruption in interpersonal relationships because of the perpetrator's power and control measures, (5) a distorted body image and/or somatic or physical complaints and (6) the issues of sexual intimacy (Hard et al., 2009).

Kaser-Boyd (2004) stresses the importance of carefully examining the battered woman syndrome because of possible malingering (intentional deception of diseases or symptoms at a physical or psychological level in order to guarantee something in return) and the implications on criminal statistics as well as custody of children. The author (Kaser-Boyd, 2004) states that women who learn about the battered woman syndrome via television or books can fake the effects of mistreatment.

Follingstad (2003) warns us of the serious problems that have been raised concerning the validity of the battered woman syndrome. The question that arises is whether there is sufficient evidence to establish battered woman syndrome as a genuine syndrome. Morse said in 1999 that in medical terminology a syndrome is the collection or objective setting of subjective symptoms that together constitute the description of a recognizable pathological condition (Follingstad, 2003). In 1994, Schopp et al. asserted that a psychological syndrome is a significant clinical pattern of a psychological functioning impairment (Follingstad, 2003).

Also according to the writings of Schopp et al. in 1994, women who suffer battered woman syndrome should be qualitatively and quantitatively different in a group of psychological variables as a way of showing that this entity is distinct from the others. This type of validity was not established on battered woman syndrome (Follingstad, 2003).

Morse wrote in 1998 that, by definition, a syndrome is pathological (Follingstad, 2003). Battered woman syndrome has never been designated as a diagnostic category in the DSM-IV-TR or even in the DSM-V. Therefore, the ambivalence between mental health professionals and lawyers has been evident in the decision to label the battered woman as a pathology or a result of abusive actions. Follingstad (2003) assumes that it is difficult to conclude any other distinctive thing that supports the syndrome as a clear and valid concept.

Battered woman syndrome seems to fail every test of a true syndrome. Namely, the absence of specific criteria, the unclear etiology, the lack of explanation on how some women develop symptoms and others do not, the lack of clarity about whether women with the syndrome should display all of the suggested features, the difficulty in proving that the presence of symptoms is different from other nosological entities and, finally, it has not been established that professionals can safely diagnose a woman with battered woman syndrome (Follingstad, 2003).

According to McMahon's thoughts expressed in 1999, the empirical key that is the basis for syndrome at hand is characterized by methodological flaws, conceptual inaccuracies and internal inconsistency (McGrath, 2009). Follingstad (2003) believes that the confusion surrounding the use of battered woman syndrome must be addressed and decisions must be made about its use.

However, in the view of McGrath (2009) Walker's works on battered woman syndrome help describe some victims of domestic violence, but not all and probably not most of them. However, despite the identified limitations, McGrath (2009) considers that Walker deserves credit for having brought the problem of domestic violence into the social domain.

Another important aspect that the syndrome we are looking at brings to the discussion is the reference to the cycles of violence.

## CYCLES OF VIOLENCE

Walker (2009a) believes that one of the most important research findings from the battered woman syndrome was the identification of cycles of violence. In 1979, Walker understood that for a woman to be seen as battered she had to go through an aggression cycle at least twice (Follingstad, 2003).

The author (Walker, 1979, cited in Kaser-Boyd, 2004) said that violence is not constant in cases of battered woman syndrome. It occurs in cycles and with violence peaks and periods of peace, ie, the abuse is episodic and unpredictable, alternating with adjusted behaviors. This fact usually contributes toward the victim not considering the behaviors she suffered as abusive, making her believe in the offender' s regret and dedication. Thus, their ability to report the abusive situation and ask for help is impaired, which is extremely important to understand this cycle and aiding effectively (Magalhães, 2010).

Walker (1986) believes that violence occurs in identifiable cycles through three stages, which is why Antunes (2003) states that the cycle of domestic violence is also commonly called the "Theory of the Three Stages of Family Violence."

The first phase (increased tension) is the critical tension period, where the abusive incidents occur discretely (Walker, 1986). For the victim, it is an added difficulty for the already difficult distinction between abuse and family conflicts. It is common for the occurrence of conflicting situations in families with more fiery discussions. The line between family conflicts and abuse is sometimes very thin. However, you can point out the molds that behaviors assume through time as a significant difference between both situations. As a rule, family conflicts tend to be resolved with somewhat consensual compromises to cease the conflict. In turn, regarding the occurrence of the abuse, the situation evolves in terms of violence where any detail, even if considered irrelevant serves as a trigger for the abuser to escalate the intensity of the aggression control over the victim. In this context, it is likely that the offender sees any behavior the victim has that he condemns or even makes fake pretexts such as hefty expenses or adultery as a reason for aggression (Magalhães, 2010).

The same author points out this first phase as the longest. The beginning of the tension is a phase that usually goes unnoticed to people outside the victim's family where "a mental darkness begins to fall on the ... clarity [of the abuser]" (Walker, 1979, cited in Garrido 2002, p. 137). We would add that from our clinical experience, the same mental darkness also falls on the clarity of the victim.

Samson (2010) draws attention to the fact that the brain structure influences the ability to speak of the event that we like or dislike. We name it metaphorically as the "garden of resentment" when someone does not talk about the events, allowing these to grow and take up a disproportionate amount of the event. Therefore, this enables the increase of tension.

The second phase (outburst of violence) is where violence is more severe and most likely to get someone's attention. It is a brief period, usually less than 24 h, and may cause severe damage, especially if it is not reported. This explosive danger stage ceases when the aggressor lowers his levels of tension (Walker, 1986).

It is common for physical abuse to end with damage, some of which may require medical help. In this situation, the abusers sometimes prevent the victim from going to a doctor in order to contain the disclosure of the abuse, which at the same time, increases the risk toward the victim's lack of treatment. Other possible scenarios are the abuser accompanying the victim to the doctor as a means of coercion in order to stop the victim from reporting the abuses. The abuser can also make fake promises to silence her. Magalhães (2010) also points out cases where the victim, even when seeking health care, conceals facts when she is asked questions that require compromising answers, making fake explanations why she has those injuries.

This phase assumes great relevance since it is many times during this period that health professionals are faced with the possibility of detecting abuse and helping victims to state the facts and/or report. If the victim does not want to do it or perceives it as impossible to do so, it is the professional's duty to report the case and start the necessary arrangements, including the victim's protection process (Magalhães, 2010).

At this stage the abuser, realizing the contours of the damage done, starts presenting explanations for his assaults. He can justify through his own issues (eg, excessive alcohol consumption or work-related stress) or blame the victim through facts (eg, unadjusted behaviors). Although they are inadmissible justifications, they are usually well received by the victim, which initiates the third phase of the cycle (Magalhães, 2010).

The third phase is the period of peace and kindness (reconciliation or honeymoon). In this period there are many gifts, gentle conversations and promises that the violent behavior will not happen again (Walker, 1986).

The abuser tries to give his justifications for the abuse some credibility by saying that he is sorry. Additionally, he makes promises stating that the assaults will no longer happen and declares his love for the victim. In this situation, the victim normally accepts the apology, believing in the offender's remorse and his promises of no more violence. This dynamic is reinforced by the victim's desire to believe in the aggressor's transformation and the desire to maintain the relationship (Magalhães, 2010).

This way, you enter a rich stage in terms of affections, similar to passion. This is a reality that thwarts the victim to submit the complaint or makes her deny the existence of spousal violence if it was previously declared, stating she lied on the origin of the facts (Magalhães, 2010). Therefore, if the victim chooses to present a new complaint in the future, the perception that others (eg, experts and nonexperts) will have of the situation will most likely leave them skeptical.

In the repentance phase, the abuser may also direct his attention to the family and the victim's friends so that they can convince the victim to forgive him. Thus, the woman believes that the attacker has changed since she feels external support (Walker, 1984, cited in Sanchez and Sierra, 2006).

This phase tends to disappear with the repetition of the cycle and the violence becoming more serious. It is therefore possible to say that "as time goes by, the risk and danger toward the victim increases, leaving them increasingly vulnerable and impaired in their ability to react, feeling powerless to break this cycle of violence" (Magalhães, 2010, p. 94). In other words, with the continuous submission to the cycle of violence, it has been noted that with time the cycle is shorter in duration while the explosions become more common. Honeymoon periods cease to exist and aggressions are increasingly impetuous because the offender believes in the idea that the victim only understands his intentions through brute force (Samson, 2010; Walker, 1986, 2009a).

Esplugues (2008) considers that, on occasion, the cycle stops only when the aggressor kills the victim. So Samson (2010) believes that the best alternative is to end the relationship as soon as possible. Walker (1986) argues that men or women are more likely to take control and put an end to the relationship precisely when they become aware of the cycle they are living. Samson (2010) advocates the need for an active role of the victim to stop the cycle of violence. Hirigoyen (2006) considers the opposite, stating that the cycle can only be stopped by the man himself.

Similar to the controversy surrounding battered woman syndrome, the theme of domestic violence cycles has also been surrounded by discussion. According to Follingstad (2003), Walker's 1984 study sample does not provide consistent support for the idea that aggression is a cyclical phenomenon. In 1986, Faigman conducted a review of Walker's data and determined that only 38% of cases experienced three phases of the cycle of violence. This means that there is no evidence to suggest that any aggressive relationships go through the cycle of violence, since there is little support for such a theory (Follingstad, 2003). McGrath (2009) still underlines the usefulness of the theory of cycles of violence as a way to describe and understand domestic violence.

We do not want to end this chapter without mentioning two additional relevant aspects to this discussion.

The first is that the consequences of abuse can be severe not only for the victim (eg, injury, depression, posttraumatic stress, job loss, homelessness, even death by homicide or suicide), but also for the perpetrator (eg, prison), for the children (eg, emotional scars, parental responsibility) and for society (eg, medical costs, loss of productivity and legal costs) (Karmen, 2010).

The second aspect is that there is a myriad of domains that are affected, such as the relational (eg, moving and/or forced separations, interpersonal difficulties), maternal (eg, how much did the violence affect the motherhood role, how it affected the children and their future life goals), professional (eg, absence from work, reduced productivity, being fired), sociocultural (eg, compliance with benevolent beliefs toward certain abusive attitudes), interpretations associated with victimization (eg, dominant feelings, fake claims of accidents, beliefs in traditional stereotypes of domestic violence and the woman's role, fear of stigmatization and occurred changes) (Matos, 2011).

# Chapter 5

# Characterization of Spousal Violence Victims

As an introductory title, it is clear that we share the position of Turvey (2009b). According to him, the victims are not just theoretical, ideological, or archetype constructions, but people. This view is contrasted with the Medieval and Absolute Monarchy Law and Order (XVI–XVIII), which attributed a guilty role to the victim in a degrading and inhumane manner (Herrero, 2007). Due to the sensitive nature of this chapter, we also took into account Herrero's (2007) warning, stating that extremes do not belong in proper science.

The word *victim* is from the Latin *victima* and has its origins rooted in the concept of sacrifice (Burgess and Roberts, 2010), where there is no crime without a victim (Herrero, 2007). The status of being officially recognized as a victim is socially constructed. It is determined by players in the criminal justice process (eg, criminal police bodies, public prosecutor) and is greatly influenced by the legislators and the media that shape public opinion regarding certain incidents (Karmen, 2010).

The concern with the role of victims in the genesis and development of the offense starts with the work of Von Heting, "The Criminal and His Victim: Studies in the Sociobiology of Crime," 1948, cited in Verde, 2005.

The word *victim* is used in modern criminal justice to describe anyone who has experienced loss, injury, or deprivation due to illegal actions of another individual, group, or organization (Ferguson and Turvey, 2009). In 1990, Manzanera said that in general the victim is the individual or group who suffers damage by their or others' actions/omissions, or even due to random events (Herrero, 2007). Rocañin, Forneiro, and Iglesias (2007) note that, according to the United Nations (n.d.), a victim is someone that has suffered a loss, damage, or injury to their person, property, or human rights as a result of a conduct that constitutes a violation of national criminal laws, a violation of the principles on human rights that are recognized internationally, or an abuse of power by political or economic authorities.

A thorough understanding of the victim and their circumstances allow an accurate reading of the nature of their injury or loss as well as provide information regarding the aggressor. We point out that "the less we know about the victim, the less we know about the crime and the criminal" (Ferguson and Turvey, 2009, p. 22).

Forensic Psychology of Spousal Violence. http://dx.doi.org/10.1016/B978-0-12-803533-7.00005-3

Exploring the dynamics between the victim and the aggressor is the key to understanding a large number of forensic and research issues. This involves the examination of the role played by the victim in her own victimization (Diaz, Petherick, and Turvey, 2009). Verde (2005) emphasizes that domestic violence includes an interactive process between the victim and the aggressor. González (2010) considers that studying the victim provides more information about the process of violence and its proper answer than actually studying the offender's behavior. Garrido and Sobral (2008) stress the importance of not forgetting that one of the direct consequences of the existence of crime is the victim as a major player required in the criminal context. Burgess and Roberts (2010) consider that there does not exist a typical profile for victims of crimes. People of all ages, population affinities, and socioeconomic levels are targets of crime one way or another.

In the first chapter of this book, marriage is defined by psychological science as a space for development and sharing for those involved. When violence erupts in the union of two married adults, we witness a negatively charged space and, in some cases, containing traces of said love by convenience that existed several centuries ago. Thus we witness the rising issue of women who are victims of domestic violence who remain in a marriage that, rather than providing personal fulfillment, is a source of suffering and destruction.

There are several studies that focus on the length of remaining in an abusive relationship and the findings are indeed worrisome. In Mota et al. (2007) sample, the average time of union between the victim and the aggressor is approximately 12 years. Plana (1999) notes in their casuistry a case of a 65-year-old woman who was beaten for 40 years. The victimization situation lasted more than 5 years in half of women surveyed by Baptista et al. (2003, cited in Matos, 2006) and half of them mentioned an experience of 15 years or more. Interestingly, victims with higher educational level recorded lower victimization periods.

In the Service Manual for Women Victims of Violence, published by the *Associação Portuguesa de Apoio à Vítima* (Portuguese Victim Support Association [APAV], 2010) there are four advanced explanatory models about the decision to terminate or not terminate the violent relationship: (1) psychological impediments (the victim remains in the relationship by virtue of individual handicaps); (2) learned helplessness (the victim assimilates an attitude of passivity and blame); (3) theory of change (the victim experiences a dilemma between staying in the relationship and the unknown, fear of a female single-parent education, economic issues due to lack of staff and community support); (4) theory of planned behavior (despite the internalization of not taking action, the victim accommodates to the bully's behavior and expects that he will change).

Several investigators have focused on the reasons why the victims are unable to abandon a sentimental relationship characterized by abuse (eg, Matos, 2003;

Markowitz et al., 2006b; Thapar-Björket and Morgan, 2010). However, in very similar conditions (eg, subject to the same cultural heritage, economic conditions, children), there are women who can stop the aggressor–victim dynamic through separation or divorce. This liberation movement carried out by some victims suggests the need to place greater emphasis on the victim's personality study, without undermining the sociocultural dimension of the problem. Zeigarnik (1981) states that a person's attitudes are related to their personality structure and needs, as well as emotional and volitional characteristics. We understand personality as the corollary of a brain's organization, structured throughout its development. It is what characterizes us as individuals and is responsible for the way we perceive the world, others, and ourselves, and the way we deal with the world. Therefore, personality is important in how we organize a response to be carried out by our behavior, as in what we want at any given time and in a given situation (Aires, 2009b).

Personality is the organizing agent or individual governor. It contains functions like integrating the conflicts and limitations the individual is exposed to, satisfying their needs, and making plans for future goals. In the words of Henry Murray, personality is located in the brain and with no brain, there is no personality (n.d., cited in Hall, Lindzey, and Campbell, 2000). In other words, personality is essentially the notion of a person's integrative unity with all its permanent differential features and unique modes of behavior, integrating in a biological, environmental, and cognitive dimension (Serafim and Marques, 2015). Thus, "loving or not…is more dependent on the characteristics of our personality than any destination written somewhere else…" (Aires, 2009b, p. 8).

## PERSONALITY CHARACTERISTICS

It is important to take into account that the victim's personality characteristics have an influence on the domestic violence phenomenon (Garrido and Sobral, 2008).

Regarding the personality of women victims of spousal violence, they appear with common features such as low scores in affection and emotional instability. They are easily affected by feelings and are described as dependent, insecure, introverted, shy, depressed, and anxious, with various somatic symptoms that have their genesis in the events of experienced violence (Arroyo, 2004).

In a more controversial stance, Alexander said in 1993 that a woman that remains in an abusive relationship and restates the love of her husband after being assaulted does so because she enjoys the whole situation or she is mentally ill (Matos, 2003, 2006). Zeigarnik (1981) states that it is possible to talk about pathological personality modification when, under the influence of the disease, it decreases the victim's interests, needs and she remains indifferent toward things that once troubled her. Zeigarnik (1981) also mentions the absence of objective and pondering in the victim's actions, as well as when they cease to regulate their behavior, not being able to adequately assess their capabilities, changing their attitude about themselves and the world that surrounds them. Esplugues (2008) thinks it is important to consider in the equation the idea that whoever truly loves them, they will respect and attempt to not make them suffer.

In this sense, the expression "women who love too much" (Norwood, 2002) is curious, referring to the obsession with a man, which is confused with love. Thus, they give the male figure room to control their behavior, and while acknowledging this obsession as a negative influence on their health and well-being, they are unable to release themselves from it. This means the greater the suffering, the more they love the aggressor. Also related to this topic, Aires and Bulha (2012) add that those who love too much love a fantasized image of the other person and not who is real without ever being aware of this incident.

The victims mistakenly believe that love and pain go hand in hand and the power of their love will be able to solve their issues. They tend to unconsciously establish a correlation between jealousy and love. In other words, jealousy breeds more love. This aspect shows that the human brain, as well as being an important resource, can jump to conclusions if left drifting, contributing toward accepting behaviors that are clearly not acceptable (Samson, 2010).

Women who report more psychological abuse show a greater preference for partners with characteristics associated with abusive personalities. On the other hand, men who inflict more psychological abuse show greater preference for partners with anxious features (Zayas and Shoda, 2007).

Similar to what happens in every romantic relationship, in 1986 NiCarthy noted that relationships with an abusive man are due to the fact that something in him attracts the victim or there is something about the victim that attracts him, stressing the importance of the psychological characteristics of family members (Zayas and Shoda, 2007). As a result, many professionals involved in domestic violence argue that in order to interrupt the abuse, a change in the pattern of preferences when choosing a partner is necessary (Kirkwood, 1993, cited in Zayas and Shoda, 2007).

There is evidence to suggest an association between abuses in the past and preferences for subsequent partner choices. In 1998, Jacobson and Gottman mentioned that the abused woman shows preferences for romantic relationships described as "on the limit," unpredictable and potentially dangerous, suggesting a link between partner preferences and victimization (Zayas and Shoda, 2007).

Research and psychological theory reinforce the ability of individuals seeking partners to confirm their relationship expectations, even if those are negative (Zayas and Shoda, 2007). In this direction, Hirigoyen (2006) alludes to the notion of psychic complementarity of the protagonists.

According to studies by Zayas and Shoda (2007), women characterized by high patterns of anxious attachment report major events of emotional abuse and physical abuse, preferring potentially abusive partners. Women who reported higher rates of psychological abuse are three times more likely to choose a potentially abusive partner. Those who had a greater psychological victimization exhibited a strong preference for partners described as impulsive, jealous, possessive, aggressive, hostile, and violent. The aggression and jealousy in male partners are attractive ingredients for a woman who experienced psychological abuse in the past and has an anxious attachment style.

Plana (1999) says that women who have endured more than 20 assaults before reporting the facts show a lower level of intellectual performance, lower determination, emotional instability, submission, and easy accommodation toward exterior factors. They show little confidence in themselves, dependency, little concern for practical issues, and end up being conservative and apprehensive. They tend to want to keep the family situation, wanting to keep their companion, not feeling the violence as such or devaluing its seriousness. They rationalize the fact that they are assaulted, do not defend themselves, and are afraid of the perpetrator.

It is essential to mention the emotional dependence of the victim toward the abuser, since strong emotions are involved (Magalhães, 2010; Plana, 1999). Thus, the way they explain the abuse is rationalization through the verbalization of conclusions where they assume:

1. That the mistreatments are a sign of the abuser's concern (eg, he is very fond of me and beats me because he is jealous);
2. That the offender is not responsible for their actions (eg, he just hits me because he's very stressed);
3. The victim is guilty of everything (eg, I behaved badly).

Therefore, the victim assumes the abuse. She will not report it and might even deny it to defend the abuser. Magalhães (2010, p. 86) adds that "it is often more painful for the victim to accept the removal of the abuser (because he is getting arrested or because she is forced to leave her household) than the continuity of the abuse."

According to Esplugues (2008) and Falcón (2004), what mainly contributes to some women supporting an abusive situation is not the economic dependency on the abuser but the emotional dependency. Arroyo (2004) states that one-third of abused women reveal an emotional dependence on the perpetrator and continue to live with it. Dependency will eventually contribute to a feeling of anxiety after separation. Additionally, the confusion between dependence and love intensifies the anguish felt by the victim because she does not understand how she can wish well to someone who mistreats her (González, 2010).

A person is especially vulnerable when direct dependency criteria is detected (eg, emotional, economic, professional), reducing capacity criteria (eg, cognitive deficits) and dependent personality traits. Consequently, the existence of one of these aspects assumes that a person's ability to freely decide is committed (Plana, 1999).

---

**Diagnostic Criteria for 301.6 Dependent Personality Disorder [F60.7]**

A pervasive and excessive need to be taken care of that leads to submissive and clinging behavior and fears of separation, beginning by early adulthood and present in a variety of contexts, as indicated by five (or more) of the following:

1.  Has difficulty making everyday decisions without an excessive amount of advice and reassurance from others
2.  Needs others to assume responsibility for most major areas of his or her life
3.  Has difficulty expressing disagreement with others because of fear of loss of support or approval. Note: Do not include realistic fears of retribution.
4.  Has difficulty initiating projects or doing things on his or her own (because of a lack of self-confidence in judgment or abilities rather than a lack of motivation or energy)
5.  Goes to excessive lengths to obtain nurturance and support from others, to the point of volunteering to do things that are unpleasant
6.  Feels uncomfortable or helpless when alone because of exaggerated fears of being unable to care for himself or herself
7.  Urgently seeks another relationship as a source of care and support when a close relationship ends
8.  Is unrealistically preoccupied with fears of being left to take care of himself or herself

---

Husmann and Chiale (2010) identify a number of features of people vulnerable to abuse, particularly the difficulty of imposing limits, hearing only what they want to hear (selective and distorted perception), high level of demand that leads to frustration when the results are not the desired, fear of conflict, of being abandoned, of being deceived (chronic indecision, not by lack of information or training but by lack of trust), and believing too much in the capabilities of others. However, the authors emphasize the excess of empathy (the ability of someone placing themselves in another person's situation without voiding their own identity) to the extent that the victims tend to forget themselves, ending up being a victim of its distorted empathic thinking in the first place. Therefore, this behavior allows abuses against people that are identified as vulnerable.

In a more extreme position, González (2010) argues that there is a need to address the conduct of the victim, since she can also be considered a controlling partner.

Matos and Gonçalves (2001) report that women with greater tendency to cling to the past remain in abusive relationships. The category of women who left abusive relationships shows a significant change process, including their narrative of the past, the present, and also the future. This approach allows alternative self-images (eg, self-esteem, confidence), images of other people, the problem at hand, their marriage, and the victimization experience. The contributions of Vygotsky (2001) on the richness of the language enabling the human to bring the past and the future to the present provide the basis for understanding these results, as well as Luria (1977) on the brain structure involved in planning and its confrontation with the results.

A fragile mental health is a risk factor for a woman to be abused in a spousal relationship (Walton-Moss et al., 2005, cited in Sierra and Buela-Casal, 2009). In 2000, Riggs, Caulfield, and Street said that in the absence of longitudinal studies, it is difficult to determine whether psychopathology is a result of domestic violence or part of its etiology (Sierra and Buela-Casal, 2009). Swan and Snow wrote in 2003 that the personality of the women involved in these relationships is also very characteristic. There is victimization of both partners through the use of abusive emotional-oriented strategies targeted at men (Matos, 2006).

According to research published by Buzawa and Buzawa (1996), women who are condescending with intimate violence suffer pathologies for their incapability of learning and for their inaction attitudes. According to the same authors, there are plenty of bibliographies that refute the idea that women victims of violence universally present a psychological numbness and that there is a homogeneous response pattern toward the abuses (Matos, 2006).

In terms of searching for help, it turns out that the five most common precipitating events that lead battered women to seek help from an aid program for domestic violence are: (1) an acute aggressive accident with serious body injuries; (2) a sharp escalation in the level of violence (ie, from shoving and slapping to attempted strangulation or stabbing); (3) an impairment in hearing and/or vision as a direct result of a serious assault; (4) a history of watching many news reports of women being brutally murdered by their partner after suffering silently for several years; (5) a serious assault on the victim's child (Roberts and Roberts, 2005).

## THE VICTIM'S UNDERSTANDING OF THE PURPOSE OF VIOLENCE AND ITS SURROUNDINGS

After presenting the main aspects related to the personality of the domestic violence victim, it is worth discussing how the victims understand and position themselves against violence and their surroundings, such as the sociocultural or economic aspects.

As evidence of the importance of reflecting on the understanding of the victim about their situation, Turvey (2009a) reports that women victims of domestic violence do not always see themselves as victims because, as in many other social problems, denial serves as a psychological means of survival.

Sociocultural aspects justify the fact that the victim could not identify violence as such or be able to resign and submit themselves to the same. Thus, a person can be abused without being able to identify said abuses and therefore not perceive themselves as the victim. Take as an example the fact that many consider acceptable the aggression of men toward women as a result of the exercise of a male-empowered culture. Magalhães (2010) lists in his work a lot of myths and proverbs whose origins are lost in time and facilitate or devalue victimization.

It is crucial to take into account the victim's perception in relation to the aggressor's acts, ie, the meaning that the victim attributes to the abuses, possibly considering them as violent or not (Ali, 2003). Sometimes victims assimilate norms and cultural speeches that blame the victim and legitimize the behavior of the offenders (Machado et al., 2001).

Victims and nonvictims are different regarding their understanding of the legitimacy factor through normalizing small assaults. Being victims of physical violence in general means that they are more tolerant of those assaults than nonvictims. Victims try to minimize violence in order to have a reason to do so and survive their spousal status (Machado et al., 2001). In the study of Matos and Gonçalves (2001), the group of women who remained in their marriages reveals more difficulties in making significant changes. The linguistic characteristics of their speech are more focused on the problem and present legitimating beliefs of domestic violence (eg, it is part of fate). Additionally, they share the idea that the attacker is moved by external influences, such as alcohol or an extramarital relationship.

In this regard, with the understanding that beliefs (religious or not) limit a clear understanding of violence, interfering as mentioned earlier. Due to the way we react to this phenomenon, we present in the following table some of the most common beliefs about domestic violence and their respective explanation (Table 5.1).

There are multiple reasons that contribute to the victim remaining in a violent relationship such as love, fear of loneliness, fear of retaliation, pride, shame, loyalty, economic barriers, difficulties with a child's custody, low self-esteem, or a combination of all or part of these. Other reasons that play a role in maintaining the relationship or marriage are cultural, religious, and related to personal beliefs and standards (Antunes, 2003; Baccino, 2006; Husmann and Chaile, 2010; Regehr and Roberts, 2010; Sánchez and Sierra, 2006). Markowitz et al. (2006b) point out some reasons for victims to stay in the relationship despite the abuse, namely the fear for their personal safety, their children's or other relatives' safety, economic matters, hopes of the abuser changing his ways, cultural or religious perceptions, family pressure and uncertainty about the viable options, especially with women with children.

Machado and Dias (2010) highlight the association between domestic violence and the patriarchal organization of the family.

Edelson, Hokoda, and Ramos-Lira pointed out in 2007 *machismo* and *marianismo* as dominant traits of the Latin culture that contribute to women enduring abusive relationships. The first is related to the sexual domain and male aggression. The second is related to the glorification of submission and female sacrifice (Machado and Dias, 2010). Pais (2010) states that in the people's culture, the weight of tradition is rooted. It makes it difficult to change and is the reason why a change of mentality represents a challenge to overcome.

One aspect often mentioned in the literature is the economic issue. Once again at this point, the core lies in the understanding of the victim facing this issue. If there are authors who claim that the economic dependence of the victim on the abuser limits her autonomy, preventing her from trying other alternatives to free herself (Magalhães, 2010), there are others that mention the fact that some women have a better professional and economic status in relation to their husbands, moving in contexts of financial independence, but even so, remain in

## TABLE 5.1  Beliefs Regarding Domestic Violence

| Beliefs | Explanation |
|---------|-------------|
| A slap every now and then doesn't hurt anyone. | Hitting is never a sign of love. It is an illegitimate and abusive exercise of power/control. Moreover, domestic violence is not from time to time but is rather a continued pattern of various violent acts committed against the victim in order to control and dominate. |
| Violence and love do not occur at the same time in families. | Even in the most serious cases there are stages where attacks do not occur, especially in the early days of the relationship. The behavior will alternate between the expression of positive emotions and acts of violence. These changes may occur depending on the domination and doubt that you wish to impose on the victim. That is why often and usually many victims continue to feel a positive affection for the aggressors even when the violence has set in, not realizing that they are harming themselves and their children. |
| Violence only happens in lower socioeconomic strata. | Victims and perpetrators come from every socioeconomic stratum, which comes across different cultural, religious, economic, and professional patterns. The difference is the visibility of violence. That is, it can occur due to an effect of stronger cultural and educational factors that legitimize violence in the lower sociocultural strata or simply an effect of the increased visibility that the victims and the perpetrators of these strata have. As a lack of economic and social alternatives, they tend to seek more public institutions for victim support, official instances of social control, and less avoidance of the monitoring of instances of social support and legal regulation. |
| Domestic violence only happens because of alcohol and other drugs. | Alcohol and other drugs are not the cause of violence. Saying they are not is not a sign of immaturity, as a lawyer once said (sadly) to an aggressor of a teenager who was institutionalized in a shelter, but a lack of discernment, and a follow-up scientific ignorance. One thing is to say that the abuse of alcohol and other drugs appear associated with episodes of domestic violence, another is to consider it as a cause of violence. It is true that the use of alcohol/drugs can be at times a facilitator or trigger of domestic violence, but it is incorrect to consider that violence occurs only because of these circumstances. There are offenders that don't drink alcohol and most of them don't attack under the influence of alcohol. Most people who get drunk or use drugs does not harm their partners. The consumptions serve as an excuse/rationalization strategy to avoid responsibility for violent behavior. In addition, the attackers, even when under the influence, do not attack random people. Usually, they get drunk away from home but wait to get home to attack their wife and/or children. |

*Continued*

**TABLE 5.1** Beliefs Regarding Domestic Violence—cont'd

| Beliefs | Explanation |
|---------|-------------|
| Domestic violence is a result of mental health problems. | Only 5–10% of offenders have some sort of psychopathology/associated mental disorder. It is difficult to recognize the idea that continued violence patterns can be committed by "normal" individuals in the eyes of society. Such knowledge means we must recognize that one of us can be an offender. |
| Domestic violence does not happen very often. | All of the existing statistics contradict this idea. Violence is common and has high costs for society. It is considered a public health problem that is the leading cause of death and disability among women ages 16 to 44, surpassing cancer, road accidents, and even war. |

a violent relationship (Aires, 2009a; Matos, 2003). If, for some women, the economic issue is the reason for accommodation and conformity, for others it does not constitute an obstacle to terminate a marriage of suffering and destruction.

Although some women suggest their children as an excuse to stay in the relationship, there are others who do not see them as impediments to rebuild a life outside a violent spousal relationship. But even if the children are singled out as an excuse, they do not wish that their parents continue together when they assault each other and cause suffering. Parents who mention the children as the reason to keep a marriage that only leaves them unhappy can be truly guilt-inducing for children (Aires, 2009a). I remember one case that I followed and have written about (Paulino and Matias, 2014), in which a teenager verbalized as follows: "Sometimes I was afraid he could kill my mother. I would just be waiting, waiting for that not to happen, waiting for time to pass, but I know that waiting for time to pass does not solve anything. We have to do something. Sometimes, I'd say I had enough of what was going on and wanted to go away. I did not want my mother to give my father any more chances."

Vilanova (2011) mentions the possibility of an actual selfish need to have a child in order to constrain her husband. However, when the birth of the child is looked upon as the wedding salvation, the only change that occurs is one more person suffering (Aires, 2009a).

When the decision to abandon the relationship is made, the children do not constitute an obstacle to divorce, but an excuse. It is important to retain that "being only a mother and not a woman does not make anyone happy…[In addition to] the weight that this emotional dependence will have on the children" (Aires, 2009a, p. 180). Thus, depending on their personal sense of life (Aires, 2012), victims can see children and fear either as inhibitors or as boosters of decisions (Baptista, Silva, Silva, and Neves, 2003, cited in Matos, 2006).

Another important element of consideration, which reinforces the importance of taking into account the understanding of the victim, lies in the management of the report, since not all victims maintain the reports until the end of the process (Rojas et al., 2002). In some cases, they return to the abusive relationship (Esplugues, 2008). The increase in complaints per se does not qualify as an effective measure to prevent the risk (Garrido, 2002). Matos and Gonçalves (2001) state that a complaint has little impact in making substantial changes in the lives of women.

Dutton-Douglas and Dionne reported in 1991 that a significant number of women who have been in a shelter returned to live with their companions and many suffered further aggression (Karmen, 2010). Hirigoyen (2006) says that leaving does not mean that women are determined to divorce. They house for a long time the hopes of getting their partner to change in a fantasy world where the rupture produces an electroshock effect, changing the aggressor's attitude. González (2010) says it's often that victims withdraw the complaint because they expect their companion to change or due to emotional dependency and the self-denial that they experience.

According to Matos (2006), the multiple occasions where the victim backs away from ending the relationship contribute to the family, friends, and professionals experiencing feelings of disappointment, disillusionment, incredulity, and even some offense. Consequently, these reactions can further compromise the victim's social support such as, for example, when a woman chooses to retry leaving the aggressor. On the other hand, a woman who reports the violence and then intends to withdraw the complaint or does not testify against her attacker reinforces the hypothesis being contemplated by the penal system as a person who does not know what they want and is unreliable (Carbó, 2006).

Women victims of more severe attacks tend to look for social institutions, while the victims of more situational family conflicts turn more frequently to neighbors and friends (Johnson, Leone, and Cohan, 2007, cited in Turvey, 2009a). A large proportion of victims does not resort to public institutions for help, but more regularly to friends, family, and religious leaders (Walker, 1986).

Regarding the resort to religious leaders, Walker (2004) states that some faith-based groups propose forgiveness as a recovery mechanism, but most mental health professionals do not consider it appropriate nor effective.

Falcón (2004) points out that when women decide to leave the abusive relationship and request help from family or friends, they are faced with various difficulties, including pressure to keep the couple together so that the children do not grow without the father and to forgive the perpetrator in order to fulfill the age-old tradition of preserving the family. In this process of understanding, only when the costs of the relationship outweigh the benefits is when the abused woman activates herself to finish the relationship. However, if her needs for dependence and obsession prevail, the end of the relationship is hindered (Walker, Needle, Hard, and Nathan, 2009a).

According to Ferraro and Johnson (1983, cited in Verde, 2005), there are six rationalizations made by the victim to stay in the abusive relationship, namely

(1) believing in an ethical salvation, (2) denial, (3) denial of damage, (4) denial of victimization, (5) denial of the available options, and (6) appeal to higher religious entities.

The appeal to an ethical salvation occurs when the victim perceives the perpetrator as affected by multiple problems (eg, alcoholism, stress), trying to save him from sources that act upon the aggressor in a pernicious way. As a complement to this situation, Aires and Bulha (2012) allude to women who, based on a serious disturbance in the perception that they have of the aggressor, engage with problematic people with the unconscious intent of saving the aggressor and the illusion that the person they love needs them, serving only their need to take care of, love, and protect him, but without ever questioning if he truly wants her.

Denial involves not taking responsibility for resolving the issue. In this way, the situation is beyond their control and even to the perpetrator.

By denying the damage, the victim does not recognize the physical or sexual abuse that she is the target of by defining the act as tolerable, normal, and legal.

Denial of victimization is characterized by self-blaming due to the received aggression, neutralizing the responsibility of the offender.

Regarding the denial of the available options, the access to legal resources and the idea of getting a new companion are seen as out of their reach.

Finally, appealing to high religious entities is part of maintaining her relationship in a sacrifice based on traditional or religious principles that the victim undergoes.

The acceptance of traditional religious values, a greater psychological impairment regarding the relationship, and the expression of positive feeling toward the relationship are favoring elements for the victim to stay in the relationship (Matos, 2006).

Because of cultural and religious traditions, some women fear the stigma of having left their husband or being part of a failed marriage. They believe they should stay in the relationship and help it change, blaming every situation on external causes such as alcoholism, unemployment or work-related stress (Karmen, 2010). We again stress the issue of the victim's understanding, that is, if the victim values the phrases "married till death do us part" or "Christ died on the cross to save her from a life of suffering," forgetting whether it is a truly uplifting relationship or not.

Matos (2006, p. 127) says in his doctorate thesis that "in summary…the decision of a woman to stay or leave an abusive relationship depends essentially on the judgment that they make of their needs, alternatives and resources perceived in each moment." We would state this based on his understanding of violence and its surroundings.

## THE IMPORTANCE OF ACCOUNTABILITY: FROM SUBMISSION TO A POSITION BASED ON ACTING UPON

As Turvey (2002) points out, blaming the victim adds nothing to the investigative effort. However, our goal, based on scientific evidence, is to emphasize the importance of blaming the victim of domestic violence who should be seeking its own autonomous posture of an adult with emotional and cognitive skills rather than the submission and conformity that facilitate the perpetuation of aggression. In this way, we avoid slipping into blaming the victim, since we are aware of the harmful consequences it might bring.

In addition, Magalhães (2010) states that the presumed fault of the violence's victim can be understood in two ways. One way argues that the victim is at fault because they acted wrong and therefore deserve a punishment under specific ways of thinking and cultural practices. Another way says that the victim is guilty because she got abused and did not move to stop the abuse, revealing ignorance and lack of information about the process of victimization. Although the victim is an adult, she does not have the capacity to react and protect herself from the aggressor or report the situation without stepping back (Magalhães, 2010).

It is in this second thought process where our understanding is related to the role of victims in the dynamics of domestic violence. However, it seems too strong to use the word *blame* due to the negative charge it socially represents. Accountability is a polysemic notion regarding the status of a subject who is admittedly guilty, as well as the feeling of guilt connected to the infringement of a rule or violation of a moral norm (Selosse, 2001).

Turvey (2009c) alludes to the term "learned helplessness" to refer to the psychological condition in which a person believes that they have no control over the situation and that any effort to change is futile. The result tends to be passivity and apathy, despite the suffering and ongoing damage caused by something that can change. Matos (2006) considers that a passive attitude predominates in victims toward their condition. Women set limits to a potential change and the construction of a new narrative in which they have rights and powers (Matos, 2003).

Regarding the accommodation of the domestic violence victim, Samson (2010, p. 68) tells the story of when certain scientists put a frog in a pot of boiling water. Immediately, the animal jumped off to save itself. In a later experiment, they inserted another frog in a pan of warm water, putting it on low heat. The frog eventually got cooked without ever trying to escape. By comparison, "in an oppressive loving relationship, violence gradually increases and the victim finds herself swept into a spiral without thinking of escaping."

Husmann and Chiale (2010, p. 20) say in a nonaccusatory way but as a warning tone that the victim is coresponsible for the maintenance of the bond, and "only after discovering this responsibility can the victim work towards abandoning that role." Aires (2012, p. 38), based on his clinical experience, says that although it is women who suffer greatly to the point of putting their life at risk, they end up "…often being accomplices for the other person's behaviour."

In terms of accountability, Garrido (2002) argues that the victims must view their safety as a personal issue and not an issue for the police, government, or courts, despite the important contribution of social support. Accounting women for the violent situations helps them face their fears (Matos, 2003).

In conflictual spousal relationships, the domain requires two protagonists, namely the one who orders and executes, gives and receives, and exercises control and the one who is manipulated. However, manipulation does not uniquely depend on the abuser's intentions. The victim plays an important role, having accountability for the situation throughout the process. Husmann and Chiale (2010, p. 96) state that "this is perhaps the best example that can be seen more clearly of the co-participation of the people we call victims."

Building yourself as a victim means you build yourself as an effect of someone else's action, reducing the ability to take responsibility for one's actions and become an amorphous agent. Blaming the aggressor is the option of placing the violence outside the relationship, but the victim must be analyzed and include herself in this relationship (interpersonal processes with the aggressor, dominant speeches) in order to change herself (Carbó, 2006). For Vilanova (2011), the woman becomes a victim when she gives up her power of decision-making facing external circumstances. Victims are sorry for themselves, they are passive, they feel helpless, and believe they are not major characters when it comes to getting what they want (Kohlrieser, 2006). When the victim considers herself as one, the woman grows the desire for the other person to change, believing that this is the sole cause of her unhappiness.

Samson (2010) stresses the importance of the victim taking an assertive role in order to communicate her disposal as a final decision, without having to defend or explain it. Garrido (2002) highlights the need for the victim to make a firm decision in order to tear off the shackles of an abusive relationship. The end of the relationship does not hurt more than the constant suffering caused by it (Esplugues, 2008).

For Samson (2010), the victim's difficulty of her terminating the relationship resides in the fact that she is still in love with the man that she idealized in the first phase of the relationship (passion), implying that she has to mourn the fantasized person that in reality never existed, as well as face the partner's real image. In the view of Husmann and Chiale (2010), the victim's difficulty is the feeling of necessity that the abuser incites on her, either by fear, low self-esteem, or through the effort of being accepted and worthy of his love.

When you have to end a relationship, it is necessary to sacrifice a few things that the victim is not willing to. To achieve this, it may be helpful for the victim to draw up a list of pros and cons about the lived relationship, with additional comments for each point (Samson, 2010). Overcoming the inertia of the subdued lifestyle of the victim requires courage and a tremendous effort. In order to end unhealthy relationships, it is critical that the victim recognizes their vulnerability and becomes aware of their responsibility for the abuse. Becoming aware of the dysfunctionality is the first step (Husman and Chiale, 2010). And remember the words of Luria (1976, p. 23) on consciousness, which is considered "…the highest form of reflection of reality…" which is not given a priori, nor is it immutable and passive, but constructed through acting and is used by humans to relate with the environment.

Consciousness as a differentiating element between the animal and man (Vygotsky, 1996) is relationally structured (Vygotsky, n.d., cited in Shotter, 2006). Without consciousness, the victim will sustain the violence in the illusion of a miraculous change of the other person or the situation. It is crucial to realize that only she can be the true promoter of change (Husmann and Chiale, 2010). Or, if one prefers, it is essential to build awareness that she is the one who pushes forward life changes. For that to happen, it is essential to point out to the victim that it is illogical to remain in relationships of abusive and annihilating characteristics, in order to promote an active attitude based on acting upon. This simultaneously influences the building of awareness and change. It is important to retain that human action is the transforming agent of nature and humans themselves (Aguiar and Ozella, 2006; Marx, 1990).

Therefore, it is then possible to see the difference between doing and acting upon in psychological terms. On one hand, the former changes the exterior, what is outside. On the other hand, acting upon incites change on the person itself, beyond changing the exterior (Aires, 2011, 2012).

In line with the aforementioned, Hussmann and Chiale (2010) state that, generally, consent is not aware and has its genesis in the victim's vulnerability, with fear starting to lose effect only when the victim begins to act upon. The authors consider that only through acting is it possible to weaken the feelings of fear. There is no other alternative.

To Esplugues (2008) and Garrido (2002), the victim needs courage to face the fact that someone is mistreating her. She must activate herself for her protection and therefore increase her alternatives, as well as accept that the person who she lives with does not love her.

Savater (2004) alludes precisely to the courage needed to choose, which is the ability to decide and make up actions. In addition to changing the reality, it transforms ourselves and distinguishes us from animals.

If the victim has sufficient firmness to tell the abuser that violence is unacceptable in any of its forms, it's possible that in some situations, the relationship ends. However, if the limits are not placed, an escalation of emotional and physical attacks is most likely (Markowitz et al., 2006b).

Women who are assertive are more likely to cease an abusive relationship, as in the ones who demand their right to be treated with respect (Garrido, 2002), because women, as Hirigoyen (2006) says, prove to be too tolerant, not knowing how to establish the limits of abusive behaviors to their companions and not knowing how to verbalize what is acceptable and what is not for them.

It is necessary for the victim to understand that the feeling of well-being due to ending the relationship and having a decent life justifies all efforts. Women who managed to end the relationship overcame many obstacles. The first step was becoming aware that there was no reason to remain loyal to a partner that assaulted them (Garrido, 2002).

A woman's choice to stay or end the relationship must be understood in terms of contextual factors and specific life circumstances that influence her decision.

Victims should be considered as those that have the opportunity to change their lives and adapt to the situation and have to seek a solution for the problem (Thapar-Björkert and Morgan, 2010). The time when women make the decision of terminating the relationship is, in most cases, the moment of greatest physical violence from their husband, says Hirigoyen (2006). Baccino (2006) complements this idea by mentioning that women who are in a divorce period report three to four times more abuses, arguing that the separation stage is a high-risk period for violence.

However, on one hand, if a woman leaving the house and relationship increases risk and severity, on the other hand, remaining in a violent environment is no solution. Victims should prepare to leave under protection (Pais, 2010). Hirigoyen (2006) points out that if the victim does not give in, the perpetrator has no power.

The strategy most reported by women who can stop the abuse is leaving the relationship (Matos, 2006). Women who ended the relationship and are no longer harassed allude to a sense of relief and peace in their lives since leaving the aggressor (Walker, 2009b).

According to research by Matos and Gonçalves published in 2002, it is possible to identify two different processes in terms of leaving a violent spousal relationship. One of the leaving patterns is the result of a gradual process—a decision built through a cautious plan with the possibility of it being supported by a professional. Another pattern is the choice to forcibly leave after a violent event involving a severe risk to the physical integrity of the victim (Matos, 2006).

Walker (2004) and Husmann and Chiale (2010) underline the importance of the victim owning her own life, being creator of her projects and the architect of her decisions—in short, the architect of her life, enjoying the "…wonderful ability to walk with her life in her hands" (Aires, 2009b, p. 10).

## STOCKHOLM SYNDROME

In a moment when one feels trapped, powerless and helpless, they become a hostage. It is particularly evident in interpersonal relationships when power, authority, or positions are abused or wrongly feared (Kohlrieser, 2006).

The Stockholm syndrome is one of the most interesting bonding and connection phenomena. It is a survival mechanism by which the hostage, in an intense shock of fear of death, starts to feel gratitude for being allowed to still be alive (Kohlrieser, 2006).

Esplugues (2008) and Hirigoyen (2006) use the Stockholm syndrome as a way to explain the victim's permanence in the relationship, since the abuser kidnaps the will of the victim, who reacts as defined by the syndrome. The victim becomes, as Garrido (2002) states, psychologically dependent on the abuser.

## BRIEF NOTES ABOUT SPOUSAL AGGRESSORS

Although the approach to spousal attackers escapes the scope of this work, we believe that a look at them, even if short, allows us to infer some information about the victims of domestic violence.

The attackers come from all cultural, educational, and socioeconomic arenas (Antunes, 2003; Baccino, 2006). They are not part of a homogeneous group, as some may suffer from mental disorders (eg, dissociative disorders), related or unrelated to the abuse of substances. Others can be carriers of personality disorders (eg, antisocial, borderline, or psychopathy) and others may still present cognitive distortions, low self-control, gaps in terms of communication and problem solving, and low self-esteem. Finally, there are still a remarkable number of offenders who are considered as adjusted and functional from the psychological point of view (Echeburúa et al., 2008, cited in Gonçalves, Cunha, and Dias, 2011).

Davis (2008) warns that many spousal abusers exhibit a different behavior in a private environment than the one they show in public. Therefore, they are seen as two different people. One is revealed to the victim while the other is presented to other people (Husmann and Chiale, 2010).

In Cuba, the perpetrators are mostly men between 25 and 34 years old. They are mostly heads of households, workers, and have an alcohol consumption habit (Rojas et al., 2002). In Spain, Arroyo and colleagues presented a different picture, in which the age of the offenders varies between 28 and 64 years, with a statistical average of 42 years old (Arroyo, 2004).

The aggressors tend to show insecurity, immaturity, instability, and low self-esteem (Plana, 1999). Most of the attackers are comprised of individuals described as violent. They present chronic alcoholism, jealousy, cultural differences, precariousness; the partner's pregnancy and the birth of a child are also triggers to incite violence (Baccino, 2006).

The abuser is usually a suffering subject, often in denial. They present relationship problems and strong tensions with a very low threshold for inciting violence (Baccino, 2006). They are described by Garrido (2002) as a "paper tiger," as he can attack and/or kill the companion, but is a coward and a loser. Narcissistic, antisocial, schizoid, and borderline traits are identified as common characteristics of spousal aggressors (Poirier, 1999). A few general factors are also brought up, such as poor socialization, irresponsibility, sexist, and compulsive behavior (Burgess and Youngblood, 1988, cited in Poirier, 1999).

The power of the aggressor is based on the cultural heritage of a patriarchal society that is justified based on the different roles assigned to men and women, which start from an erroneous principle of the capabilities and responsibilities of each person (Magalhães, 2010).

In 2007, Scott and Strauss emphasized that men tend to minimize conflict and blame the partner when they report their recent involvement in a violent act (Ely and Flaherty, 2009). Covell and colleagues expressed in 2007 that offenders with high propensity for violence experienced difficulties in recognizing the perspectives of others and in dealing with the negative nature of other people's emotions, suggesting low levels of empathy (Ely and Flaherty, 2009).

Generally, offenders with a past history of violence present an increased risk of harming their partner, even though the violence has not been directed to intimate partners or family members. Violence outside the family context is also cited as a recidivism risk factor for domestic violence and death threats (Campbell et al., 2003, cited in Saavedra and Fonseca, 2013).

Magalhães (2010) considered being young and male, developing addictive behaviors (eg, alcohol and drugs), suffering from physical or mental illness (eg, personality or mood disorders) having an immature and impulsive personality, having low frustration tolerance, high vulnerability to stress, low self-esteem, unrealistic expectations, and inability to handle responsibilities as risk factors of the abuser. She also points out as important factors the sociocultural and economic gaps, being unemployed, difficulty in establishing positive relationships with family members due to an intense professional life, presenting a history of deviant behavior and/or personal family history of violence, and misunderstanding of real needs and the possible clinical situation of the victim.

Matos (2003) notes that research in terms of risk factors for single events versus ongoing events is sparse. The few existing research works mention that there are few differences between the occasional offender and the one who is constantly aggressive. The latter category designs, with less accuracy, prison and social condemnation as a severe effect. The attackers who have violated parole, imposed coercive measures, or compliance with injunctions are more likely to reoffend than other offenders (Andrews and Bonta, 1996, cited in Adams and Soeiro, 2010).

Samson (2010) points out a number of indicators considered relevant to identifying potential attackers or the dangerousness of these, namely the derogatory way they speak of previous companions, how easily they lose control, cruelty to animals, excessive planning, lack of mutual sharing of biographies, intentions to isolate the victim, imposing life perspectives, abrupt mood swings, among others.

Garrido (2002) found that 20–40% of physical abusers of women are psychopaths.

In 1992, Saunders divided the offenders as dominant (eg, violent, impulsive, anxious, hostile) and as dependent (eg, depressed, jealous) (Álvarez, 2007). According to the publications of Holtzworth-Munroe and Stuart in 1994, spousal offenders can be understood in three dimensions, namely the severity and frequency of spousal violence, the focus of violence (eg, intrafamily or outside the family), and psychopathology or personality disorders. As such, they pointed out three subtypes: (1) exclusively family related (least violent subgroup and with a low risk), (2) dysphoric (affective state dominated by irritability, inner tension, and discomfort)/borderline (instability in interpersonal relationships, self-image, and affections with marked impulsivity) (moderate to severe violence), and (3) violent and antisocial (most violent group containing severely violent behaviors) (Gonçalves et al. 2011).

Becerra-Garcia (2015), in view of what he termed as neuropsychology of domestic violence, approached the executive functions (multifaceted construct related to the activity of the frontal brain areas including different cognitive processes such as cognitive flexibility, selection of responses, processing speed and attentional control), which are essential for the achievement of effective and adapted social behaviors. He concluded by applying the Trail Making Test (properly validated neurocognitive task). Both domestic aggressors as well as sex offenders have an executive function characterized by low performance on cognitive flexibility and executive control. Thus, the uncompromising standard of cognitive functioning is particularly important in domestic violence and sexual assault, in that it may help explain the interrelationships between both forms of aggressive behavior and psychological processes that underlie certain cognitive beliefs (eg, women are objects). Such findings raise the importance of equating the benefit of neuropsychological therapy of executive functions to enhance adaptive social responses. This intervention approach can be a complementary part of psychoeducational and cognitive-behavioral programs, usually used to treat domestic abusers and sex offenders.

Another niche that deserves special attention is the families of the police officers. Officers may present a greater tendency to mistreat their families because of their more authoritative type of work, misusing the knowledge that was given to them (Davidow and Teichroeb, 2003, cited in Turvey, 2009d). In this context, colleagues tend not to reveal the abuse for fear of being ostracized by their community and being labeled as informants, a.k.a. snitches. Those who report can be seen as unreliable. Trust is essential between police officers, especially because they must protect each other in situations that may endanger their lives. Turvey (2009d) suggests that by virtue of the fact that the offender has a firearm, a badge, and the power that comes with it, the victim fears that whomever receives the complaint is connected to the offender. The offender may have greater access to shelter networks and, finally, there is the risk that the testimony of the victim is devalued due to the accusation against an officer of the law. This is considered as an aggravating situation.

## THE CONTROVERSY SURROUNDING ALCOHOL

Matos (2006) states there is no consensus in studies about the association between alcohol and violence. Wilson wrote in 1997 that although the two variables can coexist, the truth is that they are distinct problems. The consumption of alcohol is especially harmful to the health of the individual, but the violence that may occur from its consumption mainly causes damage to the victim (Matos, 2006). Schifrin and Waldron found in 1992 that the force that is used to defend the alcohol–violence association stems from a reluctance to conceive of domestic violence as a social problem that occurs in a significant number of families (Matos, 2006).

Sometimes alcohol is suggested as a possible explanation for domestic violence. However, according to Garrido (2002, p. 144), it is important to understand that "…the aggressors hide behind something they do consciously—drinking—so they have a reason in their own view…and in the eyes of justice."

Finney alluded in 2004 to the consumption of alcohol as an important contribution to domestic violence, to the extent that beliefs can encourage the person to drink in order to gather the courage for assaulting the victim (Thapar-Björkert and Morgan, 2010). Field, Caetano, and Nelson also added in 2004 that the social and individual beliefs that alcohol generates aggression can encourage violent behavior after consumption, using alcohol as an excuse (Thapar-Björkert and Morgan, 2010).

The fact that the aggressors drink helps them to bear the burden of their negative ideas, their hostility, and their aggression. However, when they drink, their control over their behavior decreases (Garrido, 2002).

It is important not to confuse a cause with a supporting factor. Thus, Esplugues (2008) considers alcohol as a contributing factor. The educational level is considered the deeper cause of violence against women in general and violence in the couple in particular settings.

If the only reason that exists is an alcoholic addiction, violence would be exercised against all members of the family and would always coincide with the drunken state of the subject (González, 2010).

Although there is no simple relationship between alcohol use and domestic violence, it is important to note that alcohol assumes an important symptom in men with a tendency to use violence than a mere direct causal factor of aggression (Matos, 2003).

In terms of prognosis on the outcome of a therapeutic intervention in a typological or categorical division based on the differentiation within these parameters (the violent dynamics and violent acts perpetrated by spousal aggressors), it enables the identification of the attackers who can benefit from treatment and succeed, and those whose probability of success is low (Holtzworth-Munroe and Meehan, 2004, cited in Gonçalves et al., 2011).

# Chapter 6

# Spousal Homicide

Today what we consider a spousal homicide was a case of domestic violence in the past (Mullender, 2000; cited in Garcia, 2010; Liem and Roberts, 2009). Matos (2005) states that a significant number of spousal homicides imply years of violent episodes. It could also happen when the victim makes the decision to abandon the abusive relationship.

The Crime Classification Manual (Douglas et al., 2006) referred to domestic homicide as a murder that occurs when a family member or household kills another member of the household. There are two subcategories of this type of homicide, including spontaneous domestic homicide and staged domestic homicide.

Spontaneous domestic homicide is triggered by any recent stressful event or the cumulative effects of stress. There tends to be a history of prior abuse or conflict with the offender. On the other hand, a staged domestic murder is planned and can occur due to the same stressing agents as a spontaneous domestic murder. The biggest difference between the two homicides is the crime scene. The domestic homicide crime scene of staged homicide reflects an organized and controlled crime. The way the crime is perpetrated is planned and the evidence is usually removed (eg, gun, fingerprints) (Douglas et al., 2006).

It is in the context of spousal homicide that the concept of femicide arises, which corresponds to a form of lethal violence that presents a particular context because the target is a woman and the perpetrator is their intimate/romantic partner. This form of lethal violence is committed particularly in the context of domestic violence. It may involve a recent break-up of the relationship between the offender and the victim. Homicides tend to be planned and premeditated as opposed to those deaths that result from an incident of physical abuse and result in the death of the wife.

Regarding the murder of women by the aggressor, it is important to consider the existence of weapons at home, severe aggression in previous situations, death threats, obsession, addiction, jealousy, male domination, threats of homicide or suicide, depression, addictive behaviors, and access to the victim (Matos, 2003, 2005). Walker et al. (2009b) emphasize the presence of guns at home as a risk factor in the occurrence of lethal incidents.

The following table lists the main risk factors associated with the risk of spousal aggression and spousal homicide (Gonçalves, 2004; cited in Gonçalves et al., 2011, p. 235).

Forensic Psychology of Spousal Violence. http://dx.doi.org/10.1016/B978-0-12-803533-7.00006-5

| Spousal Violence Risk | Spousal Murder Risk |
| --- | --- |
| Alcohol abuse | Alcohol and drug abuse |
| Low tolerance to frustration | Access or possession of weapons |
| Low self-control | Threats with weapons |
| Low educational levels | Death threats |
| Low monetary income | Suicide threats |
| Gaps in verbal and behavioral assertiveness | Extreme dominance and power attitudes |
| Antisocial personality disorder | Obsessive and ruminative behaviors/ attitudes |
| Different religious orientations in the couple | Excessive jealousy |
| Accidental factors (eg, early marriage, unemployment, unwanted pregnancy, separation) | Generally violent behaviors |
| | Serious injuries in past incidents |
| | Psychiatric morbidity/psychopathology |
| Psychopathy | Forced sex with the victim |
| Academic and/or professional superiority of the woman | Psychopathy |
| Violence toward children | Usage of weapons in past incidents |
| Violence toward family | Violence toward family |

Another element of risk is related to the fact that the tolerance or censure toward violence may differ according to social/cultural background, or belonging to a minority or practiced religion (Campbell, 2001; cited in Saavedra and Fonseca, 2013).

Based on the main risk factors identified in the literature, Saavedra and Fonseca (2013) emphasize that the use of guns and death threats appear linked to episodes of severe and repeated violence. Men who have made credible death threats have an increased risk of recurrence of violence and offenders who used or threatened to use weapons have a higher risk of recurrence of violence and increased risk of spousal homicide.

Women threatened with death are 15 times more likely to be killed than other women victims of domestic violence.

It is known that the likelihood of attacks is further increased the longer the history of aggression remains. Studies indicate that women who are victims of strangulation attempts are 10 times more likely to be killed (McPhail, 2015; Badenes-Ribera et al., 2015; Knight, 2015; Baker et al., 2013; Klein, 2009; Dobash et al., 2009; Campbell et al., 2007).

There are studies indicating that when there are lethal outcomes for victims, often violence had increased frequency or severity in the month preceding the murder. This is a reason for that it is necessary to determine whether the episodes of violence have occurred more frequently in time or have increased in severity over time, especially in the last month.

When the partner appears to be very controlling, including situations of stalking, showing intense, obsessive, or unhealthy jealousy, we are faced with clear factors that significantly increase the risk of homicide.

The presence of violence during pregnancy and after the recent birth of a child are high-risk indicators. The aforementioned studies indicate that pregnant women whose partner assaults them are four times more likely to be killed, and if this pregnancy was unwanted by the offender, the likelihood of recourse to violence is even greater.

Research indicates that in cases of murder-suicide, there are higher rates in cases where there is alcohol abuse, history of violent behavior, and personality disorders. Other studies indicate that the victims are four times more likely to be killed in situations where perpetrators abuse or have addiction problems with alcohol and drugs (legal or illegal).

Thus, it is important to specify the presence of drugs/alcohol, which should indicate if we are dealing with illicit drug consumption (eg, hashish, crack, heroin, cocaine), alcohol, or prescription drugs (medicines), which are indicators that may increase the risk.

It is particularly important to consider a possible total eviction of the aggressor. The aggressor's difficulty in holding a job or activity due to their interpersonal/professional relationship difficulties are the reason for their partial or full availability due to not having anything on which to focus.

Control and isolation simultaneously constitute high-risk factors, being strong predictors of repeated violence. The victim distances themselves from friends and family, and the destruction of relationships and control of friendships undermine a woman's ability to get help and leave the violent relationship. As such, the existence of psychopathology by the offender can increase the degree of isolation of the victim, who may fear that family members, friends, and/or professionals do not understand and judge them for abandoning the companion as a "mental illness." Personality disorders characterized by anger, impulsivity, and behavioral instability are also associated with increased risk of domestic violence (Dutton and Kropp, 2000; cited Saavedra and Fonseca, 2013).

Garrido (2002) identifies two time periods when it is more likely for a murder to happen, which are when the woman is willing to end the relationship and shortly after the separation, extending the biggest risk period up to 2 years later. However, with the progression of the couple's separation time, the risk decreases and eventually ceases to exist as the years go by. Studies from several countries indicate that one-third to half of all women killed by partners had separated or had intended to separate at the time of the murder.

Women are particularly at risk in the first 2 months after the abandonment of an abusive relationship (Wilson and Daly, 1993; cited Saavedra and Fonseca, 2013). A survey in the United Kingdom shows that, after separation, over 75% of women had suffered harassment and violence by an ex-partner and that contact with children represented a particular point of vulnerability for both (women and children) (Humphreys et al., 2005; cited Saavedra and Fonseca, 2013), which raises the urgent need to reflect on the patterns of regulation of parental responsibilities in cases of actual domestic violence. Given these findings, the conclusion is that ending the relationship is dangerous, but so is staying.

Women are the main victims in spousal homicides (Silva, 1995; cited in Matos, 2005). Women register seven times more probability of being the victims of spousal homicide in an intimate relationship than being murdered by a stranger (Garrido, 2002). According to Liem and Roberts (2009), several studies point to the fact that spousal homicide is the only lethal form of violence where women are the main victims. Studies done by Matos (2003) pointed found that 90% of women murdered are killed by their husband or ex-partner and two-thirds of these women were physically abused before the murder.

Garrido (2002) argues that the killings within intimate relationships are much more crimes of dominance than crimes of passion, to the extent that the killings do not occur due to a sweeping attack of passion but because the murderer decides in advance the goal of the final assault, viewing it as inevitable. Thus it "is not the killer's amorous passion that guides him to commit the crime, but his inordinate self-centeredness that makes him believe that there are people who belong to him, even if said people do not want him ..." (Garrido, 2002, p. 58).

The crimes perpetrated by men are more numerous than the ones perpetrated by women. With the exception of infanticide, murder is a form of typically masculine violent behavior (Parent, 2010). Men who kill their women, partners, or dating partners premeditate their final assault for a long period of time (Garcia, 2010). Although men commit more murders than women, women commit more homicides in a domestic context than in any other sphere. In other words, men generally kill more than women in spousal homicide. However, when women kill, it is targeted toward the husband or partner (Parent, 2010).

With regard to murder perpetrated by women, most women who have committed said crime intended to put an end to spousal mistreatment. Thus, women who kill do it usually against a spouse or ex-partner with a history of associated domestic violence (Pais, 1998; cited in Matos, 2003). Wilson and Daly said in 1992 that women commit acts of lethal violence to escape from prolonged physical abuse or protect their children (Liem and Roberts, 2009). There are women who kill their husbands in order to prevent physical or sexual harm to their children (Walker et al., 2009b). However, many of the women who killed their husbands did not do it while they were being attacked (Regehr and Roberts, 2010).

In a sample of 50 women who killed their offending husbands, 38 of them used a weapon. Of these women, 78% used the same weapon with which they had been threatened (Walker et al., 2009b).

Compared with other assaulted women, the ones who killed their abusers suffered more severe attacks and experienced an escalating level of violence (Karmen, 2010).

For Matos (2005) the frequency of violent incidents, severity of injuries in women, death threats by the partner, drug use by the partner, a state of intoxication by the partner, female suicide attempts, and sexual behavior forcing the victim are all elements correlated with the killing of the aggressing husband.

Liem and Roberts (2009) stated that spousal homicide, being the most common type of domestic homicide, is also the most dominant in homicides that are followed by a self-destructing act like suicide or suicide attempt. Unlike men, women appear to choose between murder and suicide rather than a combination of both as an escape method.

Studies show that the suicide rate is four times higher among spousal or intimate relationship murderers and that the murders followed by suicide/ suicide attempts are strongly correlated with intimate relationships. It is emphasized that in this context of domestic violence, threats of suicide have been reported as a potential homicide indicator, whether they murder children or other family members. Thus, a suicidal subject should also be considered a potential killer.

In Portugal, in 2008 and 2009, spousal homicide accounted for 13% of all homicides recorded by official statistics (Ministry of Internal Affairs, 2008, 2009; cited in Matos, 2011). In 2009, there were 29 murdered women in Portugal. In 2010, the Observatory of Murdered Women counted a total of 43 murders, with greater representation in the age range between 24 and 35 (*União de Mulheres Alternativa e Resposta*, a Portuguese Women's Union, 2011). The year 2014 was marked by the death of 42 women in a domestic environment, of which 35 died at the hands of current or former husbands, partners, or boyfriends. The seven other women were also murdered in a domestic environment, but by their fathers, uncles, or in-laws. On average four women died per month, with one registered death every week. In about 30% of cases, the woman died after already being separated from the abuser, and, in many cases she was already divorced and the crime occurred when the victim started a new relationship (Anjos, 2015). Firearms and knives were the most used means for the consummation of the crime, and within the decade of 2004–14 there were 399 femicides and 464 attempts. In the analysis on the children of those victims who participated in any way in these crimes, the results indicate that 24 witnessed the murder and 11 of them had also been victims of direct physical aggression (one fatal) (*União de Mulheres Alternativa e Resposta*, 2015).

It is emphasized that in most situations there is a history regarding the crime of domestic violence. It is possible to register cases with ongoing criminal proceedings (Women's Union Alternative and Response, 2011).

Given the previous discussion, risk assessment emerges as a crucial and unavoidable issue. It is an ethical imperative, as one of the first tasks the expert has to do is assess the risk and conditions of the situation (Matos, 2006). Paulino and Matias (2014) found in one of their studies that it is critical that experts consider the issue of risk assessment and respective preparation of a security plan as mandatory in their daily work routine. However, the action of risk factors or protective factors regarding behavior cannot and should not be perceived as a causal action but a correlational one. Such correlation can be static if we focus on factors that do not change over time (eg, family history, prior history of violence), or dynamic if they treat factors predisposed to change (eg, social or psychological status). The identification of the presence or absence of these factors is essential to assess the likelihood of recurrence of violence (Campbell et al., 2003; cited in Saavedra and Fonseca, 2013).

Most risk assessment instruments of developed violence act to minimize the likelihood of a new act of violence, as in reducing recidivism or victimization. Risk assessment is based on the assumption that the knowledge of the risk factors associated with a particular problem allows us to manage them and handle them, reducing the probability of the event repeating. The risk is a dynamic and multifaceted character, so its evaluation should not be static, which forces a permanent revaluation of every situation. Thus, it should take into account the changing risk factors that contribute to the performed analysis (Hart, 2008; cited in Saavedra and Fonseca, 2013). The growing development of risk assessment tools acts a premise that certain personal and environmental characteristics can be employed in order to predict the risk of future occurrence of criminal acts (Pimentel et al., 2015; Payne et al., 2015; Chamberlain and Wallace, 2015; Rydberg et al., 2014; Makarios et al., 2010; Meredith et al., 2007).

The evolution of risk assessment tools allows us to define four generations, categories, or approaches for assessing the risk of violence. These reflect the trends in the development of risk assessment in general, beginning in the first half of the 20th century to the present day, defined as: (1) nonstructured clinical, (2) actuarial, (3) structured clinical, and (4) systematic and comprehensive (Table 6.1).

We can say that today the competence of various risk assessment tools is empirically established in order to predict criminal behavior with minimally reasonable accuracy as superior in relation to traditional clinical judgments (Pimentel et al., 2015; Ægisdóttir et al., 2006).

Thus, risk assessment in domestic violence comprises an information-gathering process about the people involved with the motive of making decisions according to the risk of recurrence of violence (Kropp, 2004; Kropp et al., 1998, 1995, 1994). It is necessary to use of risk assessment tools that allow us to address violence at the individual level and prevent it from recurrence. The main goal of these tools is prevention, namely to establish what steps should be taken to minimize risks.

The risk assessment in domestic violence includes and involves five basic principles:

1. the use of multiple sources of information
2. identifying risk factors supported in the literature
3. the informed consent of the victim

**TABLE 6.1** Summary Table of Four Generations of Risk Assessment Tools

**First Generation**
**Nonstructured Clinical Evaluation**

- During the first half of the 20th century, a first-generation risk assessment was born (Bonta and Andrews, 2007), based on a medical basis.
- Nonstructured clinical evaluation for risk assessment is intuitively based on decision-making.
- It is based on an unstructured clinical trial, usually regarding the psychopathological sphere (Pimentel et al., 2015).
- It is an inconsistent approach, since different experts can focus on different information sources and obtain well-diversified conclusions. They might end up with decisions that end up not being supported by empirical data (Feiteira, 2011; Pueyo and Echeburúa, 2010).

**Second Generation**
**Actuarial Evaluation**

- It is characterized by the use of actuarial factors, based on the empirical link between risk factors and outcome measures, with particular emphasis on criminal recidivism, emerging from the 1970s (Pueyo and Echeburúa, 2010; Andrews et al., 2006; Andrews and Bonta, 2007; Harris and Rice, 2007; Luong, 2007).
- The essence is based on the prediction of a specific behavior within a given period of time (Wang, 2014; Messing and Thaller, 2014; Kropp, 2004).
- It is possible to use statistical methods, actuarial tables, or algorithmic programs to predict future behavior (Grams and Magalhães, 2011; Feiteira, 2011; Douglas and Skeem, 2005; Grove et al., 2000).

**Third Generation**
**Structured Clinical Evaluation**

- It begins in the late 1970s and early 1980s (Andrews and Bonta, 2007).
- It overcomes some limitations of the previous categories by serving dynamic risk factors and criminogenic needs that are theoretically founded (Kang and Lynch, 2014; Kroner et al., 2007; Harris and Rice, 2007; Luong, 2007; Andrews et al., 2006).
- In this valuation model the emphasis is switched from risk prediction to risk management. This approach benefits from a flexibility that is not evident in the exclusively actuarial valuations, however being more strict than the unstructured clinical assessments (Logan, 2014; Pritchard et al., 2014; Lewis and Doyle, 2009; Doyle and Dolan, 2008; Douglas and Kropp, 2002).
- The results obtained with this approach have shown greater reliability and a satisfactory predictive validity (Feiteira, 2011).

**Fourth Generation**
**Systematic and Comprehensive Evaluation**

- It has only recently been developed and presents instruments linking the risk assessment/criminogenic needs and case management by integrating the process of risk management/criminogenic needs, selecting modes of intervention, and evaluating the evolution of the subject (Bonta and Andrews, 2007).

*Continued*

**TABLE 6.1** Summary Table of Four Generations of Risk Assessment Tools—cont'd

- It uses instruments that combine intervention and systematic monitoring with the evaluation of a broader range of offensive risk factors (which were never measured before these instruments) as well as other personal factors for treatment (Pimentel et al., 2015; Azevedo, 2013; Feiteira, 2011).
- In order to evaluate, integrate, and treat the subject, these instruments outline underlying interventions: (1) risk management process, (2) the selection of intervention methods and targets for treatment, and (3) the evaluation of rehabilitation development (Andrews and Bonta, 2010; Campbell et al., 2009).
- This approach suggests that assessments are scheduled for one to obtain information regarding the individual's development before, during, and after the intervention (Ávila et al., 2014; Feiteira, 2011).

4. the use of instruments with guidelines
5. risk management (Messing et al., 2015; Banman, 2015; Gonzalez-Mendez and Santana-Hernandez, 2014; Cho et al., 2012; Ménard and Pincus, 2012; Grams and Magalhães, 2011; Feiteira, 2011; Bowen, 2011; Almeida and Soeiro, 2010; Kropp, 2008a, 2008b, 2007; Kropp et al., 2002; Kropp and Hart, 2000).

The first principle of risk assessment requires that the evaluator/expert get multiple sources of information through different methods. Ideally, intimate partner violence risk assessment should be based on interviews with the offender, the victim, consulting the criminal record, psychological assessment, as well as other sources of information regarded as relevant by the examiner.

The second principle is based on the care that the evaluator should have in consideration of risk factors, basing his results on theoretical and empirical support that can assimilate and identify multiple information (eg, history of violent behavior against family members, history of physical, sexual, and emotional abuse against intimate partners, use or access to weapons, attitudes and antisocial behaviors; unstable relationships, which includes a history of separation or divorce; agent in stressful life events, which are part of the financial problems, unemployment or recent losses, victim/witness of violence during childhood; mental problems/personality disorders; resistance to change and motivation for treatment, etc.).

The third principle points to the relevance of the risk assessment schemes for management and risk reduction, promoting itself as a major caution when it performs risk assessment based on interviews with the spousal aggressor. This process can minimize or even deny their responsibility. Thus the information provided by the victim is essential. It is information that during a trial should enable comparison with the information presented by the offender. In this context, the victim should be informed of all evaluation parameters.

The fourth principle is related to the requirement of the evaluator to use risk assessment instruments containing guidelines. At this stage the evaluator should be able to communicate the reached conclusion. It is important that this process of communication might facilitate and specify an action based on a notion of the degree of risk involved and plan strategies that will minimize said risk.

In the fifth principle, we enter a phase in which the decision process is susceptible to review and explanation based on risk management. This should be documented in detail as well as reach various experts. Here assessors should properly select what risk management strategies should be used based on four basic categories:

1. monitoring/surveillance
2. evaluation/treatment
3. control/supervision
4. the victim's security plans

Take as an example specific instruments of risk assessment on domestic violence, including the Spousal Assault Risk Assessment (SARA), Spousal Assault Risk Assessment: Police Version (SARA:PV), Domestic Abuse, Stalking and Harassment and Honor-Based Violence (DASH), Danger Assessment Scale (DAS), Domestic Violence Screening Instrument (DVSI), Ontario Domestic Assault Risk Assessment (ODARA), Domestic Violence Risk Assessment Guide (DVRAG), Brief Spousal Assault Form for the Evaluation of Risk (B-SAFER), and Level of Service—Case Management Inventory (LS-CMI).

Risk assessment tools for spousal relationships are used in various professional fields, including justice, criminology, health, psychology, social work, or police. However, due to the first intervention being carried out by the police, there has been a need for allocation of specific instruments for these professionals in recent years.

In this context we highlight SARA, which began to be used over time by professionals of the security forces. However, this instrument does not seem to be an entirely appropriate one to be used by police, except for those working in specialized units of domestic violence. This view is based mainly on it being based on 20 risk factors and requiring specific assessments related to mental health (eg, mental disorders and personality), which as noted, is not an analysis that is generally within the expertise of the police force (Kropp, 2008b).

It was in order to address these gaps that the authors of SARA (Kropp et al., 2005) developed a new tool for the police, B-SAFER, which would come later to be adopted and known as SARA-PV.

The SARA emerges as an important tool for systematic guidance and understanding for assessing and managing the risk of violence in intimate relationships. It is a checklist of predictive factors of domestic violence developed from a careful review of the literature on risk of violence, with moderate levels of internal consistency, good validity with respect to other measures related to risk in general and violent crime. The administration time is approximately 60–90 min. It comprises 20 risk factors grouped into five areas/sections, namely:

- Criminal record
- Psychosocial adjustment
- Domestic violence record
- Transgression index
- Others

SARA requires specific assessments related to mental health, such as mental and personality disorders. It aims to assess people aged over 18 years regardless of gender or sexual orientation who have a known or suspected history of violence in their intimate relationships.

It also may be useful in the evaluation of adolescents who have a known or suspected history of ongoing violence. However, users should be cautious when evaluating adolescents, because scientific research is relatively limited for this specific age group.

In a favorable environment, information collection should be based on different sources, including interviews with the perpetrator, interviews with the victim, interviews with family members and friends of the offender and the victim who can provide additional information, additional records including police reports, victim's testimonies, testimonies made by the offender, criminal record, etc., as well as psychological or psychiatric evaluation when it is suspected that the offender has a history of mental health problems.

The SARA:PV presented an assessment of 10 risk factors divided into two sections. The first section covers five risk factors related to the offender's history of violence:

1. violent acts
2. threats or violent thoughts
3. violence intensification
4. violation of court ruling
5. violent attitudes

The second section covers the remaining five risk factors related to psychosocial adjustment (eg, psychological and social functioning history of the offender):

6. other crimes
7. relationship issues
8. professional issues
9. drug abuse issues
10. mental health issues (Almeida and Soeiro, 2010).

| Spousal Assault Risk Assessment (SARA) | Spousal Assault Risk Assessment: Police Version (SARA:PV) |
|---|---|
| 1. Violence against family members | 1. Violent acts |
| 2. Violence against strangers or acquaintances | 2. Threats or violent thoughts |
| 3. Violation of parole or community supervision | 3. Violence intensification |
| 4. Recent relationship problems | 4. Violation of court ruling |
| 5. Recent professional problems | 5. Violent attitudes |
| 6. Victim or witness of domestic violence | 6. Other crimes |
| 7. Recent abuse/addiction of substances | 7. Relationship issues |
| 8. Recent suicidal or homicidal ideation/ intentions | 8. Professional issues |
| 9. Recent maniac and/or psychotic symptoms | 9. Drug abuse issues |
| 10. Personality disorders (rage, impulsiveness, unstable behavior) | 10. Mental health issues |
| 11. Past acts of physical violence | |
| 12. (Past) sexual violence and extreme jealousy | |
| 13. (Past) weapon use and/or credible death threats | |
| 14. Recent intensification of violence regarding frequency and severity | |
| 15. Violation against prohibited permanence or absence of contact in the past | |
| 16. Extreme trivialization or denial of domestic violence history | |
| 17. Attitudes that support or attenuate domestic violence | |
| 18. Severe violence and/or sexual violence | |
| 19. Weapon use and/or credible death threats | |
| 20. Violation against prohibited permanence or absence of contact | |

A lack of investment in risk assessment and management can lead to neglecting protection policies, insensitivity, and professionals who lack technical skills for intervention in these matters. This would also include the lack of specific assessments and interventions that are particularly focused on vulnerable victim groups and, for obvious reasons, also included in cases of fatalities and severe victimization (Saavedra and Fonseca, 2013). In short, risk assessment and management are not without challenges, limitations, and ethical dilemmas, as well as risk assessment in domestic violence, particularly in spousal relationships. It is essentially an information-gathering process about the people involved with the purpose of making decisions according to the risk of recurrence of violence. These existing instruments, underpinned by the support of justice and police, are presented as very important milestones in the prevention and combating of domestic violence.

# Chapter 7

# Explanatory Models of Spousal Violence

Magalhães (2010) states that the behaviors we do not approve of today regarding spousal violence have always existed throughout our human history. They were, in many eras, culturally legitimized. Still today there are societies in Africa and Asia specifically that consider violent behaviors as correct, while Western laws consider these acts as criminal. Changes are registered in terms of sociocultural characteristics, values and paradigms that are dominant in today's world, since "the ways we perceive these acts have changed. Due to the understanding that we have regarding legitimacy and legality, we now consider them as abusive according to what we now respect and consider as Human Rights" (Magalhães, 2010, p. 30).

Pérez and Martínez (2009), based on the 2003 writings of the World Health Organization, refer to the multidimensional nature of gender-based violence. Said violence is the corollary of the complex interplay of individual, relationship, social, cultural and environmental factors. Campbell and Landerburger wrote in 1995 that domestic violence is a phenomenon of great complexity in the diverse domains that it partakes (eg, psychological, social, cultural), to the extent that the mistreatment of women is a multicontextual problem (Matos, 2003).

Matos (2006) states that today the understanding we have of the reasons for family violence is not consensual. For Davis (2008), the causes and consequences of domestic violence must not and cannot be limited to a single ideological theory or a one-size-fits-all intervention. Specific gender and age studies that ignore or minimize the vast exploratory and explanatory contribution of other variables result in only partial and imperfect answers. Removing the violence committed against women from all the efforts to understand the causes, consequences and prevention of violence has proven to be counterproductive.

Assuming that there are causes and multifaceted consequences of domestic violence, it requires different and distinct interventions. Given the context and circumstances of a singular event, Davis (2008) briefly shows in his work three models, namely the Duluth model, the model of family conflict and the psychological model.

According to the Duluth model, domestic violence reflects a patriarchal organization of society. It is the man who uses violence to create a dominating role in the family. The male behavior is the result of sexism, as well as standards and customs that are learned culturally, with violence committed by men against women being considered as tolerable. This emphasizes the need for the victim's legal protection

Forensic Psychology of Spousal Violence. http://dx.doi.org/10.1016/B978-0-12-803533-7.00007-7

and criminal penalties for the offenders. According to Davis, most of today's criminal justice and social service interventions are based on the Duluth perspective, which assumes that all incidents of domestic violence involve power and control, and that all the assaults are not separate or different from others' family conflicts.

In the model of family conflict, abuse is the result of family tensions or the acceptance of conflict to resolve disputes, both in the family and in other social contacts. The abusers strive for an important or predominant role in the family. Any family member or intimate partner can contribute to escalate the conflict. This model emphasizes the importance of providing services to recognize the intervention needs and aspirations of the various family members while keeping the perpetrator accountable.

In the psychological model, personality disorders, premature traumatic experiences or other individual dysfunctions predispose some people to resort to violence in family relationships. Therefore, it emphasizes the need for a psychiatric and psychological intervention, sometimes for both victim and aggressor. We believe that in addition to the victim and aggressor, children should also benefit from psychological counseling.

For Davis (2008), since spousal violence is a complex and multifaceted issue, the context and the circumstances of each incident should dictate the appropriate intervention for the individuals involved. The author warns us of the risk of a limited investigation regarding gender issues, which creates a set of actions based on incomplete information, instead of creating a complete set of actions and information. It is counterproductive and irresponsible to expect that arresting and punishing the man without exploring the context and circumstances of the event or evaluating him individually will solve the problem.

There are many authors who refer to three theoretical methods that aim to explain spousal violence, namely the intraindividual, the interpersonal and the sociocultural (Antunes, 2003; Falcón, 2004; Matos, 2003). The approach to the first one focuses on the individual characteristics of the offender, as well as the personality of the victim, in an attempt to identify psychological traits and a variety of private individual issues of the women who put up with the assaults. Defenders of this type of approach assert that women who consent to violence are also pathological. Hyden (1995, cited in Matos, 2003) mentions that Gayford in 1983 sees women as fragile victims, a factor that facilitates victimization. In 1995, Campbell and Landerburguer believed that as the degree of physical attack increases, the greater the probability of relating to a dysfunctional personality structure or psychopathological disturbance (Matos, 2003).

Matos (2006) states that focusing on individual factors is one of the most widespread and particularly useful methods in order to assess the situations that involve increased risk of severe and/or lethal violence from a clinical and forensic viewpoint.

In 2000, Jasinski pointed out that with the support from the perspective of individual factors, we have developed distinct intervention hypotheses from a psychotherapeutic, medical and pharmacological point of view adjusted to the specificities of the aggressor (Matos, 2006).

With regard to the dyadic-family perspectives, we highlight the experience of child victimization as facilitator of perpetuation, especially in the greater probability that the individual will become an aggressor in the future (Matos, 2003).

In these perspectives, violence is seen as a family dysfunction product, as in poor communication, scant expression of feelings, strict rules, secrecy, lack of boundaries and isolation toward others (Machado and Dias, 2010). Through this perspective, violence is due to a family that is dysfunctional, presenting with a lack of mutual communication, emotional distance and indifference, inability to manage conflicts and talking about them as frequent changes. We can also consider poor or no coexistence capabilities, rigid and authoritarian relationships, inability to adapt to changing situations and inflexible expectations of others as other violence-inciting factors (Falcón, 2004).

Matos (2003) states that the international research suggests that women who were battered during their childhood tolerate aggressive partners more easily. The exposure to parental violence during childhood increases the risk of women's victimization during adulthood, in that it contributes to low self-esteem and believing that love can legitimize violence perpetrated by her husband. González (2010) considers that educational factors continue to be the means of transmitting gender violence from one generation to another. The relationship established with parents during childhood shapes future relations, as these models orient interpersonal relationships, whether they are family related or external (Figueiredo et al., 2003).

In 1995, Cicchetti and Toth reported that individuals with a history of abuse tend to develop an insecure bonding model as well as choose a partner with other insecure bonding models, with which they can develop a relationship where they find their negative bonding stories (Figueiredo et al., 2003). Growing up in a violent family is an element of risk for similar violent behavior in the future (Rojas et al., 2002). However, for Matos (2003) a violent past does not always correspond to a violent adult, especially if there are other mediating factors. We take as an example the contact with nonviolent male figures.

Magalhães (2010) considers that the typical behaviors of domestic violence that are part of conjugal violence differ from ordinary assaults, mainly with regard to the particular intimacy and trust of the relationship between the victim and the abuser. Therefore, the author states that it is the interaction conditions between the people involved that make it especially critical to implement measures for the identification, diagnosis, treatment and prevention of violence. Finally, the sociocultural perspectives take into account historical, social, cultural and political factors that legitimate control and male supremacy over women (Antunes, 2003; Falcón, 2004; Matos, 2003).

Authors who fall in this area place the emphasis of their research in patriarchal families, gender representations, socialization processes, as well as conflict resolution models (Matos, 2003). In addition to playing an important role in explaining the etiology of violence and its social approval, culture influences how victims experience and manage aggression (Machado and Dias, 2010).

The theories of feminist nature are frequently referred to, which suggest that men attack women in order to gain power, based on a patriarchal structure of society that teaches men to be dominant. Davidson said in 1978 that religion reinforces male supremacy and encourages women to support and pray for the salvation of their partners (Walker, 1986). This category takes into consideration that there are rigid socialization patterns on the gender role that contribute to the stereotypes found in aggressive relationships: an aggressive man and a passive woman (Walker, 1986).

The criticisms directed at the feminist approach claim that it limits its cultural approach on the gender domain (Machado and Dias, 2010). According to Davis (2008), intervention in domestic violence should be free of gender stereotypes and should become more positive and inclusive to all victims and less negative and exclusive. It should promote equality and eradicate gender stereotypes and should remain the core of the feminist movement.

Another alternative referred to by Machado and Dias (2010) is the ecological perspective, according to which the violence is a result of a complex web of influences ranging from individual conditions to the macrocultural. In this light, the understanding of family violence should cover "the developmental-psychological context of the subject (ontogenetic level), immediate family interactive context (microsystem), formal and informal contexts that influence family life (exosystem) and cultural context (macrosystem)" (pp. 18–19).

Álvarez (2007) also presents theories called rationalist, namely the theory of costs and benefits exploited by Pfouts in 1978, the theory of psychological dependence and the theory of rational investigated action by Strube in 1988.

The theory of costs and benefits states that the victim carries a weighting of the pros and cons related to keeping the relationship, deciding to go for the pros. In the theory of psychological dependence, the victim shows her commitment to believing that she can save the marriage. The theory of rational action argues that the victim perceives that leaving the abusive relationship has its advantages (social life, independence) and disadvantages (loneliness, economic difficulties), and the stance taken facing the offender will depend on the positive or negative perception of the overall results (Álvarez, 2007).

In short, this chapter emphasizes that when talking about spousal violence, it is relevant to consider the weight of stereotypes regarding gender and the differential socialization of men and women, beyond the factors of the individual or relational domain of indubitable importance. It is important to analyze as well their relation with the disposition of power inside a family frame (Machado and Matos, 2001, cited in Matos, 2003). It is counterproductive to minimize, marginalize or ignore any victim or permanently perceive a victim as passive and the aggressor as always aggressive. The will of both genders blaming each other has proven to be dangerous and divisive. It is more productive for the safety of all victims to determine in a specific incident which specific individual initiated the causes or started the violence and afterward provide interventions based on these incidents (Davis, 2008).

# Chapter 8

# Considerations Regarding Spousal Violence Intervention

Magalhães (2010, p. 138) advocates "(…) an articulated multidisciplinary inter-vention. Isolated interventions, even if well-intentioned, can cause more harm than good [however] (…) it is always better to intervene than to be waiting for a natural resolution of the case."

Machado et al. (2001) argue that research projects should be developed in order to cover the scientific, social, and clinical domains as a way to contrib-ute to new and improved work paths with this population and their social and cultural contexts. This idea is similar to other researchers' positions, pointing to medical, judicial, police, and social intervention (Álvarez, 2007; Krug et al., 2003 cited in Pérez and Martínez, 2009; Plana, 1999).

Another important aspect refers to the essential protection for the woman who reports the abuses (Garrido, 2002; Matos, 2003; Regehr and Roberts, 2010; Walker, 2004), which highlights the role of shelters (Arroyo, 2004), where in order to be admitted, the woman should file a criminal complaint (Matos, 2006).

As is the case with any aspect related to health and safety, Corsi and Bonino (2003) suggest strategies that focus on health promotion (eg, development of cooperative behaviors), primary prevention to reduce the probability of prob-lems appearing, secondary prevention in order to detect the problem in its ear-lier stages and intervene effectively before the violent episodes, and, finally, tertiary prevention to reduce the effects of problems and prevent relapses of recovery and rehabilitation.

From the point of view of Machado et al. (2001), we must defend pri-mary prevention programs targeting all of society and not just the supposed risk groups. González (2010) also refers to the multidisciplinary approach and the strategy to combat this issue that is plaguing world society, and Robinson (2006) emphasizes the benefits of a coordinated community response. An effec-tive intervention strategy must encompass various levels, including the victim, the accused, the family, and the dynamics of violence (Antunes, 2003; Garcia, 2010). Magalhães (2010) considers that the intervention is aimed at two essen-tial goals: victim protection and the criminal investigation. It must be done in a structured manner to prevent secondary victimization.

With regard to the criminal investigation, it is a public crime, with man-datory reporting if someone is suspected of perpetrating domestic violence.

Forensic Psychology of Spousal Violence. http://dx.doi.org/10.1016/B978-0-12-803533-7.00008-9

Through the legal molds, public or equivalent employees must report these cases, for it is their duty (Magalhães, 2010).

It is understood that secondary victimization is a situation in which the victim becomes the victim of experts and of the system that is supposed to help her (Matud, Bermudez, and Padilla, 2009; Paulino and Matias, 2014). It is imperative to have qualified working experts, which improves the effectiveness of interventions (Portuguese Council of Minister Resolution No. 100/2010) and safeguards essential ethical aspects of the process (Matos, 2005, 2006; Poirier, 1999).

Garrido and Sobral (2008) present a number of components of secondary victimization, namely: (1) the system investigates the objective reality of a crime, focused only on pursuing the perpetrator, treating the victim in a cold and inhuman manner; (2) the lack of information provided to victims about the development of the proceedings or the sentence; (3) the absence of an environment that strives for intimacy and protection; (4) the use of excessive legal technicalities, hindering the understanding of the victim; (5) the lack of knowledge about the different professional roles (eg, difficulties in identifying the relevance of certain questions and intentionality, the sense of certain participants' positions in all legal and criminal scenarios); (6) the agonizing slowness of the judicial process that interferes often in an untimely manner in the victim's process of recovery and rehabilitation; and finally (7) the destruction of speech and credibility.

For Davis (2008), many victims, regardless of gender, are victimized twice. First, they are victimized by an attacker and then are again assaulted by an unfounded and overloaded criminal justice system, characterized by procedures, protocols, and laws rather than individual needs. They also add that hurdles to progress have been created regarding domestic violence because most participants and many policy makers see domestic violence as just a problem for heterosexual women and their children. However, the total number of children, men, elderly, and homosexuals is greater than the number of heterosexual women abused by a straight male adult.

Any intervention must be coordinated to be effective and save time in the process (González, 2010). The most promising short-term intervention should include 24-h hotlines, support groups, shelters, and treatment programs. Battered women confirm that the support phone lines, women's groups, social workers, and psychotherapists are useful.

## SPOUSAL VIOLENCE COSTS

According to the Council of Ministers Resolution No. 100/2010 (2010), a key concern with regard to domestic violence is related to the high social and individual costs, particularly in the physical (hospitalizations, development of chronic problems, and eating and sleep disorders) and psychological domains (Machado et al., 2008a), whose calculations are important to demonstrate the impact of such violence in society (Chan and Cho, 2010).

Various studies that have addressed this issue present inconsistent results, particularly because of the methods used and the included costs (Chan and Cho, 2010).

Collins and Lapsley proposed in 2003 that the tangible costs refer to the costs that can be evaluated in the market, which usually means medical care, mental health, property damage, use of legal and social services, and lost productivity. Mental health care includes responses such as pastoral counseling and marital or family therapy. However, in lost productivity, we include the loss of salaries and lifelong earnings, as well as increased costs for labor entities, which translates into lost revenues for the state (Chan and Cho, 2010).

Intangible costs are those that can only be measured indirectly, including pain, suffering, loss of quality of life, damage to self-image, and decreased motivation and morale (Krug, Dahlberg, Mercy, Zwi, and Lozaro, 2002, cited in Chan and Cho, 2010).

According to the National Association of Crime Victim Compensation Boards, the financial costs related to the health of the victims of crimes are escalating. In the United States, the numbers reached $165.9 million in medical and dental expenses, $55.4 million for mental health expenses, $73.5 million in lost salaries, $40.3 million for funeral expenses, $8.6 million for forensic rape examinations, close to $105,000 for cleaning crime scenes, and "other" expenses estimated at $23.1 million (Burgess and Roberts, 2010). Still the same institution reported in 2002 that 28% of adults who received compensation during the previous year were victims of domestic violence (Burgess and Roberts, 2010).

In 1999, Wisner and colleagues had concluded that the direct cost of medical treatment of abused women was estimated at $1.8 billion annually (Burgess and Roberts, 2010), and in 2003 the National Center for Injury Prevention and Control published data indicating that the cost of medical care, mental health, and lost productivity resulting from violence in close relationships had been about $5.8 billion in 1995 (Stampfel, Chapman, and Alvarez, 2010).

According to Chan and Cho (2010), some studies point out that the fact that children witness interparental violence is associated with a high propensity for youth crime and adulthood. This represents additional costs to the criminal justice system and government services in the future. Public policy cannot turn a blind eye to this reality.

The clearance of expenses allows us to study in greater depth the advantages and costs of intervention programs (Chan and Cho, 2010), which should include training and preventive intervention that raise people's awareness of abusive patterns and allows the possibility of an impact in reducing recidivism because, as Baccino (2006) said, one of the objectives of the intervention must concern avoiding and preventing recurrences, insofar as these are generally more serious. When those in power are aware of the high costs of this social problem that continues to be treated and supported by public funds, there is more likely to be an effective discussion on the matter (Chan and Cho, 2010).

More recently, a new study by the European Institute for Gender Equality (EIGE, 2014) has shown that in addition to its human toll, gender violence also has high economic impact on the European Union (EU), estimating that member states spend more 109 billion euros a year in costs related to this, representing about 0.8% of gross domestic product (GDP) of the European Union. According to the same Institute, violence entails economic losses affecting the victim, their immediate family, society, and the economy to such a degree that they manage to slow down its normal functioning. The fact that EIGE estimates that "only" about 3 billion euros is spent on prevention of gender violence in the EU is paradoxical.

We believe that the development of prevention programs, rather than reactive, in addition to avoiding victimization, would be an engine for new jobs for mental health experts (therefore more money for the public treasury and fewer unemployed receiving state funds).

## FAMILY AND SCHOOL CONTRIBUTIONS

Like most of the health and social problems, the best intervention in domestic violence is prevention (Poirier, 1999). In this sense, the educational factors should, in González's perspective (2010), be understood as the basis of prevention of domestic violence.

Preventing domestic violence in the broad sense involves the preparation for social life with implications in many spheres such as family, school, social action, and the media (Antunes, 2003). Karmen (2010) considers that preventing aggression means, in addition to preventing the outbreak of violence before it starts, that there are interventions for those who have suffered.

In terms of prevention, Samson (2010) stresses the importance of a parental model that meets the capacity to deal with conflicts and the ability to assess a loving relationship. In view of this task, Aires (2007, p. 18) mentions that love should be contemplated as a learning experience, as we are "not born knowing how to love. We are merely born in need of love." Therefore, we can talk about emotional illiteracy, resulting from the fact that society fails to ensure that all children learn to deal with emotions (Goleman, 2010). To Garrido (2002), the core of intervention is an education that teaches young people the contours of violent relationships and how to identify partners with the greatest potential risk in order to know the dysfunctional dynamics installed in a pathological relationship. This will help women understand the idea that they should not accept someone who mistreats them as their partner.

It should be noted that "educating for equality implies seeing the person in the light of human diversity, structuring the educational process around the person's integral development" (Resolution of the Council of Ministers No. 100/2010, p. 5767). Another important intervention strategy is to help promote resources within each child to develop feelings of self-efficacy and self-confidence (Walker, 2009c).

In the field of prevention, it is critical for people to be alert to more subtle forms of violence, learning to detect and reject abusive situations (which requires an intense awareness intervention), through information and education (Hirigoyen, 2006).

Together with the family, school is the ideal context of socialization for children and young people, not only for curricular learning related to the regular classes, but also covering key social skills to learn how to conduct oneself in society and in groups, and facilitating self-efficacy of students to the demands of life. Durlak (1995, cited in Saavedra and Machado, 2010, p. 147) says that "school is a natural environment for conducting prevention programs, because most children attend school and all the underlying infrastructure allows affecting a high number of children during the formative years." In 2002, Avery-Leaf and Cascardi ascertained that the programs built in schools have a better chance of success the longer they are presented in the classroom. The more qualified the teachers are and motivated to reflect the theme, and the greater the administrative support that the school provides, this will also increase the chances of success (Saavedra and Machado, 2010).

Gracia (2009) stresses the need for the expression "zero tolerance" to no longer be a cliché and become a reality.

## THE IMPORTANCE OF A SPECIALIZED EXPERT

Magalhães (2010, p. 105) states that "anyone can identify abuse (…)", however, some have more competence and responsibility than others, particularly professionals with greater proximity to the phenomenon. A skilled professional who understands the dynamic components of domestic violence will be better able to recognize abuse compared to a citizen without any knowledge in this field. Health professionals should be aware of the phenomenon and its mutations, recognizing and signaling the situations when there is a reason to suspect, even without having seen in flagrante delicto, with the victim concealing or not wanting to report.

Similar to Magalhães' (2010) concerns on professional responsibilities are the considerations of Markowitz et al. (2006b). These authors report that the lack of professional attention can also be a barrier between the health professional and the victim of domestic violence. There are numerous professionals who fear being implicated in a legal process in the form of court hearings or proceedings before judges.

A Portuguese study that used a sample of 352 National Health System doctors of general medicine and family practice from the country's north showed that 60% had completed a training curriculum on domestic violence, but the presence of training curriculum on the subject appeared unrelated to diagnostic factors and guidance of cases; 72% did not address the issue in a routine way by means of consultation, and 40% felt "somewhat" or "not comfortable" with these consultations. The main factors that hindered the diagnosis were the denial/nonconfirmation of the diagnosis by the patient, the lack of medical knowledge in this area, the absence of intervention protocols, and also the fact that the patient does not see the doctor as a participant in any role in the matter. The results show the periodical and provided training needs with practical and concrete sense of resolution of situations, making use of resources to develop in their workplaces and to work with community resources. It also became evident that the conflict between legal obligation of reporting and the deontological aspects (which are solved in favor of the latter, not acting without the consent of the victim), putting in their hands the resolution or need to proceed to social referral. This raises the need for debate because of families where there are children exposed to violence and that have to be protected (Paulino and Matias, 2014).

It is highlighted that in the area of intervention, it is important to make the distinction between identification and diagnosis. The first term alludes to suspecting that certain facts may give rise to an observer as to whether, in that particular situation, the victim in fact experienced abuse. However, this suspicion may or may not be unfounded, requiring specialized technical intervention in order to make a clinical diagnosis for insurance, and, in Portugal, the legal responsibility of the National Institute of Legal Medicine and Forensic Sciences.

To aid the identification of attacks, it is useful to meet indicators, which are signs or symptoms that can be more or less suggestive of abuse. The first indicators are certain injuries, referring to certain pain complaints or certain behavioral changes. However, the existence of these indicators is not a condition sine qua non that abuse exists, and their absence should not be translated as the nonoccurrence of violence. Consequently, even though the indicators are an important warning, a firm diagnosis requires a combination of these indicators, their context, the analysis of risk factors, and, whenever possible, the testimony of the victim. Thus, an indicator serves only as a warning and may or may not warrant further investigation, as in professional and specialized analysis of the situation.

It is also essential to take into account other possible etiologies that can justify the injuries or symptoms, such as accidents, illnesses, malformations, morphological conditions, injuries from alternative medicinal practices, or even self-inflicted and simulation injuries, reinforcing the need for a specialized professional search for an effective differential diagnosis (Magalhães, 2010).

Magalhães (2010) addressed an alert to professionals that it is safer to report and investigate, even facing the possibility that violence is not confirmed, rather than tolerate the evolution of the case, in anticipation of new evidence or if the victim chooses to disclose, with the risk of ending a life or allowing irreversible damage.

Thus, the professional should be aware of certain details and suspect violence, namely:

1. When the injuries suggest features that were produced at different times, revealing that they were not a single act, but cyclic acts like the case of various bruises with different colors;
2. The location of the injuries in unusual areas in accidental injuries (eg, inner thighs or arms, neck region or behind the ears, mouth, genitals, or buttocks) in conjunction with meager explanations regarding them as accidental and possibly being caused voluntarily;

3. Multiple injuries confined to distinct and different zones, pointing to the existence of more than one traumatic mechanism and possible continuity of trauma throughout time, characteristic aspects of injuries produced intentionally;
4. Injuries with defined contours that suggest, for example, a belt, rope, iron, hand, teeth, cigarette butt, or footwear;
5. The injuries were not presented to medical treatment in a timely manner, stating that the victim, the perpetrator, or both, sought to conceal the abuse committed, dodging the exposure of injuries and therefore not having to explain anything to the experts;
6. The lesions present certain specific types and patterns, strongly suggestive of the mechanism that caused them, such as the strangulation standard;
7. The existence of intoxication, especially more than once, and the accidental explanation is not consistent;
8. The inconsistency between the involved explanations about the traumatic agent and the period from the production of injury, or changes in the justifications, or even avoiding clarification of how the injury was caused;
9. The existence of a history of repeated injuries, even if the explanation appears to be logical (Magalhães, 2010).

In this mission, the expert must have to consider, as a first step, consulting the medical history concerning previous visits to the hospital to rule out the existence of the same signs and symptoms of injury patterns or indicators of violence (Markowitz et al., 2006b).

Clinical indicators of existing abuse in the medical history to take into account include previous medical visits due to an unexplained source of injury or because of poor reasonable grounds for professionals, multiple visits due to anxiety issues, patient's concerns due to pain (eg, headache), a history of suicidal thoughts, depression or substance abuse, strange behaviors relating to consultations (eg, canceling scheduled sessions without previous warning, showing up without a scheduled session), trauma history or mutilation of breasts or genitals, burns, muscle/skeletal injury or other bruising and trauma, observation of an excessive submissive/passive posture or very evasive responses, and finally, a history of unwanted pregnancy and abortion, premature birth, birth of children with low weight, and bleeding in the first or second trimester of pregnancy (Markowitz et al., 2006b).

Follingstad (2003) states that the informed clinical experts who are aware of the scientific literature are able to ask more pertinent questions in order to probe more effectively and bring to light aspects that the woman might not consider significant. This is fundamental because most people who go to a hospital or health center will not want to reveal the cause of trauma or will seek an unlikely cause in the light of presented injuries and medical knowledge that professionals hold. Some of the most common stories given include falling down the stairs, hitting a door, and slipping in the bathtub. Some of the most important questions and indicators to identify/synthesize a possible case of domestic violence are the following (Paulino and Matias, 2014):

1. Many scheduled sessions because of several complaints and vague symptoms or habitually going to health services with similar physical and injury complaints;
2. Missing appointments, delays, and frequently canceling consultations;
3. Injuries incompatible with the descriptions provided by the victim;
4. Common injuries in the hands, face, head, neck, chin, chest, and abdomen;
5. Evidence of multiple injuries in different stages of healing;
6. Attempts to minimize the severity of injuries and/or try to hide them by covering them with clothes;
7. The victim seems frightened, overly anxious, or depressed;
8. The victim is constantly being accompanied in consultations by partners or family members, being too passive or seeming to be afraid of her partner, who tends to answer questions instead of the victim;
9. The companion seems aggressive or manipulative and reluctant to let the woman speak or be alone with health professionals;
10. Refers to marital problems but without specifying situations of violence;
11. History of miscarriages or premature births.

If healthcare professionals only focus their attention on the treatment of injuries without asking their causes, they will do little to help the victim. The screening of domestic violence while conducting a medical history can be done by conducting three simple questions:

1. Since last year or the last time she was pregnant, has she suffered some kind of physical injury by someone?
2. Does she maintain any relationship with a person who threatens or causes physical injury?
3. Has someone forced her to perform sex acts against her will?

Karmen (2010) considers crucial that professionals recognize the importance of sensitivity to racial, ethnic, and cultural differences in order to achieve strategies, treatment plans, and effective criminal justice policies. It is crucial that culture can be presented as a resource for assisting victims of domestic violence and not as a reason to replicate the submission processes and obtuseness that they are commonly targets of (Coelho and Machado, 2010).

## SAFE HOUSES: THE STARTING POINT AND THE INEFFICIENCY OF THE SYSTEM

Shelters are residential spaces for temporary care, safety, and confidentiality, intended for women victims of domestic violence with or without minor children and who are in a serious risk situation, including the possibility of death. They are support structures with the goal for the protection and safeguarding the physical and psychological integrity of women victims of domestic violence and the promotion of preventive personal, social, and professional skills, of any social exclusion, with a view to their future (re)insertion. Therefore, they constitute an essential context in promoting security as well as skills and resources necessary for the reorganization of a new life project. This is a temporary social reception response that solves an immediate need for accommodation. Joining these safe houses is the first confrontation with the unknown and the starting point for facing numerous challenges with the eventual goal of achieving independent living. Services (eg, victim hosting, food, basic hygiene) provided by shelters are free.

We should take into account that safe houses are not a resource for all situations of domestic violence. They must meet alternative social responses in cases where, although there is a history of domestic violence, the woman is no longer in a risk position, but as an example, she has no housing and/or economic conditions. Shelters are not an answer to housing, social and/or economic weaknesses.

If there are other issues beyond domestic violence (eg, alcoholism, drug addiction, or mental disorders), victims should be directed to a specialized therapy. Shelters should only accept women with serious problems (psychiatric/addictive) as long as they are stabilized at the entrance of the shelter. Through its partner networks, the institution is responsible for monitoring the victim right after and during her stay in the safe house.

Shelters are different from each other, but overall there are rooms large enough for a family, so that the children can also be housed with their mother. However, sometimes a family may have to share the room with another family.

The first line of intervention with victims of domestic violence is to ensure their safety and, accordingly, the houses provide shelter for victims of violence as a place of refuge and anonymity. They have security measures such as confidential location and liaison with local police forces. To guarantee the effectiveness of such measures and security methods, it is important to maintain standards (rules) that help protect the confidentiality of the shelter. Since safety is the top priority of a shelter, the victim herself must also meet safety standards (Roberts and Roberts, 2005). Conselho da Europa (2008) warns that safe houses located in rural areas have more difficulties in maintaining confidentiality.

Roberts and Roberts (2005) report that in 1974 there were only seven house shelters in the United States, while in 1998 there were already more than 2000. In Canada, the number increased from 78 to 400 between 1978 and 1989 (Denham and Gillespie, 1998, cited in Regehr and Roberts, 2010).

In Portugal, the appearance of shelters dates back to the 1990s, which corresponds to a delay of nearly two decades compared to the European reality. A public network of houses to support women victims of violence was created only in 1999. In 2015, Portugal had 37 safe houses, with 639 vacancies (beds).

According to a Portuguese legal document dated January 25, 2006 (Portuguese Executive Decree 1/2006), shelters are a form of support especially dedicated to the protection of women victims of violence in order to pursue several objectives, namely (1) temporarily accommodate the occupants and children with a view to protection of their physical and psychological integrity; (2) to provide the users and the children the necessary conditions for their education, health, and overall well-being in an environment of peace and security; (3) promote the acquisition of personal, professional, and social skills for the occupants; and (4) provide, through appropriate mechanisms, the reorganization of their lives, seeking their family, social, and professional reintegration.

In 2011 in Brazil, the Secretariat of Policies for Women (SPM) and the Presidency drew up the National Guidelines for Sheltering Women in Situations of Risk or Violence, referring to a set of recommendations that guide the sheltering of women in situations of violence and the flow of care in network services, including the various forms of violence against women (trafficking women, domestic violence against women, etc.), and new alternatives to sheltering (such as temporary short-term shelter/"passing-by" houses, hostels, possible benefits, sheltering under consortia, etc.).

The first shelter was set up in São Paulo in 1986 and was called the Social Center for Women Victims of Domestic Violence (*Centro de Convivência para Mulheres Vítimas de Violência Doméstica*, Convida). In 1990, the Santo André shelter was created (São Paulo); in 1991, the Helenira Rezende de Souza Nazareth House (São Paulo); in 1992, the Viva Maria Shelter (Rio Grande do Sul) and Casa do Caminho (Ceará); and in 1996, the House-Shelter of the Federal District and the Sempre-Viva Safe House (Minas Gerais). In 2003, according to the Secretariat on Policies for Women, there were a total of 42 shelters in the country. When drawing up the National Guidelines (2011), there were 72 shelters in Brazil.

The Women Against Violence Europe (WAVE, 2011) urgently pleads for victim shelters to remain working despite the economic crisis. According to the recommendations of the Council of Europe, all countries must guarantee a place of shelter for every 10,000 inhabitants. In fact, there are only 27,000 vacancies (beds) in Europe and there is an urgent need to create an additional 54,000 to meet the standards of the Council of Europe.

The WAVE's 2011 Country Report shows that there are 2349 shelters for women throughout Europe, providing about 28,000 jobs for women and children victims of violence. According to the minimum standard of a place for every 10,000 inhabitants, we would require approximately 82,000 places in Europe. There are only five countries in Europe (Luxembourg, Norway, the Netherlands, Slovenia, and Malta) where the standard of providing one or more than one vacancy per 10,000 people is fulfilled. In addition, only 503 vacancies are available in the new EU countries for a population of over 10 million people. A single vacancy serves a population of nearly 188,000 people.

WAVE urgently calls on the Council of Europe and the EU and its member states to take effective measures to increase the number of shelters for women victims of domestic violence and not to accept that the economic crisis leads to new budget cuts and puts at risk the health, life, and freedom of hundreds of thousands of women and their children. Moreover the fact that, according to

Article 23 of the Council of Europe Convention on Preventing and Combating Violence Against Women and Domestic Violence (Istanbul Convention), active since August 1, 2014, with Portugal being the first EU member state to ratify, "each involved party shall adopt such legislative or other measures as may be necessary to create appropriate shelters that are easily accessible and in sufficient numbers in order to provide victims, especially women with children, safe housing, and helping them proactively."

In terms of minimum standards of safe houses, the training for volunteers and staff must be at least 30h and focus on the analysis of violence against women, communication techniques and intervention, confidentiality, child protection, access translation and disability services, effective delivery, information on trauma, coping and survival, as well as risk assessment, empowerment, nondiscrimination, and diversity (Conselho da Europa, 2008). Empowerment was considered one of the principles inherent in shelters, including information to enable service users to make better-informed choices (Conselho da Europa, 2008).

In order to achieve the aforementioned goals, from February 23–27, 2015, in Montenegro there was a mission lead by experts in shelters and domestic violence, organized by the Technical Assistance Information Exchange Instrument of the European Commission. The guidelines included various topics such as legal status, staff, financial component, organizational planning, confidentiality criteria and admission process, evaluation system, crisis intervention, emotional support, individual and group counseling, transportation, health standards and security, housing and food conditions, child care, follow-up, recruitment and training of volunteers, professional training, medication and special needs.

Although shelters only provide for a small number of women and children, their existence in the community conveys the message of zero tolerance for abuse (Walker et al., 2009d). While some shelters only offer a safe address, many offer a combination of services such as legal aid, counseling, and services for children (Conselho da Europa, 2008).

Equally important is the ability to empower battered women to move on with their lives (Walker, 2009c), preferably without incurring the same kind of relationships, because in fact most women who have been in a shelter go back to living with their mates and many suffer further violence (Dutton-Douglas and Dionne, 1991, cited in Karmen, 2010).

The intervention in shelters has to be professional, with the development of a global project of intervention with each household, planned for, with trained and interdisciplinary technical teams taking into account the needs and characteristics of victims. Fortunately, more and more shelters advocate a global project of intervention within each household planned by technical teams, which includes socioeducational and psychotherapeutic counseling of children, taking into account their individual needs (Conselho da Europa, 2008; Coutinho and Sani, 2008, 2010).

They must also model and promote respect for nonviolence in all interactions, including those between adults and children (Conselho da Europa, 2008).

For children, the shelter operating standards are perceived as a potential personal growth factor, coupled with discipline and responsibility, in stark contrast to the chaotic family environment in which they were inserted. Most children feel safe in the sheltering institutions, not fearing any new instances of victimization. Following the integration shelter, children perceive mothers as more active and autonomous people, both in personal and social life, and more available to meet physical and emotional needs of children. In addition, the support given to the children is felt by mothers as very useful, whether the contribution is from the perspective given to the psychological adjustment of children, whether as a mediator and facilitator in improving the mother–child relationship, heavily damaged by the experience of domestic violence (Coutinho and Sani, 2008, 2010).

In this context it is imperative to share the following story created by a 7-year-old boy who was welcomed in a shelter. In just a few pages we can see changes that occurred in the life of this child and how passing through a shelter that responded specifically to children seemed to have a positive effect on him and contributed significantly to the change in his emotional state.

In one of his last follow-up sessions, after having started the independence process of a mother with her two children, as in living again with his mother and brother in safety in a new city, this child said in session that he wanted to draw and write a story.

He called his story "My life" and drew many hearts on the cover (square no. 1). In the second square, he wrote that "There once was a sad family. The angry mother, angry father, sad X (name of child) sad and sad Y (the name of his brother) "(sic). In the third square, containing two pages, where she wrote: "The mother and children were in a shelter and felt sad, alone and relieved. Time passed and the family felt: happy, calm and had friends "(sic). In the fourth and last square, the child wrote, "I love living in the new house. I miss Andreia, Carina and Mauro [the first two names are examples of psychologists who accompanied the two brothers] and friends of the shelter"(sic) (Fig. 8.1).

In Portugal, pets are not allowed inside shelters. According to a report in the American newspaper *The Huffington Post* on June 11, 2015, fewer than 3% of shelters have some sort of accommodation for pets. This aspect should be urgently reflected upon since evidence shows that pets have an impact on people's well-being and, in turn, are a variable to consider in domestic violence.

On the one hand, according to the Sojourner Center—Pet Companion Shelter (2015), 71% of women who are pet owners and are looking for a shelter claim that their attackers had also threatened, injured, or killed the pet. On the other hand, according to the National Coalition Against Domestic Violence (2013), between 25% and 40% of victims of domestic violence do not leave the dangerous situation they are in because they do not want to leave their pets. The separation from their pets, even if only for a short period, is traumatic and devastating.

In the United States, some pioneering programs have been developed that already provide shelters for pets in conjunction with the safe house. Children can go to visit their pets while the coaching staff is present. It should be noted

**FIGURE 8.1**  History created by a child who was introduced in the shelter.

that children are the main users of shelters and often are the closest to the four-legged companions.

In conclusion, on one hand, it is important to defend humanization, improve and disseminate shelters in a way that they constitute an important starting point of dealing with victimization by violence. On the other hand, we urgently need to reflect on the justice and victim protection system. Women victims of spousal violence and their respective children leaving their own home is an undeniable indicator of system inefficiency. There is no logic in the victim quitting her job, her environment, her kids leaving school and friends, and the offender being allowed to stay at home without any penalty. Without reflection upon this and consequent change of practices, it seems that we are blaming the victim for what happened because it is she who leaves home and becomes a hostage of her own life.

In this regard, we must end the trend for the application of suspended prison sentences in cases of conviction for crimes of domestic violence. They are very serious crimes against human rights of women, and the aggressors increase the intensity of violence when the victim leaves home and reports the violence, as well as continue to pursue women and children in order to control them.

## Personal Safety Plan for the Victim Who Is Sheltered in a Safe House

The design of a personal safety plan proves to be crucial in that it constitutes a fundamental instrument to assist victims in distress and achieve alternative security solutions, focusing mainly on their immediate needs. Bear in mind that an effective security response depends largely on the available information regarding the risk of the victim. Thus, an appropriate personal safety plan should be drawn up jointly with the victim in order to ensure that in the event of violence occurring more than once, any negative impact on the psychological and physical functioning of the victim is minimized.

The fundamental objective is to minimize the risk experienced by each specific victim, so the defined security strategies should be evaluated and recognized with a focus on the victim's resources without increasing the risk of recurrence of violence. The victim must also be aware of their own resources. The security plan should also be regularly reviewed ensuring that it still meets the needs of the victim and remains consistent with the circumstances and available resources.

The development of this instrument should allow management of the risk of victimization and revictimization after the level of risk has been identified. It should also be realistic and able to be used, as well as to gather a list of vulnerabilities and various types of threats and dangers. Only then can it help us to know the signs that often precede a violent attack by an intimate partner and identify all personal and community resources available (information gathered from the victim).

A detailed analysis of the various issues, risk factors, and protective factors present should allow the design of management strategies more adjusted to each situation. The risk management planning involves considering whether it is possible to improve safety at the place where the victim lives, where they work, and when traveling.

Therefore with the addition that safety procedures should be adjusted to the specific situation, for example, if the instructions are different if the victim is in the relationship (eg, thinking of a safe place to protect and avoid dead ends; thinking of a set of trustworthy people who the victim may rely on; memorizing important phone contacts, defining a code word or sign so that family, friends, neighbors, or coworkers know when to ask for help) or the victim has left the relationship (eg, change phone number; save and document all contacts, messages, injuries, or other incidents that have involved the offender; change the house locks if the aggressor has a key, avoid being alone if necessary to meet with your partner, do it in a public place, change your routine, alert your workplace of the situation, and eventually apply for inclusion in a shelter for victims of violence). Even in the event of a violent act, there are some recommendations that are important to follow, namely:

- Protect head, chest, belly
- Scream
- Stay away from areas of the house where there are knives or firearms
- Know where all the doors are
- Tell the neighbors to call the police if they hear screaming
- Warn family and friends

If the victim is able to run from the house, they should consider whose house they are going to, which means of transportation, which documents to have at hand, as well as what clothes and objects to take. It is also equally useful to always be ready in case of running away, having an emergency backpack in case of having to suddenly flee (eg, clothes for yourself and/or children, money, coins, phone numbers, ID card, marriage certificate, children's birth certificates, and copies of house and car keys).

The specific questions that a personal security plan must address are:

- What are the prewarning signs/clues that indicate that the victim may be at risk?
- Which internal alarm signals does the victim identify as a sign of stress or fear? (eg, thoughts, behaviors, physical, and emotional reactions)
- What external stressful events can put the victim in danger? (eg, children, time of day, family problems)
- How can the victim protect herself and her children? (if there are any)
- How effective were the previous attempts at resolving the issue? (if there were any)

The following are examples of some items that should be included in a personal safety plan for someone who is sheltered in a safe house:

1. Not to disclose the address or location of the shelter;
2. Do not receive visitors in the shelter nor nearby. You can receive visits in a location to decide by experts;
3. Change the phone number that the aggressor knows and provide the new number only to trustworthy people;
4. Always have on hand the technical staff's phone numbers as well as numbers for the shelter, police, and other trustworthy people;
5. Do not move to the area of origin without giving prior knowledge to professionals in charge of the process;
6. Do not use ATMs, credit cards, and bank accounts in the area of the shelter;
7. Pay special attention when using services that can report the location of the victim, such as post offices or public phones;
8. Do not go to places normally used by the offender, or people known to the perpetrator;
9. Walk on busy streets, avoiding the most isolated places;
10. In the event of being spotted or followed outside the shelter, the victim must go to the nearest public place and call police as soon as possible, as well as contact the shelter professionals.

For various reasons, sometimes the victim chooses to return to their place of origin, not staying in the shelter. In such situations there may important instructions should also be provided, such as:

1. Do not go to spaces normally used by the perpetrator;
2. Do not walk by isolated places or with few people;
3. In the case of being followed, they should go to the police or nearest public place and call the police;

4. Have the telephone numbers of the nearest law enforcement agency always at hand;
5. Change the phone number that the aggressor knows and provide the new number only to trustworthy people;
6. In addition to recording the numbers on your phone, always have them available in another safe place (house of friends, family), so they can be accessed in an emergency;
7. Have photocopies of personal documents and some goods (clothes, money) in another safe place where you can access them in case of emergency;
8. Change timetables and routes to work and school as often as possible;
9. Do not have the offender visit in your home, or if you do, always have people who are your friends with you;
10. Always lock doors and windows whenever leaving home;
11. If you find it important, consider requesting a copy of the house key for someone you trust;
12. Talk with your children and teach them how to prevent dangerous situations and how to act in an emergency situation, especially someone trustworthy whom they can contact.

## BEYOND SOCIAL INTERVENTION: PSYCHOLOGICAL INTERVENTION

Regarding psychological intervention, Baccino (2006) suggests a holistic approach, covering both participants.

Berns wrote in 1999 that women's magazines spread the notion that it is the woman's responsibility to solve the problem, commonly suggesting the demand for psychotherapeutic support or ending the relationship (Machado and Dias, 2010).

In the area of domestic violence, women's safety and risk of violence is part of the psychological intervention since we seek to keep the victim in a violence-free environment (Matos, 2003). So one of the psychotherapist's first tasks is to determine the likelihood of conditions for the occurrence of very severe assaults, such as assassination attempts and use of weapons or dangerous objects (Matos, 2006).

Hirigoyen (2006) considers that the first stage of the intervention is the recognition by the victim that she is in a situation of violence.

An essential feature of the therapeutic process is asking questions in order to assist in the coconstruction of meanings. The strategy of the questions aims to involve, in a proactive manner, participants in a speech in order to empower, establishing a commitment with change (Matos, 2003).

*If a woman seeks psychotherapy at the time they decide to separate from the partner, the psychotherapeutic space can allow to rebuild some meanings associated with that stage..., continually review her needs, evaluate the benefits/risks of that option, strengthen its intentionality and the legitimacy of her choices, enable and promote the resources (personal and contextual) and to promote women's resilience (Matos, 2006, p. 141).*

Joint action of different support institutions, such as justice and psychotherapy, can contribute to overcome issues, more effectively, by the victims during the separation phase (Matos, 2006).

In Holf's view expressed in 1995, an effective model of intervention in the issue of domestic violence should cover future objectives and formulate an alternative plan for life (Matos, 2003). To Datner et al. (2003), an effective intervention should help women adopt protective changes to their lives.

Husmann and Chiale (2010) report that most people who cease an abusive relationship only do so after the intervention of an external facilitator, such as a psychotherapist or a support group, among others. The research highlights the utility of support groups for women, in that it shows statistically significant differences posttesting compared to pretesting in the areas of self-esteem, anger, and depression (Tutty, Ogden, and Whyllie, 2006, cited in Regehr and Roberts, 2010). In 1993, Tutty, Bidgood, and Rothery, regarding the clinical intervention with women victims of domestic violence, qualify that there are significant gains in regard to increasing the sense of inclusion, self-esteem, the internal control locus and decreasing perceived stress, as well as the traditionalist attitudes toward the representation of family and marriage. They also point out changes in the level of expression of affection, reduction in control behaviors and reduction of abusive behaviors, despite their nontermination (Matos, 2006).

In therapeutic terms, the research reinforces the importance of narrating what happened regarding the abusive experience (Matos, 2006). The narration of experience as a victim allows her to contain the pain and mitigate its effects, contributing to the awareness of how dominated she really was (Carbó, 2006).

Freeman and Combs emphasized in 1996 that change is possible through language and dialog (Matos and Gonçalves, 2001).

In 1992, Webb said that the purpose of intervention aims at the empowerment of battered women to respond to situations of life in a more self-valued form (Matos, 2003). The empowerment enables women to drive a power speech focused to their decision-making toward their autonomy, facilitating the understanding of how able they are to master the effects of problems in their lives. On the other hand, it directs them to an idea of conducting their lives in a preferential way. In this way, the victim is considered the protagonist in the support process and can still rely on third parties that may ultimately play an important role in solving the problem (Matos, 2003).

Garrido (2002) believes that we should not defend the idea that the hope to significantly decrease the abuse of women lies in a more severe justice, pointing to the empowerment of victims as the best alternative.

Thus, the purpose of intervention must be to reintegrate the victims to a sense of mastery and control over their bodies and their lives (Walker, 1986).

The intervention aims, according to Matos and Gonçalves (2001), at the free construction of alternative meanings that are not constrained and should focus on a transformative dialog in order to empower women to follow their preferred directions in life.

Psychotherapy, as a transforming element of the brain, whatever method is chosen, should enable the victim to free herself from an alienating relationship in order to recover their very existence (Hirigoyen, 2006), promoting the integration of a harmonious, creative, and meaningful life (Cozolino, 2010). Thus, when psychotherapy results in reduced symptoms or experiential change (changes in the life of the subject), the brain has been transformed in some way (functional modification of the nervous system) (Kandel, 1998, cited in Cozolino, 2010).

# Chapter 9

# Tips on Investigating in the Domain on Domestic Violence

According to Gil (1994), the methodology consists of describing the structure of a study, particularly the description of procedures, methods, and techniques used for the correct development of research. As Ghiglione and Matalon (2001, p. 108) warn us, "Any error, lack of skill or ambiguity will have an impact on all the subsequent processes until the final conclusions."

Based on a warning by Uexkuell (1959, cited in Leal, 2007), Zeigarnik (1981), and Matos (2006), it is important that research contemplates a quantitative and qualitative approach.

The quantitative approach involves the translation into numbers of opinions and information in order to be classified and analyzed through the use of resources and techniques of statistical nature (Vilelas, 2009).

In turn, the qualitative approach emphasizes the meaning given by the partakers of the violent situation to actions in which they are engaged, aimed at broad understanding of the phenomenon we are researching (Freixo, 2010). It focuses on how individuals interpret and give meaning to their experiences and the world around them (Vilelas, 2009). Uexkuell highlighted in 1959 the importance of understanding how living things apprehend, subjectively, their environment from their own point of view. The core of this issue lies in how perception affects problem solving (Leal, 2007).

Zeigarnik (1981) argues that one's own attitude toward a situation and the way the person faces it should be the object of study. Matos (2006) stresses the need for further studies where the subjective experience of both victims and aggressors should not be forgotten. Few investigations have given effective space for victims, as in how they experience and understand the problem and the resulting changes due to mistreatment and in the postviolence period.

Minayo defended in 1994 that both analyses are not irreconcilable, as they can both be integrated in the same investigation project (Vilelas, 2009).

Under the quantitative approach, it is often that the investigator resorts to the method of testing, using paper and pencil tests and the survey method with the questionnaire technique. The questionnaire survey covers the application of a set of questions pertaining to multiple aspects (eg, expectations, attitudes, and personal, professional, and social status) to a number of people (Quivy and Campenhoudt, 2003).

Forensic Psychology of Spousal Violence. http://dx.doi.org/10.1016/B978-0-12-803533-7.00009-0

In the field of qualitative approach, the case study method prevails, which collects the maximum possible elements of an individual for a large part of their life. Often the case study is done in a clinical setting to assess a particular behavioral problem (Hansenne, 2004).

There are two broad approaching perspectives in the study of personality, including nomothetic and idiographic. The nomothetic approach focuses on rules that can be applied to various subjects through the study of groups and universal laws. In turn, the idiographic approach includes the subject as an individual, focusing on specific cases and the individual's operating structure (Hall et al., 2000; Hansenne, 2004; Turvey, 2009d). Hansenne (2004) believes that the combination of the two approaches appears to be the most accurate.

One of the variants of case study method is the comparative study of cases in which it is possible to draw comparisons between two or more specific approaches so that comparative perspective enriches qualitative research. It consists of thorough and intensive research using the description, explanation, and comparison of the results (Triviños, 1995). For example, a comparative study between a victim of domestic violence who ended the relationship with the offender and one that still remains in the violent relationship. It is also possible to compare between the victim that remains in a safe house and one that did not react this way. We can also compare situations of a child exposed to interparental violence and another that was not subject to such mistreatments.

For the achievement of effective studies, the objective must go beyond the study of obvious reactions at first glance, to the extent that, according to Vygotsky (1996), this contributes to sterile and unjustified results.

Having made this introductory qualification on different methodologies, the next step is going through a proper determination of the studied object and problem and its consequent justification. At this stage it is important to meet the recommendation of Hill and Hill (2009), according to which the empirical part makes sense and is justified by the reviewed literature that is explained in the theoretical part.

In the case of the delimitation of the object and problem being studied, it should be noted that it is domestic violence. It is often mentioned in the news and in some cases resulting in a fatality, which highlights the timeliness and relevance the problem under study. The victimization involves real people with real lives and problems occurring in complex and internal circumstances or as a result of equally complex relations (Turvey, 2009b).

Domestic violence has taken, nationally and internationally, a worrying extension (Machado et al., 2008b), constituting a public health problem (Datner et al., 2003; Mota et al., 2007), widespread and burdensome, which has achieved a prominent place in scientific, political, and judicial domains, in literature, and in the media in general (Matos, 2006). In addition to being a serious social problem, it is a serious medical and legal problem (Arroyo, 2004).

Matos (2006) warns that we can be in the initial phase of a long crusade, as the history of research on domestic violence is only 40 years old. He notes that there is little research on domestic violence, although this problem is significantly frequent (Matos, 2003).

In addition, and even before a marriage is marked by destruction and suffering, victims remain in the violent relationship for a long time, over 10 years on average (Álvarez, 2007). According to the publication of Snyder and Fruchtman, in 1981, between 57% and 78% of battered women remained with their partners and more than 60% of those applying to shelters returned to the previous situation of abuse (Álvarez, 2007).

Sociocultural perspectives are an element of paramount importance in that "the stereotypes of gender and marriage, the differential socialization of men and women and the unequal distribution of power within families contribute significantly to one tacit tolerance of society against this type of abuse" (Machado et al., 2008a, p.137). On the other hand, beliefs can contribute to the assaulters belittling the need to change their abusive behavior and contribute to the victim not desiring to stop the relationship, viewing such occurrences as harmless episodes.

In another perspective, Doumas et al. (2008) state that a growing body of literature has identified the adult bonding style as a risk factor for domestic violence. Mayseless said in 1991 that the bonding provides aid in the understanding of violence and intimacy in a relationship (Doumas et al., 2008).

The data indicate that the most significant contribution to the mental health of adults is provided by the affective relationships established during the adult years (Canavarro, 1999, cited in Canavarro et al., 2006).

Another pertinent angle of the problem lies in the approach of coping strategies. The term *coping* involves the notion of a new behavior in the face of substantial changes that one has in mind or a problem that challenges the behavioral paradigm of the subject. They are usually unpleasant and anxiogenic situations that require adaptation in order to relieve the subject. In short, coping is related to the adaptation of the individual in arduous conditions. In the view of Serra, coping is related to the strategies used by the person to deal with stressful events, whether they are damaging, threatening, or challenging events (Rebocho, 2007). Some battered women develop positive coping strategies, while others develop negative coping strategies and are potentially self-destructive. Positive coping strategies include networks of formal and informal support, looking for additional information, and requesting housing in shelters for battered women. At the other pole, negative coping strategies include alcohol dependence, drug use, and suicide attempts (Roberts and Roberts, 2005).

In short the problem that serves as an engine and justifies the research is the obvious need to increase knowledge of the psychological functioning of the victim of domestic violence, in order to prevent the problem and promote the development of effective intervention programs.

After the delimitation of the object and problem under study and its consequent justification, we should devise a research issue. According to Quivy and Campenhoudt (1998), the best way to start a research project is the raising of one or more questions in an attempt know, clarify, or better understand a situation. For the success of the investigation, the questions should be characterized by being clear, achievable, and relevant. By extension, research objectives should be established, which must be both general and specific. Take as an example the overall objective of bringing in light of scientific knowledge a contribution to the understanding of the domestic violence victim, which includes various specific goals such as characterizing the victim of domestic violence and relationship(s) with partner(s) who was/were perpetrators, as well as typify the assaults and their extent and determine the behavior of the consequent victim to aggression.

Another important notion in scientific investigation is the idea of participants. Hill and Hill (2009) define the universe or population as the total number of cases that are intended for study and from which they intend to draw conclusions. The universe is defined by the goal of the research that will be undertaken. In view of the impossibility to collect and analyze data for each instance of a given universe, it is considered only a part of all cases that make up what is known and is denominated as a sample (Hill and Hill, 2009). One sample is composed of a group of individuals taken from a population (Ash, 2010). In all cases, we must guarantee the consent and anonymity of participants.

The nonprobabilistic or nonrandom sampling refers to the process by which all elements of the population do not have the same probability of being part of the sample (Ash, 2010). This way it reveals a pragmatic character (Vilelas, 2009).

Accidental or convenience sample consists of people or elements that are easily accessible and present in a given time. In other words, the elements are chosen based on their presence in a particular place and period (Ash, 2010; Vilelas, 2009).

In order to appropriately define the sample, the criteria for inclusion and exclusion of participants should be rigorously defined. In the case of questionnaires drawn up by the investigator, they must have aspects referenced in the theoretical framework and the questions should be guided by the achievement of specific objectives. The wording of those questions must be properly designed to avoid difficulties of understanding the issues (Hill and Hill, 2009).

When the choice involves the preparation of a questionnaire, one of the first steps is to conduct a pretest of the new questionnaire so as to ensure that it is truly applicable and that it responds effectively to the required information (Ghiglione and Matalon, 2001). The pretest aims to highlight possible flaws in the construction of the questionnaire. Take as examples the complexity of the questions, inaccuracy in the writing, or participant constraints (Gil, 1999; Vilelas, 2009). To conduct the pretest, you can apply some questionnaires (variable number according to the size of population and resources) to a small sample of people in the population that the survey is intended for, but not part of the selected sample (Vilelas, 2009). Notably, the questionnaire pretest is only applied to a limited number of elements, so that in the end it does not compromise the final sample size. Normally, it is a step that, regardless of its complexity, proves to be of utmost importance to reach the final version of the questionnaire.

Another option goes through resorting to semistructured interviews that constitute one of the principal means available to the researcher to obtain data. This interview format values the role of the researcher and simultaneously allows all possible optics for the informant to get freedom and naturalness required in order to enrich the study (Triviños, 1995). It is advised that the interviews contemplate topics on personal functioning and spousal functioning (Matos, 2005, 2011, 2012).

It is essential that the investigator ensures the formal authorization of any official institutions and services. In some cases it may be necessary to have physical meetings to present the study's objectives. After issuing the proper permits, it is useful to the whole process to seek and establish close contact with a professional reference in order to promote speedy interviews and/or application of the assessment tools.

If the investigation includes the application of psychometric assessment tools, they should be selected in line with the aspects highlighted throughout the literature review and taking into account the theoretical and psychometric foundations. We speak of battery instruments when it is directed to a selected set of instruments specifically designed by psychologists to use in a particular context and with a particular goal (Urbina, 2007).

We synoptically describe some psychological evaluation tools that can be used as a way to illustrate that dimensions can be evaluated.

We will start with beliefs associated to spousal violence. In Portugal, Machado et al. (2008a), during 2000, developed a Beliefs Scale of Spousal Violence, allowing the evaluation of beliefs regarding the physical and psychological violence committed in the context of spousal relationships. It is composed of 25 items. Each item is a phrase that expresses legitimacy for the use of violence. Individuals have to answer each item on a Likert scale of five points. One means "strongly disagree" while five means "completely agree." High values indicate high levels of acceptance of the use of violence (Machado et al., 2001).

This assessment tool resulted from the need for an adjusted instrument to the Portuguese population to assess beliefs regarding violence in close relationships, enabling a better understanding of the reactions of the individuals involved in them and understanding of the broader cultural context in which these attitudes and practices happen (Machado et al., 2008b). The tool enables measurement of the degree of legitimacy against domestic violence, as well as the factors or specific beliefs that could contribute to such a stance. Factor 1, designated as *legitimization and trivialization of minor violence*, includes a set of beliefs that normalize and trivialize small violence such as slaps and insults, which is understood as common, normal, and not very serious. Factor 2, referred to as *legitimization of violence by the conduct of the woman*, refers to the legitimization of violence by the conduct of the victim, that is, the breach of duties, infidelity, ideas of a bad wife, being slanderous, and/or provocative. Factor 3, entitled *legitimization of violence by its attribution to external causes*, includes items that locate the source of spousal violence in a number of factors outside the abuser's behavior (eg, addictive behaviors, unemployment, economic difficulties, and extramarital affairs). This design is apologetic toward the aggressor and simultaneously assigns it to certain social or behavioral statements, vulgar dysfunctional families, denying the spreading of these issues throughout society. Finally, the fourth factor, called *legitimacy of violence for the preservation of family privacy* covers items that legitimize violence by invoking the notion of privacy and the need to protect families from outside intrusion (Machado et al., 2008a).

The usage of the scale can be for individuals or targeted at a group without time limits. The total score of the scale is obtained by the direct summation of the responses to each item. It is even possible to calculate the score for each factor through the sum of the scores of the items that constitute it. The total score of each scale assesses the level of tolerance/acceptance of the individual with regard to domestic violence (physical and/or emotional). The score of each factor enables a better understanding of the type of particular beliefs involved in this tolerance toward violence (Machado et al., 2008a).

Another useful tool is the usage of a spousal violence inventory. Portuguese researchers have developed the Inventory of Spousal Violence, a listing of psychological, physical, and sexual mistreatments. It assesses the level of perpetration and physical and emotional victimization in the spousal context. It enables us to typify forms of violence perpetrated and suffered in spousal relationships and their regularity, filling a void in the range of assessment tools available to the Portuguese population (Machado et al., 2008b). It consists of two parts, the first being related to behaviors that occurred over the past year in the current affective relationship and the second is dedicated to past romantic relationships. The second part is of optional administration (Matos, 2011). Each part consists of 21 questions covering physically abusive behaviors (eg, kicks or slaps), emotionally abusive behaviors (eg, insults or slander), and coercive/intimidating behaviors (eg, prohibiting contact with others, breaking objects to intimidate) (Machado et al., 2008b). The items were constructed based on the reports of battered women as well as other questionnaires and surveys on domestic violence (Machado et al., 2000, cited in Machado et al., 2001).

In order to ascertain the impact of domestic violence, we must consider that in Portugal there are, for example, the psychopathological symptoms inventory (BSI), a Portuguese adaptation of the Brief Symptom Inventory (BSI) created by Derogatis (Canavarro, 2007). It evaluates psychopathological symptoms at a level of nine dimensions of symptoms and three global indices, which are summary reviews of emotional disturbance. It is composed of 53 items. The nine primary dimensions on which Derogatis leaned upon in 1993 are somatization, obsessions-compulsions, interpersonal sensitivity, depression, anxiety, hostility, phobic anxiety, paranoid ideation, and psychoticism. The items that make up the nine dimensions of psychological symptoms assessed by the inventory are, as a whole, relevant components of psychopathology (Canavarro, 2007). The CID-10 considers the relevant aspects for the development of diagnostics of the first five categories (F00 to F49) (Canavarro, 2007).

Bonding is another important variable in the context of domestic violence. In this regard, we should refer to the *Escala de Vinculação no Adulto*, which is the Portuguese version of the Adult Attachment Scale-R by Collins and Read (Canavarro et al., 2006). It consists of 18 items; factor analysis allowed the identification of three factors, each of which consists of six items. The first factor is called *Anxiety* and refers to the level of anxiety felt by the person, being associated with interpersonal aspects of abandonment of fear or not being wanted. *Comfort with Proximity* is factor 2, relative to the level at which the person feels comfortable with closeness and intimacy. Finally, factor 3, *Trust in Others*, reports to the level of confidence that individuals have in others and the availability of these when you need them (Canavarro et al., 2006).

The items integrated in the scale are numbered 1–5, with special attention to the fact that some of them are quoted in reverse. After listing the items we proceed to the sum of the number of items of quotations that make up each dimension, making the average score obtained (Canavarro et al., 2006).

In terms of coping strategies (mechanisms used to deal with a stress-inducing situation), we should refer to the Problem Solving Inventory. It is a Likert scale with five categories, which can be given a score to each question from one to five. In order to banish response trends, some questions are designed in a positive direction and the others in a negative sense. To assess coping strategies, the inventory shows the individual three types of stressful situations, representing threat of damage and difficulties, exposed to give the notion that can extend in time and tire a person.

It is also important to mention the interest in assessing the scale self-esteem, as well as the personality of the participants, which contain a vast range of possibilities in the latter context. As examples, we have the Eysenck Personality Inventory, Rorschach, Personality Inventory NEO Reviewed, Minnesota Multiphasic Personality Inventory-2, Millon Clinical Multiaxial Inventory-III, and the Personality Assessment Inventory.

At the end of the application of the techniques chosen by the investigator, we should proceed to the statistical treatment of collected data using the software itself (eg, Statistical Package for Social Sciences).

# Chapter 10

# Reality

## CASE 1

Portuguese Caucasian participant, 58 years old at the time of the collaboration, of which 36 years were involved in a spousal relationship, "36 years of violence" [sic]. Self-identified (personal identity) and externally (location, time and situation).

Coming from the central region of the country and the oldest of four sisters. She states that her childhood "was normal. I do not remember dealing with hunger nor walking barefoot. I spent a lot of my time taking care of my younger sisters" [sic]. She studied up to the ninth grade, having failed to pass once.

Regarding family matters, she states they "were always very good. That is why I felt weird at my home. I did not grow up in an environment like this [referring to the violence committed toward her] and I don't remember my father saying a swear to my mother. We would always have pots on the table and my father would always find the nicer bits of food to put on my mother's place" [sic]. She denies any history of violence between couples in the neighborhood where she spent her childhood.

Regarding the relationship with her parents, she says that it was "good, very good indeed. My relationship with my father was good, but I think the one I had with my mother was better. She was like a friend, but I would never go to parties with her like my friends used to do with their mothers. I was never interested in that either. Also, the early pregnancy compromised my freedom. They were a little strict. How can I explain it? They were not violent. My mother had a bigger tendency to get physical. I remember my father hitting me once. One day, I had a tantrum because I wanted to sleep with them and my father took off his belt. The day after, my mother showed my father that I was covered in bruises and he held on to me crying and saying that he would never do that again" [sic].

She states that "it was a different time. My mother assumed she had to stay home and take care of the kids. My mother used to work at farmlands and would help my father farming while I took care of my sisters. I had to learn how to be a woman, a housewife" [sic].

When questioned about her first romantic relationship, she said that "it was one of those short-lived teenaged relationships. I only met him after he came back from the Colonial War in Africa. At the time, soldiers would have Madrinhas de Guerra (War Godmothers—women who would write back to soldiers during wars in order to give them moral support, sometimes without

Forensic Psychology of Spousal Violence. http://dx.doi.org/10.1016/B978-0-12-803533-7.00010-7

knowing him personally). However, when he came back, he saw nothing of what he idealized in me and we stayed friends. It was a paper love. Meanwhile, I was working for a couple at their house as a housekeeper. One of their sons would visit very frequently. I was still studying, but we were getting along nicely. I found out later that he was a bit of a womanizer. He got interested in me and would sometimes say that we should go for a walk and things were developing until the day that it happened. We were not dating, because I knew what he was and I thought nothing would come out of this. They were only temptations. We tried having a relationship three times mostly because he was willing to try and I got pregnant" [sic].

She also adds that "when I had my daughter, my mother was shocked. She would close her windows, dry out clothes by the fireplace so she would not have to put them outside simply out of shame because I became a mother at 20 years of age" [sic].

Regarding her pregnancy, she says that "nobody knew I was pregnant. Not even I knew during the first few months. I have not been with another man to this day after him. So, I got pregnant and he moved on with his life and so did I. I feel like I never really had a relationship with that person. It was, as people say, the love of my life because I never met any other man, but it was a letdown. My daughters were the only good things that ever came out of the two men I met. They were the only ones I ever met intimately" [sic].

She clarifies that "I would always vent with my mother and one day I called my mom saying 'mother, I just want to tell you that I am pregnant.' It was immensely shocking. At the time, there were no cell phones and I would call the operator to put my mother on the line and she would refuse to go to the phone. They rejected me. My daughter was born and they never wanted to meet her at first. I was hospitalized for about a month because I was anemic and they never came to visit. However, one day my father saw the state I was in and told my mother. My father really enjoyed to meet his grandchild. So much that my daughter is obsessed with her grandfather and has always rejected her grandmother because she wanted me to give the little girl to the father" [sic].

Regarding the beginnings of the relationship with the aggressor, she mentions that "we met during the holidays when he came back from the Colonial War. Back then, we would have to go to a fountain to get fresh water and one day, he was there. Afterwards, he went back to war and from then on, we started trading letters. We would only communicate through letters and that is how the flirting began. It wasn't even a relationship, we were just writing. We would say that we were the perfect couple. You have a son and I have a daughter, we will be happy together. But the son never lived with us, my parents-in-law would not let me" [sic].

She states that after the return of her ex-husband he ended up getting a job in another part of the country and proposed to him to come live in the house of an acquaintance that the aggressor knew outside the village. "Then we started to take care of our wedding, but at the time he already showed some signs of aggression towards me. We dated for two or three months, resulting in an aggressive marriage that lasted for 36 years. He assaulted me sexually right after our wedding, but in those two or three months we dated, he slapped me and I said I didn't want to marry him, but my parents rejected me and my daughter was with them at the time. I told them that there was not going to be a wedding after all because he hit me and their answer was 'we told you so. Just because you have a daughter doesn't mean you can't get someone nicer. We always warned you not to get involved with him.' They already warned me that the people who knew of them would say that they are not very recommended people" [sic].

She adds, "my father-in-law would always hit my mother-in-law. For example, at a coffee shop, if she would say something wasn't pleasing her, he would hit her no matter where they were. One time when I was having lunch at their home, my mother-in-law didn't make coffee the way my father-in-law liked, so he picked up the coffee machine and threw it at her. I was the one who stood in the middle. I said, 'hello? you see your dad hitting your mum and you don't say a thing?' and he answers, 'Me? I might get hit with a chair.' He always lived in a very aggressive environment. Afterwards, we got a house we could live in and one day at three in the morning, my mother-in-law knocks at our door, saying that her husband hit her. She was completely bruised up" [sic].

In terms of the first suffered aggression, she states that "we were having dinner and I don't like rabbit meat, but he forced me to eat it. I said, 'I don't like rabbit meat' and as I said that he answered 'if you don't eat it I'll shove it down your throat.' I told him to watch his mouth and he immediately slaps me across the face. He even cut my lip in the process. This happened in front of the couple who lived in the same house as us. They said that 'if she doesn't like it, why are you forcing her to eat? If she doesn't like it, she won't eat it. We can make something else.' And during our dating period, there was another incident. He said he was only joking, but when we were at the table he hit me with the butt of the knife on my hand and I got a hematoma. I don't remember why he did that" [sic].

After telling her mother of the two aggressions during their dating period, she clarifies that "my mother would say to me at the phone 'this is what you do not? You come and go?'" [sic]. She states that "40 years ago, my situation [being a single mother] would not be well accepted in villages. It was the first person that appeared in front of me and I took the opportunity to run away so I could stay with my daughter. I never really liked him. I gave him the straight truth and told him that I was living with him because I respected him and liked him, but I never loved him. I just remained there, finding my comfort" [sic].

Regarding sexual activities, she states that "my ex-husband said that 'since you weren't a virgin when you got here, you have to compensate somewhere else.' So, he ended up ripping me open. I had to get stitches at the hospital. It was sexual, verbal, physical violence, everything. I never had a pleasurable sex life with him. He wanted to do things I didn't want to. Anal sex, it disgusts me just talking about it. He wanted to ejaculate in my mouth and he would put almonds and chocolate squares in my vagina. Everything against my will. He would say 'bring me a glass of milk with no sugar.' He would say that my vagina was very dry. He would fill his mouth with milk and would spit it all over my vagina to make it moist. Just the thought of going to bed with him and going through those things would leave me shaken. It happened many times" [sic].

She also says that "my breasts were always swollen because he would twist my nipples. He would pinch my legs. My daughters would sometimes ask what was wrong with my legs and I would say that I hit a bench or some similar excuse. At the time I was ashamed to tell them the truth, but they know today. Furthermore, he would offend me constantly, calling me a bitch, I could never answer back because I would get beaten" [sic].

When she describes her so-called family vacations, she states that her ex-husband would not stop being aggressive. "There was one or two occasions where he told me to pack things up because we were going back home earlier. He would place his wedding ring on his keychain and would disappear at the beach, probably meeting up with some girlfriend he had at the time. I would stay alone with the girls. These are things that I'm thinking of today" [sic].

Regarding her reactions to the violence, she said that one day she tried to defend herself by fighting back, but ended up subdued by the force of her ex-husband. "My daughter saw the beating he was giving me and tried to defend me" [sic].

Even so, after 26 years, she ended the relationship with the goal of becoming independent. "I wanted to get a job, win my own money. During our marriage, I worked as a doorperson for 31 years, but he would not let me do anything else. He would not let me go out because he was jealous. So those were my jobs: taking care of one or two kids, cleaning the stairs and the building to see if I could gain more money. I wouldn't get a lot of money as a doorperson. The money I would get from the kids went to him" [sic].

But the goal of independence wasn't the only thing that led this victim to gain courage to turn her back to an abusive relationship. "I also saw betrayal with my own eyes. One night the phone was constantly buzzing with a text message alert and since I'm not an idiot, I checked it. Looking back, I shouldn't have done that. I got up while he was asleep and sat on the living room floor checking the sender of those messages who was unidentified. In the pictures, you could see him having sex with another woman. She had her face covered up with a pillow. He is living with her now. I noticed that when he was angry with her, he would look for me. I confronted him and he hit me saying that I shouldn't have touched his things. After that incident, I contacted the police. When the report was sent to our house, he told me: *Bitch, if I find out you were the one who filed the complaint, I'll fuck your life up, I'll kill you!!!* I was ironing and he kicked the ironing board away, held on to the door jambs and kicked me so hard I hit my back on the kitchen counter and fell on the floor. At that time, he was about to drip a pan full of boiling oil all over me but he ended up burning himself, dropping the pan on the floor" [sic].

She talks about two public aggressions. "Me and another friend went to visit another friend that at the time was recently undergone surgery. At the time there were no cellphones. My husband got home and I wasn't there. When I came back he, he kicked me and slapped me all the way down the street. He kicked me yet again. People saw what he did from their windows" [sic].

She states that in some moments, aggressions were predictable. "It was not unexpected because if I didn't obey him, he would hit me. He would leave for work, come back home, eat a sandwich, leave again for a drink, and he would say to me: *I'm going to have a beer, I'll be right back. When I get home, I want you naked and in bed.* That was terrifying for me and, since I wouldn't obey him, he would hit me. He wouldn't even eat afterward. He would just throw the plate on the floor and complain about nothing." Moreover, she points out that the act of breaking plates and other objects was the most typical aggressive behavior her ex-husband perpetrated. "He would destroy everything that I liked" [sic].

She suffered so many aggressions throughout these 36 years that she does not remember the first one. "I just remember the one that hurt me the most. When my mother died, he called me a son of a bitch many, many times (knowing that it was hurtful)" [sic].

"The last or nearly the last assault was when he tried to asphyxiate me with a pillow. It was at the time we were in the same house, but had separate rooms. I would come back home and I had the obligation of coming in, going to the bathroom and going to my room. We would still call me a 'son of a bitch' and I would reply 'shut up, for God's sake.' And he would say: *shut up, or else I'll shut you up for good.* I wouldn't even push back the bed sheets. I would just lie there fully clothed in case something happened. That way, I could run away. So, he came in with a pillow that was on the couch and, thinking I was asleep, he mounts on top of me to asphyxiate me. I couldn't even lock my room door because he would kick my door, as it happened many times, yelling: *I don't want any fucking doors locked in my house!!!* This was the only vocabulary used at home. I couldn't lock my door, but he could have his locked" [sic].

The aggressions, as she says, "were almost daily," but the aggressor never apologized. "What hurts me the most is that he knows what he did was wrong. He said that to our children and other people, but never directly to me" [sic].

Fear was what drove her to endure the punishment for nearly four decades. "He would say that if I left the house, he would kill me. I'm not sure anymore, but back then he would say that when he would catch me, he would run me over with a car and feed me to the dogs" [sic]. Her three sisters knew of the assaults against her. "They say I endured a lot. They told me many times to let go, but he would always say that he would kill me if I did. My daughters would also tell me to leave him." It was in fact one of her daughters that got her out of the house. "One of the days he hit me, he called my daughter and said: *Come over and get your whore of a mother, or else I will kill her.* My daughter came over terrified and told me I could live with her. I said I wouldn't leave, but she was fed up with these incidents and told me that I would leave one way or another. I ended up going with her. At the time, if I had a job like the one I do now, everything would be much easier. Although life is hard right now, I'd rather eat stale bread and a cup of coffee or a glass of milk as long as I am at peace" [sic].

After proceeding with the divorce filing, she got beaten again. As an example, she describes a situation where the ex-husband came across her and their daughter inside their car. "He passed us through the right lane. He was with his partner. He drove in front of us, provoking us. Kisses, patting each other on the head, they would speed up and hit the brakes abruptly. We pulled over and let them get ahead before going back on the road" [sic].

Today, she is living in the house they both lived in, stating that it is emotionally "difficult." "I think about it a lot and it is hard for me to lose something I fought so hard to get. There are certain [things] that I personally had a great sentimental value to me because they belonged to my mother. He already broke one of them and I fear for the rest because we might end up having to split everything together" [sic].

She says that she is living in constant fear. "I changed the lock on my door and sleep with a gas canister and two chairs behind the door, one on top of the other. Basically, the only way I've managed to fall asleep for the past three years was with the use of antidepressants. It's been like this since my mother died. She was my anchor. I've always had a tough life and things got worse after she died. I ended up resorting to a psychiatrist. I would cry a lot and talk about killing myself, so my daughters thought it would be best for me to go to a psychiatrist" [sic].

When asked to describe the aggressor, she only highlights that he "was a great stepfather, he always cared for both." She explained that he protected his stepdaughter more than their shared daughter. "But he was not an affectionate parent. He never went to any school meetings and would only care if they passed or not. But he had no problem in beating me in front of them" [sic].

She describes the support given from the center that aided her as the "family" [sic] that she had. "They have been impeccable with me" [sic].

## Brief Considerations for Case 1

The results point to a person who has experienced some anxiety related to interpersonal issues of abandonment, fear or not being accepted, feeling less comfortable with closeness and intimacy, and having less trust in others. There is evidence of a worrisome bonding pattern, characterized by a discomfort with closeness, low trust in others, and fear of experiencing abandonment (Canavarro et al., 2006).

She describes herself as not very optimistic and positive regarding herself, with a predominantly negative assessment regarding her body and sexual attraction. She expresses anxiety and uncertainty with regard to the sexual dimension. She tends to have a kind attitude toward others. She perceives herself as somewhat impulsive, nervous and tense, feeling insecure in relation to herself (Tap et al., n.d.).

She reveals a general tendency for poorly handling stressful situations, especially at the level of a confrontational attitude and active problem solving, as well as an internal/external control problems. She shows herself to be a vulnerable person with a bigger tendency to be inefficient, to get angry, and possibly to blame herself in times of stress (Serra, 1992).

She is preoccupied, nervous, emotionally insecure, with feelings of incompetence, prone to emotional decompensation, and inadequate coping strategies. She displays a tendency to experience negative emotions such as sadness, fear, embarrassment, and guilt. She is characterized as being reserved, distant, shy, unconcerned, apathetic, and with weak willpower. She is a hopeless, sad, embarrassed person with feelings of inferiority, nervous, unable to control and to resist certain desires, as well as dealing with tension. She has a weak opinion regarding her capabilities and frequently believes she is incapable of doing things. She acts upon or says things frequently without thinking about the consequences (Costa and McCrae, 2000).

## CASE 2

At the time of registry, this participant was a 34-year-old Portuguese Caucasian. She states that she was victim of two violent relationships, one with her boyfriend and the other with a de facto relationship partner.

Self-identified (personal identity) and externally (location, time, and situation).

She grew up in a city environment, describing her childhood as "happy" [sic]. She is the youngest of three siblings. Although she studied in college, she did not finish her academic studies, only presenting her high school degree as such.

She lived with her parents and siblings and states that her educational framing was based on time-outs rather than physical punishments. "Physically, the only memory that I have is one time my dad slapped me hard when I left high school and went to a friend's house and coming home late. My mom would slap me sometimes because I was very stubborn. I wouldn't dress what my mom would like me to dress and was very conflictual" [sic].

The participant described her parents' relationship as "conflictual" with a lot of arguing. "What I remember the most was that both yelled at each other. It was never my dad just yelling at my mom. There has always been some heat between them, but no beatings. My dad would drink a little and would be with other women. My mum always suffered with that but I never had that idea of my dad. To me, it didn't make sense that my dad would be with other women. My brothers were older and were already independent, so I was the one who stuck with my mum the most. When I wasn't at school, I would spend the weekend with my mum. I remember seeing her always very depressed. She even got hospitalized because of her depression caused by her relationship. My dad would always be absent during the weekend" [sic].

Regarding family vacations during her childhood, the victim states that every time her parents had the chance, they would leave her with her aunt and uncle and would travel abroad. "Nowadays, I feel that I was abandoned. I feel that my mum would always help so I'd stay with my aunt and uncle because she was jealous and wanted to be with my dad alone outside of the daily routine. But looking back now, I was basically deposited at my aunt's house until I was 17/18 years old" [sic].

She claims that she was "daddy's little girl" in terms of the relationship with her parents. "I don't know if I was like that because I came later than expected, but my dad was always more present than my brothers. My brothers would spend a lot of time with our grandparents when they were young. I would spend the holidays with my aunt and uncle, but every other day I would spend with my parents. I've always been daddy's little girl, but I used to be a tomboy. I would go with my dad to football games, I'd go running with him and ride bicycles together. I've always had a 'boy' relationship with my father and I liked it. Also, my friends and building neighbors were all boys that did not want to do girly things. That is also why I enjoyed being with my dad rather than my mum. At the time she was always depressed and my relationship with her would always be striking" [sic].

She states that "my mother was always hard working and an active person. There were many times when my dad would come home earlier and make dinner. My dad would always iron clothes. In fact, I remember when I would be eating breakfast, my dad would be ironing his shirt for the day" [sic].

She applied for college at 19 years of age, forcing her to live in a town alone, but she ended up quitting. "I ended up going through less desirable routes and it was bad for me because I had too much liberty. I started consuming ecstasy, LSD, and cocaine every weekend. It was an explosive mix and I couldn't handle it" [sic]. She asked her parents if they could pick her up. "I told them everything. They knew what was going on and always knew what happened. Their reaction was of sadness because my brother was an addict. The conversation went in that direction: *How could you do such a thing after seeing what happened to your brother?* What I can tell from that age is that I always wanted to be accepted, I wanted to be cool, and I ended up doing things I wasn't supposed to" [sic].

She clarifies that she "also took antidepressants and anxiolytics. A few years later, I moved in with my boyfriend at the time and he also consumed some pills and I went back to the same path. I was heavily depressed, I went to treatment again. It wasn't even a treatment. It would just make me sleep all day, which left me confused. I then turned to alternative medicine and went to work with my father" [sic].

She says she experienced "a very big frustration for failing to complete the objective" that she committed to doing. "I've been in three different courses and have not finished any. I never did what I wanted. I wanted to be an actress, a ballerina ... I wanted to be an artist. I was never allowed to do that. I had ballet classes and I might have not tried hard enough. However, when I told my parents that I wanted to do theater, they said that only druggies would do those things. And I thought: *I already do drugs, what's the difference?* At least I'd be doing something that would make me happy. I was never given support. I never truly carried out what I wanted to do and that held me back from growing and becoming an adult. I'm 34 years old and I don't consider myself a child because I already have one, but I think I'm a little immature. My daughter asks me what I do for a living and I tell her I work with her grandmother, as in I don't have a job" [sic].

Regarding her love life, she states that she did not have many boyfriends. "Before dating my daughter's father, I lived four years with a man that would mistreat me psychologically. We would argue a lot and he was very aggressive. He would say I was daddy's little girl and that I had everything the moment I opened my mouth. It was always like this. Sometime I would tell people to tell me no. My mother told that when I was younger, she would say to me 'no' many times but I don't remember. Later, I could not recall a single time I've been said no. So, I understand the person who I lived four years with. Then, I started working with my dad and my partner would tell me to do something with my life, to let go of my parents… he said I had my own life. He came from a very humble family. He made a lot of effort to get his degree and my lifestyle would confuse him. So, I ended up going to university again, but my parents were the ones paying the tuitions. Meanwhile, I ended up getting a part-time job at a store. It fulfilled me a lot since I got the job on my own. I was building a relationship with that person, but our drug consumptions ruined everything. I can't say we were addicts because it was not a daily consumption. We would only do drugs socially on the weekends. We would dance and do LSD. It started being a problem when we started consuming every weekend. That destroyed us, as well as jealousy from both of us. I would tell him that if he was not well with my parents providing for me, he should leave because the house was mine and he was living in it. I would cry a lot every day, it was a struggle. Those things would hurt me and I couldn't understand" [sic].

After that four-year relationship, I was alone for a year after I started working with my sister. "I've always been the family maid. That's why when I met my daughter's dad, I love the idea of 'getting out of there with him.' I already knew him, I knew he was aggressive, addicted to drugs … but I felt seduced. We already knew each other at a distance. We would start going out and after a few weeks, he started living with me. He had addiction problems, but I would just close my eyes. Afterwards, he started living with me and I started consuming less, including on the weekends. I felt that I could be this man's savior and that I should give the example showing him that I could live without drugs" [sic].

She says that her family didn't react too well to her relationship. "I was robbed during the first month of dating, but I believed in him. He stole my motorcycle. He said someone stole it and I believed him out of love. He was also very pretty. I never considered myself as a gorgeous woman and having someone like him looking at me as a fulfillment. We grew a very maternal relationship as I would take care of him. I noticed he has trouble controlling his bladder, especially when he drank a lot. It would confuse me and I'd think I could never leave this man because he needed me" [sic].

The victim describes that thanks to her partner she knew more of the world. "We were about to celebrate our 7-year anniversary. It was a fulfilling life. He was a very handy and knowledgeable man. He spoke five languages, was very smart and he also seduced me. He had a charming side, he was not only a bad person. When he was bad, he would be very mean and violent.

During this relationship, I accepted that there are good things and bad things in relationships. I'd say that to give me strength to stay by his side and endure everything. I had a feeling he was sick. It is impossible to save someone and I made my goal saving him. I could not fail or abandon him. I didn't want to feel frustration again. I would think that if I would leave, he would die. I would think that he would suffer an overdose and never wake up. I had to intervene a few times or else he would die" [sic].

She states she was assaulted for four hours. "It was the first time he beat me. When I told him I kissed the person I got involved with when he was abroad, he ended our relationship and left the house. At night, he came back, knocked at the window as I was living on the ground floor and said he had to talk to me. As soon as I opened the door, he started to beat me. I was barefooted and he would step on my feet with his boots, kick my legs, punch me, tell me to hit him back so he could answer. He would hit me and insult me. Afterwards, he picked me up and cuffed me to the bed. I don't know if he wanted to rape me. He ripped my clothes off, but he was so high that he fell asleep and I managed to get the keys out of his pocket, open the cuffs and ran to the middle of the street. I tried to stop some cars, but they didn't. Meanwhile, I remembered that a friend of mine was living behind my house and I went there. He took away my phone. First, I went to talk to his parents and showed them what he did to me and afterwards I called my parents to pick me up. I went to the hospital and I went with my parents to the police station to file a complaint. Although I was staying with my parents, I wanted to be with him and try to understand why he beat me that way" [sic].

The victim states this was the hardest assault she endured. "But I liked him. I was sick and I would forgive him for his alcohol and drug consumption. I would tell him many times that his twin brother would be here often because he seemed a completely different person" [sic].

She continues by saying that she was attacked before when her partner was drunk. He promised that he would never touch her again. "He took care of my bruise, apologized, and said that he would never touch me again, so I forgave him. I met up with him without my parents knowing and slept with him during that week. I was completely obsessed with him, I wanted to be with him even though he hurt me. I just wanted to be with him. I ran away with him. At first, we were living at his parents' house. Then, we fled the country. At the time, I was beaten at his parents' house. Pushing, grasping my arm … he punched me once. His mum hid me in her bedroom, but she eventually turned me in and he forced me to sleep on the couch. He would say I didn't deserve his company and that we would leave the country because he would let me because my father sent him a message saying they didn't care about me anymore. This means I was only going with him because he felt sorry for me. While we were on the road, he hugged me and apologized, saying he loved me very much and that I was the woman of his life. He got a job abroad and it was very difficult because he would drink every day. The beatings persisted, but they were softer, mainly pushing and squeezing. When he would drink a lot, he would remember that I cheated on him and would start insulting me. I got pregnant during the time we were outside of Portugal. It was not planned. When he got home, I told him I was pregnant and he started crying, saying that we was going to work harder and that we would manage because I asked him if we had the means to raise a child. I wanted to understand if we had the conditions to raise a child. I didn't want to be a single mother. Either we would raise the child together, or we would have no child. Four months later, I had the abortion planned but I gave up because I didn't know what was going to happen. There was a night where I drank a lot because I thought I was going to abort, but the next day he held onto me and begged me not to abort, saying that we could have a family and give the child stability. I believed him. I had a very emotionally unstable pregnancy. I cried a lot. I felt that the mattress was wet, but I couldn't pick it up and take it away, so I would sleep in the floor because he kept drinking and urinating himself. However, during pregnancy, he didn't stop doing drugs. In fact, he would insist that I would smoke with him" [sic].

When questioned about her understanding regarding the violence in the relationship, she answered that it started poorly. "I knew he was tricking me and I would fake it. He was violent, but love changes everything. In women's heads, love solves everything. Alcohol was also added to the violence. I remember during the worst assaults that he was drunk and not high. Heroine would calm him down, even stabilize him" [sic].

She clarifies that the birth of her daughter changed her relationship with her parents, making them more present again. However, the daughter witnessed some aggressive behaviors between her parents. "She witnessed an assault when she was one and a half years old. Her father punched me in the chest when she was on my lap and he almost hit her. I dropped her on the floor. I was literally paralyzed on the floor, I couldn't move. The baby came up to me and for hours she would only say, 'mommy, mommy, mommy.' And he left me there, he didn't even help me get up" [sic].

She claims the attempted strangulation was the reason for her to cease the relationship. "He started drinking in the afternoon and I went to university because in the meantime I started studying again. Suddenly, my dad called me saying that my front door had a broken window. I didn't even think that it was my daughter's father inside my house. Meanwhile, my dad went over to see what was going on. He reaches up the stairs, sees blood and then saw him sleeping on the bed. My dad called me saying that he couldn't wake him up because he must've drank.

He would later go out to find a solution for the broken window so I wouldn't have to stay up all night with a broken window. I picked up my daughter and when I got home, the repairer was doing a lot of noise, but even so he wouldn't wake up. At that time, my daughter was about to turn three. I tried to wake him up and I see blood on the bed which made me panic. He wakes up and I then understood what happened. He was very, very drunk. I put my daughter in the living room watching cartoons and told him to get up and talk to my dad. At least explain why the glass was broken. He explained to my dad, but as soon as he left he started arguing with me. I was taking care of the girl and he lied down next to her, covered in blood. Suddenly, he grabs me by my scarf and pulls me down the hallway. I thought he was going to throw me down the stairs and it would all be over then. I held on to the door and he starts strangling me as I start losing my strength. I started screaming and afterwards, my daughter started screaming too. He was holding on to my neck with his bloody hands and as soon as my daughter screamed, he said: *you fucking bitch, see what you did? Go tell your daughter everything is okay.* The physical violence stopped there and then the psychological violence started. He called an ambulance and told me he was going to get everything straight by making me say I stabbed him so that they wouldn't take her daughter away from him. Meanwhile, I managed to call my dad. He then threatens my dad and brother of killing them. We waited two hours for the police to arrive. When they came, they registered what happened and left. This wasn't the first complaint, but I canceled the previous one" [sic].

She also says that "he did not want to leave the house, so my parents stayed there sleeping. The next day, he was still drunk and said he was taking my daughter to school. I sneaked out of the house and never returned. Meanwhile, he kidnapped my daughter, I ran away for three months because he would not leave the house and I had nowhere to go with my daughter. His goal that night he strangled me was to take my daughter, but I didn't let him. Over my dead body. We waited three months for the regulation of child custody from the juvenile court. He gained the right to see his daughter every fortnight and picking her up from school once. He even got to kidnap her and take her to another country. With the help of the police from that country and an online private detective, we managed to find my daughter and I picked her up. A week later, he was arrested and was imprisoned for eight months. I don't know why. He has already been released" [sic].

The evidence of imminent aggression "was when things got too calm" and he would complain about everything. "I tend to answer back a lot and I was always expecting the day he would beat me. It was a constant psychological violence and the aggression was severe twice a month. In other occasions, he would push me, throw stuff, that kind of incidents. But I would trivialize that because I realized couples arguing is a normal, according to my friends" [sic].

She states that the most frequent aggression was theft. "I would no longer bring money home. I had a euro in my wallet and when I would go to a café to drink some coffee, the euro was no longer there when it was time to pay" [sic].

Regarding the aggressor, he says that "as the man of the house," she had no complaints. "He would bring me breakfast in bed and help me with my daughter when he would do heroin because that was like being sober for him. He would cook food and put up clothes to dry. Because of that I would think that he was lucky he could treat me like he did because he was very good in the other things he did" [sic].

For the victim, the relationship survived because they depended on each other. "It was an obsession and we would isolate ourselves from everything. He manipulated me and made me distance myself from my friends because they were 'stupid' and I was ashamed of him. I couldn't have dinner with my friends because he would start drinking and mess things, as he was very provocative. On my daughter's first new year's celebration, he fell on the floor completely drunk. He fell asleep in my nephew's bed and pissed himself. He was lost without me and I didn't want to feel the frustration of not being able to help him. However, I feel really stupid today. Of course my daughter is lovely, but I don't know how I could get pregnant in those circumstances. I don't know how I was able to sleep with a man who would pee in bed. I don't know how I went through being robbed constantly. I completely erased myself. I let him make me feel like trash, thinking that no other man would ever look at me, that no other man would love me like he did because I was worthless. I would sometimes feel guilty for not being able to build a life of my own, even without him. Maybe if I had a life as a single woman things would have gone in a way that would have let me be human and wouldn't let my self-esteem drop like it did. This frustration of never achieving a final goal is the reason people abuse me. I end up letting people harass me just to please them" [sic].

She states that what she feels for her daughter's father "is complicated." "In this relationship, I created an illusion of a person who did not exist and created the idea of a family that could be happy if it didn't do this or that. Today I know it was a mere fantasy. I feel something I don't like feeling. I feel sorry things got to this point, that he got arrested, that I couldn't put my daughter's needs above his. I haven't seen him in a long time and what scares me the most is what my heart will feel when I see him again. I'm not afraid of going back to him since I consciously know I wouldn't do it even if my heart would say I still like him. I know that if I did that, I would be a victim again and that the aggressor would never help my daughter having a stable life" [sic].

She affirms that "I was an accomplice in this relationship. I would allow him to do what he did and would always find excuses. Many people knew what was going on and would ask me how did I tolerate everything and say that I was worthless, but I would never move on because I kept minding my own business. I would always find excuses to tell my family and friends" [sic].

When talking about the eventual effects on her daughter, the participant admits that she fears the child sees violence as a regular thing in a relationship. "That's why I decided to not tell her he hit me or strangled me, but I felt it was necessary to say mum and dad were angry [with] each other. She raises her hand and screams at me because that's what dad used to do" [sic].

When asked about a possible future relationship, she states she isn't looking for a serious loving relationship for now. "I'm too busy building a stable relationship with my daughter so that she can trust in me. If I'm thinking about another relationship, I can't focus on the present and gain that stability. I don't exclude that possibility as I am still young. I might even have another child in a few years" [sic].

She criticizes some situations that she has dealt with for being a spousal violence victim. "They told me to call their support line, but they had a schedule. That meant I could only be a victim from 9 am to midday and from 2 pm to 4 pm. I thought it was funny the police didn't arrest him right away the night he strangled me. They should've taken him because the house was mine and my daughter was sleeping there. That man has signs of heavy drug use and still had blood on him. Instead, they wanted me to talk to him. If I wasn't here [referring to the institution that provides support to her at the moment], it would be much more complicated. The doctor calls me and is worried about me. She wants to know if everything is okay so she can help me move on. Other institutions don't call me asking if I'm okay. They never wanted to know how the case is developing in court and they knew about the last aggression and the fact that they took my daughter. I know there are much more serious cases than mine, but I'm still part of a case" [sic].

She also adds that despite all she did, no parental powers were removed from the ex-partner. "My daughter's dad was arrested for eight months and I don't know why. He could have stabbed someone and I wouldn't know. In this very moment he has the same parental rights as me. He can see his daughter every fortnight and can pick her up from school once a month. How is it possible for the juvenile court to allow her dad to see her still? I'm still his victim. Yesterday he called me twice with the excuse that he wanted to see his daughter. Then, he ended up in prison" [sic].

Currently, she suffers from a viral disease and can't sleep. "Ever since I reported him a year ago, I got a hold of sleeping pills and anxiolytics, but I refuse to take any. I told them to give me something weaker because I had a child. It's very confusing for me to think that my daughter might call for me and I can't hear her or move. It is a fear I have" [sic].

## Brief Considerations for Case 2

The results point to a person who has experienced some anxiety related to interpersonal issues of abandonment, fear or not being accepted, feeling less comfortable with closeness and intimacy, and having less trust in others. She experiences a worried bonding style, not feeling comfortable with closeness, no trust in others, and feels afraid with the possibility of being abandoned (Canavarro et al., 2006).

She describes herself as not very optimistic and positive about herself, feeling like a slightly irresponsible person who does not like to make her own decisions and carry them to the end. She perceives herself as someone who is incapable of facing life events. She feels that nobody can help her. She doesn't feel secure about herself, revealing sentiments of extreme passivity and energy (Tap et al., n.d.).

She reveals a tendency to deal poorly with stress-inducing situations, especially at the level of internal/external control of problems and facing them, and planning a strategy. She appears to be a vulnerable person who frequently resorts to the validation of others (eg, friends, family) with a higher tendency to be ineffective (Serra, 1992).

She is nervous, emotionally unstable with inadequate coping strategies, and a penchant for emotional decompensation and to experience negative emotions (eg, sadness, fear, guilt). She reveals to be a curious person with diverse, creative, and unique interests. However, she is carefree and with little willpower (Costa and McCrae, 2000).

She is a hopeless person with feelings of guilt, sad, shy, and with feelings of inferiority. She avoids overstimulation and boasts features of wide horizons and an open spirit. She tends to be guided by her feelings, particularly sympathy when assessing and deciding any behavior. She feels worthless with low self-esteem, not very ambitious, and somewhat lazy. She easily gives up in the face of frustration and acts often or speaks without thinking of the consequences (Costa and McCrae, 2000).

## Final Considerations

The results point to a person who has experienced some anxiety related to interpersonal issues of abandonment, fear or not being accepted, feeling less comfortable with closeness and intimacy, and having less trust in others. Doumas et al. (2008) found that worried and fearful patterns characterized by high anxious attachment or fear of abandonment and rejection are related to a negative self-model.

In terms of self-esteem, low values were recorded, which translate into a decrease in positive dimensions and an increase in negative dimensions. Bermúdez et al. (2009) point to decreased self-esteem as one of the main negative consequences of aggression by the partner. It should be noted that although both participants have low self-esteem, the participant in the first case study who registered a lower self-esteem remained in a violent relationship for more years compared to the second case study.

In terms of coping strategies for problem solving, both participants record the near sample value of patients with emotional disturbances, revealing a general tendency for poorly handling stress-inducing situations, especially at the level of an internal/external control of problems and facing them, and planning a strategy.

Both participants show a high degree of neuroticism and low conscientiousness. They are generally worried, nervous, emotionally unstable, and vulnerable to emotional decompensation.

In the second case, we would like to highlight the obsession that the participant has in trying to save their partner, as well as make him grow as a person. This is a phenomenon described in literature, but it deserves the criticism of Vilanova (2011, p. 60), as "there is another situation originating from the emotional immaturity of men: while they continue emotionally underdeveloped in their relationship with women, they more often act as children rather than men."

In conclusion, the opinions, actions, and reactions of an individual are not an immediate action to external stimuli, depending on the way they approach it, motivations, and needs. Such approaches are formed throughout life under the influence of education. However, once they are formed, they determine the actions of the individual or the victim.

## CASE 3

Hello. I was born in an eastern European country with my mother. I am a shy girl. I've been in Portugal for 10 years. My parents came over first looking for a job. I had to stay with my uncles I think. Or some friends, I think. They treated me well. Sometimes I miss them because we rarely talk.

When I came to Portugal, before school started, I would go to the beach with my dad. It was good. I would play with the other kids at the beach. Then we had to move away. We moved a lot and I would have to switch schools too.

I don't remember very well what happened with my parents. Or maybe I don't want to remember. He would sometimes beat my mum. I remember one time my dad came to visit and he forgot his cigarettes. Then, my mother opened the door, went outside, and my dad started beating her. I couldn't think of anything. I just went there and tried to help. I tried to separate them and my dad ended up leaving. When my mum got inside, she called the police. When they arrived, nobody was there any more.

I remember another occasion when my mother started screaming and told me to call the police. My dad stayed there with my mother and I called the police. I ran as fast as I could, I was only thinking about the police.

Sometimes when I would go to bed and try to sleep, I would think about what happened. For example, I thought what if my dad went outside our window again and make noise. Every night I would wish he wouldn't show up so we could rest. I was sad at school, but nobody would ask me anything.

The environment was always bad. I still remember the environment being good a few years ago. When my sister wasn't born yet, my [dad] would only drink one beer. Then, he started drinking more. In my head, I thought I had two dads. One before and one now. They are very different. He wasn't like this to my mother before. They would argue, but he wouldn't hit her. He was never drunk, so he wouldn't do anything to me. Then, he became different. He would get upset with me, scream at us, and complain to my mother. He was aggressive when he was drunk and he was okay when he wasn't. Until he was drunk all the time, so times were never good.

One time, my dad gave me a punishment that hurt me a lot. One day when I left school with some friends, they called my dad. When I got home he punished me by burning my fingers. I think it was for my own good, but it hurt a lot. I don't think he needed to hurt me that much. For example, I love my sister and I would never be able to do something like that to her because I like her a lot and she's my sister. So, I think the punishment was bad and he shouldn't have done it.

Things with my dad got worse and we had to go to a safe house. When we came over, things were very bad. I didn't want to come. Now, I still don't like it, but I know I have to stay here. It was good because I can sleep soundly, but everything is very jittery because there's always kids crying and we have schedules for everything. What I like the most are the activities that they organize for us because I can do things I've never done before and go places I didn't know.

I would talk to my mum about the things that were happening to my dad. Normally, I would always tell my mum everything on my mind. Sometimes I wouldn't tell her about my fear that I would think every night of my dad showing up again and bothering us. Sometimes I was afraid he could kill my mother. I would just remain quiet, hoping that it wouldn't happen. I just waited for time to pass. But I know that waiting for time to go by won't solve anything. We have to do something. Sometimes, I'd say I had enough of what was going on and wanted to go away. I did not want my mother to give my father any more chances. My mum moved once to another house, but he found out where we were and we were back in square one.

I think my dad beat my mum because of alcohol. When he wouldn't drink, he would do none of those things. I don't understand why he would get drunk. He would drink a beer and he would be okay, but then he started drinking much more. He would ask for forgiveness and later he would do the same thing again. It seemed he never wanted to stop doing those things. I remember him saying to my mum: "Oh, let me drink a beer, I'm starting to feel bad." He would drink one, then another, and another … When the violence happened, I just wished it would go by quickly.

In my head, things were very confusing because I miss him a little, but I don't want to think back about those days. It's weird. I don't think about him, but I miss him. I want to be with him for a while, with my first dad from back when. I don't know if that will ever happen because he once started a treatment but he stopped and started drinking again. He would always tell my mother that he wasn't ill, so he wouldn't do the treatment.

I've been asked if he thinks about me. I don't know, but he might. But if he does, he doesn't show it and never tried to do anything about it. I want to see my dad in the future out of curiosity to see how he's doing.

When we were all together, we still had good moments, but we had many more bad moments. I think I'll never forget what he did to our relationship and it will never be completely good ever again. The beatings my dad inflicted on my mum were very serious. The thing that hurt me the most was him burning my fingers. It's very hard for me to write about these things.

Sometimes, I would cry about the things that were happening. Today, I don't cry anymore. I cried before, but I won't cry anymore.

I was asked to write if I had dreams and what they were. I thought about it a lot, but I don't know if I have any. When I was younger, I wanted to be a fireperson, then I wanted to join the police. Now I don't know what I want to do. I've fallen in love before, but I hope I won't get married in the future. I don't want to…

I feel happy today. Last weekend, me and my mum stayed in the house she rented. We are getting things ready to leave the safe house. I feel very well there. I didn't want to go back to the safe house. I have my friends here, but that won't stop me from leaving.

People say I'm very close to my sister. I'm just trying to help her, that's it. I like her, so I take care of her. I would like her to have a good future.

## CASE 4

Today I'm an adult woman whose first child[hood] memory is of my dad beating my mum. I couldn't have been more than three years of age. I remember being on my mum's lap and my dad pushed her, arguing with her.

I think my story is special because my mum was 15 years old when I was born. She got married two months after I was born with 16 years of age and my dad 18. Due to that short time span between us and our life together, I've always been very close to my mother and have very strong memories of everything she lived. Basically, stuff she never told anyone. I was there, I saw everything!

My dad and his family would tell my memories were just ideas planted on my head by my mum, but I know that's not true because I felt those moments, I remember perfectly.

My dad always committed adultery, even before getting married. I wasn't even 10 years old when I found my dad [and] his girlfriends in our beach esplanade. I knew who they were because my dad would refer to them as his girlfriends. There were always arguments. My mum would question my dad about those relationships and those would always end in a beating.

I remember hearing an argument in the living room while I was in my room, supposedly sleeping. I would always be alert, always waiting for that sound of my dad hitting my mum. The sound of my mum being pushed against a wardrobe of simply the sound of body contact. At the time I couldn't do anything because I was too small, but I would end up not sleeping, simply waiting for the confirmation of the thing I was expecting. I was afraid my dad would seriously hurt my mother. He would hit without measuring his strength. He would hit to hurt badly.

More than just the fear of losing her, I felt the frustration of not being able to do anything. As soon as I had the right age and strength, I would place myself in front of my mum because he only beat me twice. I knew he would hesitate to hit me in order to beat my mum. Ever since the first episode I remember when I was in my mum's lap, I feel like I'm a sort of protection for her. If I was present, I knew things wouldn't be as bad. I never felt guilty because as soon as I had the right age and strength, I started protecting my mum. Unlike her, I didn't feel fear towards my dad, but anger. When I had a voice, I told him everything I felt.

A child adapts and finds a way to survive. They survive one day at a time. Until I was 10, the only issue in my family was domestic violence, but then came the drugs. When I hear about domestic violence, I think of alcohol and the fact that people are different when they beat others. However, in my dad's case, aggression would rise up naturally without other excuses. I understood that his love for my mum was obsessive, sickening. He couldn't think about losing her, but at the same time, he did nothing to keep that relationship. I wouldn't even ponder his life choices and wouldn't even let my mum contest them. When he started to drug himself, thing got worse because now violence happened because of money.

Since I witnessed all the problems with my mother, I didn't want to be another weight on her life. On the contrary, I made an effort to be origin of her happiness, so I've always been a good and never got into trouble. I dedicated myself to that mission and I was very focused on my objectives, so that's how I survived.

In my dad's head, I feel like I never was part of that equation. I think I was born as a means to keep my mother. He would only call me to talk to my mum. A few years later, he told me that if he had to choose between me and my mother, he chose my mother.

He didn't want to control me and I'm not even sure if he loved me in a weird way, so he didn't need to hit me. Still today he says that I haven't seen everything and all the things I say or remember are things in my head or things that I've been told but never happened. Now, I can still believe that his memories are distorted because he's a drug addict, his reality might not be the same, but on the other hand I think he's trying to convince himself of his own lies that end up only being true in his head.

My granddad from my dad's family ended up replacing my dad many times and as such I am very attached to him. He was probably the only family member that would protect my mother even if not in the best manner.

Violence always reigned in my dad's parents' house. My grandma, uncle, and dad were never stable, and my granddad never truly faced them possibly because of fear or unconditional love for his children, I don't know. There was always violence. I remember being at the table with my uncle and if he did not have his way, he would be able to grab the table sheet and throw everything on the ground and almost without changing expression he would attack my grandparents. My mum would pick me up and take me away from all the mess. My dad and uncle still don't accept a "no" and I think my grandma on my mother's side is responsible for that. I know there was no education or limits.

My mum always said my granddad was a coward because he never had the courage to go against her wife wanted, even though he was the only one who could do it. But, in my perspective, all those that could have helped and have responsibilities (including my grandparents from my mother's side), my grand-dad was one of the few people we could trust. Even if it's hard to admit it, I know he could have done so much more.

My dad was very jealous. A veteran adulterer, but very possessive! Later, my mum made a restricted group of friends that would come to our house and knew about our problems, but they never did anything. Looking back, I think they were all too young and it's never easy to make a decision over someone's life. At that time, domestic violence was not a public crime and we knew the process was complicated since it was nearly impossible to prove anything. The assaults would happen in front of me (and I was old enough to testify) but only after I was older and my parents separated did the real assaults that would leave bruises happen.

My friends would come on over very often. During the weekend or even after school, my house was mostly full of people! I always organized parties, like slumber parties and even Halloween. We always had motives to have friends at home. My mum was available to help and since she was younger than other mothers, my friends loved her. Still today, my friends from back then would remember those moments. Ironically for them, my house was like a refuge for them where they could have fun and "run" from more conservative parents.

Obviously, my dad would maintain an appearance while my friends were there and I knew there was never a fight or even a discussion while my friends were there. On the other hand, I never thought about him embarrassing me in front of my friends since he was rarely at home. When he was already a drug addict, the worst that would happen was getting off bed in the middle of the afternoon and show up looking terribly, but I think in that time, my friends wouldn't even bother with those details. He would keep his distance when we had visitors. Above everything else, my dad would always manage to convince people that society is responsible for his behavior. Many people thought my mother was responsible for what was going on [with] my dad. Only when his drug addiction started to physically show did people stop paying attention to him.

At the time, I never invited people over for any other reason than wanting to be with them. I'm still like that. Now that I think about it, I think I would do that because I wanted to abstract myself from what was going on when I was alone. As long as we were surrounded by people, we were safe. At the time I wouldn't think like that, it was not a reason to invite people over. Still today, I like to sur-round myself with people. I care about my friendships and I dedicate myself to them. I tend to say they are the family I chose.

At school, nobody imagined what was going on at home because I did not act differently, Maybe I was seen as a privileged person. Maybe they thought I could do everything and have everything I wanted because of the "liberty" they saw my mother was letting me have. I believe that my best friend who would come over very often would notice a few things since I didn't hide anything from her, but we never had a serious conversation about it. I never vented with her so to speak.

I remember the day I told my school friends that my household was a stage for domestic violence. I remember the place where I revealed [to] them what was happening. I didn't do it because I wanted to vent. I did it because ... I don't know, the topic was starting to be discussed more in the later half of the 90s and of course, teens have a tendency to joke about things they don't know about or make less appropriate commentary. As I was frustrated because I knew of the situation and I was appalled with what I was being said, I couldn't help myself from saying that things weren't like that.

I remember them all looking at me shocked when I told them I was living in that situation and it wasn't something recent because they never really noticed. At the time people thought that domestic violence would only happen in low income homes and in very alcohol-driven situations. Nothing changed after them knowing what was going on ... we all remained the same. Maybe with the passage of time they started to admire my mum more because she was strong and never victimized herself. We were never the stereotypes of victims because we didn't show how unhappy we were at home or that the feel of another assault was always present.

After 12 years of marriage, my parents left each other. The divorce only happened two years later. That two-year period was hell. When my mum decided to separate from my dad, he was the one who left the apartment. Although it belonged to my grandparents, they always said the house was mine. However, I think my dad felt wrong for being the one to leave. His obsession with my mum forced him to stalk us heavily. Not even a scene from a film would be able to describe what those two years were like with my mum trying to get my dad to sign the divorce.

The stalking was permanent and we had to deal with it. Every time we left the house my dad would be waiting outside or would chase us if we were driving somewhere with his headlights turned off so she wouldn't see him if it was night time. If he knew we were indoors, he would spend a night on the doormat, waiting for us to leave. Or, if he couldn't get inside the building, he would be constantly ringing our door.

One day, he hid inside the elevator and when we got home he forced us to let him in. He locked himself with us inside, shut the blinds, ripped the phone cords, held them in his hand and took off his shirt, saying we wouldn't leave that place alive. My mum panicked and could only think of a solution. On one hand, I would have to calm her down. That also implies I had to protect her because I knew my dad would think twice about doing something worse in my presence. On the other hand, I could only think about jumping the balcony in front of my bedroom's window on the first floor to the street and call my grandad that lived a block away. I was afraid to leave my mum alone and I just ... stayed. The situation didn't get worse because we managed to fool my dad and make us leave the apartment, but it was a very traumatic experience for both of us.

We never had authority support for all these episodes. One of the most surreal stories I can tell was one time when my dad chased my mum in a car and managed to block her passage, pull her out of the car and violently beat her in public. My mum ended up literally hanging from a bridge in Aveiro and nobody stopped to help or even call the police anonymously. She managed to run away once again to the moving car and my dad jumped on top of the car and held on to it. At that time, my mum thought about breaking abruptly and seriously hurt him, but she didn't have the courage. She opted to drive to the nearest police station. The police person that was at the entrance saw my mum stopping in front of the station with my dad on top of the car and they merely told her that she couldn't park there! This was only a small example of the situations we lived with members of the police force.

One time at dawn, we were sleeping and we heard a noise coming from the living room's balcony. When we got up to see what was going on, we saw my dad climbing up the balcony using a hook. He knew our balcony door couldn't lock properly and so he tried to invade our home again. My mum panicked and didn't know if she should remain in the living room where the phone was so we could call the police or lock the living room and would run to another room. She managed to call the police before my dad could climb in. The police (stupidly) decided to show up with sirens turned on and so, my dad heard and ran away. The police told my mum that they couldn't do anything because he wasn't caught in the action. After they left our house, they rang our door again, saying my mum's car was vandalized. My dad graffiti'd our car with very distinct things like symbols they used when they were dating "… …" which meant "I love you" and the word "bitch" in bold on the car hood.

We ended up being hostages of our own house because a lot of our nights were spent with the lights off so he wouldn't know we were home. When we would leave, he was always waiting for us to come back. Also, we had codes for each other to warn ourselves if he was around or if there was a problem and we weren't together.

Although we were going through some rough times, I always strived to bring some pride and joy to the family. Sometimes I would stay up all night when he was ringing our doorbell all night, but that wouldn't injure my performance the next day. Although I didn't think about this at the time, I think that I didn't want my dad to influence my life even more [than] he already did, so I never let him bother me more. So, I would arrive at school happy. I was a great student and nobody imagined the hell I was going through on a daily basis. The constant planning of the things I did, where I would go, my company and above all HOW could I not have "third degree encounters" of high psychological violence, because I was a teen. That was the right age to feel free and not "stuck" in my own world.

However, my biggest fear was my mum and that feeling that she held me down, so to speak. I asked her many times why she took so long to break up with my dad and she always told me that at the time she didn't have resources to leave the house. According to her, she would have to earn enough on her own to support both of us and that would mean she needed more than one job and so I would have to be taken care of by someone else. She couldn't do this. Besides, since she was very young she was afraid that my grandma would try to take custody of me. So, she decided to break up with my dad only when I was 12 years old and managed to take care of myself while she worked 16 hours a day.

On one hand, I understand her argument and I don't feel in the right spot to criticize her because I don't know what I would do in her place. However, I admit that part of me feels some resentment towards her for not acting sooner. Her "excuse" revolved around her not wanting to take away my security (home, being close to school) and even though it's true my grandparents on my dad's side always did the things my dad should be doing towards the family finances, my effective security didn't go through me staying at the house I grew in or being close to the high school I went to. My security would revolve around peace, having a "normal" life. I only had that "luxury" when I turned 16.

Truth be told, I think my mum endured 12 years of adultery and high degree mistreatments because she loved my dad. It's simple ... Maybe because she liked him and always hoped to recover that relationship. She only stopped doing it and had the willpower to be alone when she truly stopped loving him. But since my mum liked my dad, I like my mum and suffered because of it. If she was trying to protect me, on the other side of the story she was the only one who could prevent me from being exposed to certain situations, namely drugs. It's very easy to talk in hindsight. At the time where there was no support, I believe everything was much more chaotic in my mum's head. She did the best she could with the things she had. I know I am the person I am today because I was LUCKY to have her by my side.

The separating and the complications just stacking up and it wasn't an easy task. My mum had to rent a house for 325 euros at the time, which was what she earned at the time. So she was forced to get a job. At the time she worked 16 hours a day doing everything she could. Also, besides never truly having a father, I ended up "losing" a mother that would play both roles. At 12 years of age, I had to learn how to take care of myself. I would go to school, come back, cook lunch, go back to school ... without ever needing an adult nearby to do my chores.

But besides being good for me because it forced me to grow up and stay focused, it was a "small price" to pay for inner peace. I always said that I'd rather have peace at a different home than having my own room and things. The only thing we brought when we left the house was my room's furniture. We didn't have a washing machine, furniture, we would eat on our own laps sitting in a bed they gave my mum that would also function as a couch, but we were at peace! But most importantly ...

We didn't have money for other things beside the rent and essential goods. We knew how much we had to squeeze every cent, every month. So, I knew that not having my mum around for most of my days was a price to pay to know she was at least safe. My mum would kill herself working because of me so I wouldn't feel things changing, so I could only repay her. I would be a good girl, doing everything not to disappoint her and just being her reason to be happy. I feel that responsibility even today the same way I still have an instinct to protect her. Even today there are nights that I don't sleep just thinking about her well-being and ways of guaranteeing her happiness.

I always place my mum above other priorities, even today. I like making her happy. I know that besides work she has nothing more than me and I think she has the right to enjoy life. Since I know she doesn't do that alone, I feel the responsibility to push her forward and accompany her. We have a very close relationship that not a lot of people would understand. Not only because we have an age gap of 15 years, but because we went through the same problems, very close to each other, so I think that we can count on each other to understand our issues. Sometimes I feel like I'm more of a mother than a daughter because I often compromise my personal life to allow my mum to be happy.

I've felt many times because that I was the one that held on to her and made her live. I knew I was the reason for her existence. She dedicated her time in a 16-hour-long job so we would have a home and go to college and get a degree. Yes, I believe my mother dedicated her best years for my well-being. But now that I have my life straightened up, I think she should dedicate herself to her happiness. She should have more reasons to be alive. My dad took all of that away.

She had to play his own game to manipulate him in signing the divorce. She scheduled a meet-up where she put her life at risk and told him that she didn't know what the future held for them and, who knows, they might come back together, but at that moment she needed him to sign the divorce so she could buy a house and have peace. My dad tasted his own venom and eventually signed the papers. Still, he continued to torment us, but as soon as they got divorced, the stalking and aggressions ceased. The two years of hell stopped the day my mum could turn the divorce official. When my dad would get ready to start a mess, she would show him her ID card saying "divorced." I didn't understand why but maybe he stopped feeling like he "owned" her or maybe lost power, but at that moment we felt relieved. So, I think mum has begun to get a hold of the situation, reconquering her space … but the scars remain.

During that separation period, those two years of stalking, she was really afraid of him. She would panic and remain shocked without being able to think and being able to listen to me when I would try to calm her down. During the stalking phase, my mum decided to counterattack and took self-defense lessons. One time that my dad attacked her and tried to rape her, my mum attacked him with a jiu-jitsu move and broke his rib. He did not report her to the authorities. My mum however would report him dozens of times but I think after that episode my dad was a little afraid of my mum and wouldn't start the violence so easily anymore. In reality he was a coward.

After the divorce, the court agreed on me staying with my dad during the weekend every fortnight and would alternate between Christmas and vacations, but I was lucky that he was not really interested in spending time with me, so I wasn't obliged to the agreement. We would rarely go out and when we did it wasn't longer than going out for dinner. My father also never met with the agreed food pension, so I didn't think I had to comply with the "visits," although my mother has always encouraged us to keep a parent and daughter relationship.

In my case, I would have found [it] horrible to be with him because in reality this relationship had never existed, so I was supposed to forge a commitment and affection that he never felt on his behalf. Even the small moments we were together were very painful, just like visiting my grandma is now. I've always felt neglected as a daughter, so I will never give my dad the rights of being my dad. In my case, it proved to be an extension of my suffering and I wasn't going to create a relationship that never existed. In these cases, I think no one should force a child to be with someone they don't want to. The same way nobody should for a child NOT to be with someone they want to. I think the child even being a minor should have a say in the situation and should be assessed in the given context and by experts.

Actually, I also defend the fact that the child should also give testimony in order to understand if there really is domestic violence. I really wanted to be heard even if I was just 12 years old! I knew that I was the only witness and in order to "catch him," we needed witnesses. The thing I wanted the most was someone to punish my dad.

The truth is that although my parents were married for 12 years, I never had a dad. My mum and my grandad never stopped providing for me and ended up filling his role in my life. My mother has always been EVERYTHING for me and I never felt the absence of a father figure, but the fact that I was used by someone who should love me and protect left scars. Maybe even bigger scars than if he was NEVER present in my life. It would be best if he was just gone.

The truth is that at the time I lost full trust in the courts and the police. I remember the episode my dad was on top of the car hood at the police department's front door and they were more worried with the car parking. I remember the episode with the hood and the fact that they alerted him with the sirens and because of it they were not able to catch him during the act… JUST what we needed! I've never seen any relevant effort from the police in order to follow the situation in order to stay alert or protect us from my dad.

My mum reached a point where every time he would do something to us, she would report him. The idea was that if we actually went to court, we would have evidence of those things really happening. There was a time where a member of the police force said in an ironic tone: "You really want to put your husband in jail, don't you?"

But, even though we had these issues, I considered myself happy and optimist[ic] above all. My mother however would always look at things as a half-empty cup. I noticed that she's holding on to the past, to what it should have been, what she could have done differently (even in things that weren't related to my dad, but things about life in general) and that leaves me frustrated because she can't let herself be happy this way. The past is the past, it's time to rewrite our story without any restraints.

If I assess myself, I know I'm a needy person and maybe that need is a result of a lack of protection that I've felt all my life, even though my mum always tried to compensate for my dad's failure. I see that need in relations of all kinds, even with friends. I dedicate myself to my friendships, I'm always there if I can, if they need me, and I always go beyond, but I also need to feel loved and feel the need that they try as hard to make me happy as I try.

I feel that need in romantic relationships too. I've only had two boyfriends, but to me, they have to be men that I feel they can protect me and above everything else care for me. I've always been lucky: I'm independent, I survive alone unlike other women who show more frailty and feel problems in a more painful way, but what bothers me is being seen as a fort that will never fall. My friends and my boyfriend sometimes look at me and think I will never tumble over and so they don't value me when I'm feeling down or feeling unsure about something because they think: "Oh, that's nothing for Lua, she'll get over it." Sometimes I would like to be seen as other women, vulnerable and fragile, and I would like to be given support with the same intensity as they give to other people with not as serious problems. Simply just verbalizing their support with more intensity and more frequently. I admit that I feel that need.

Both at a personal level but also at a professional level. I (almost) always say what I think at work and it doesn't always leave my mouth in the best of ways. It's difficult for me to control myself and I found out if I keep things to myself I get sick, literally! When something is wrong with a friend or even my boyfriend, I don't feel good until I spit it out and fix things with a conversation.

Back then, I thought that I would never cross the same line my parents did because I thought if you love someone you don't argue with them, but the truth is I myself have never crossed the line, but I've stepped on it. Unfortunately, I found out that at times, we love in such an intense way that everything becomes so strong that we don't mind losing our dignity or respect as long as that person stands by our side. I'm not in favor of violence and if I'm outside of a relationship and analyzing it, I'll say that verbal violence is enough to end a relationship, but truth be told, when I'm in that situation as a girlfriend, I've been verbally assaulted on and I've assaulted someone before and didn't end the relationship.

Sometimes I would confront my mum saying how could she tolerate some things, but now after growing and loving someone, I understand her situation better. Truth is, I think she loved my dad much more than she loved herself. We've always been frail and insecure, even though we've always been seen as strong, confident, and independent women. Maybe it was because of that fact that she reduced herself into an unhealthy relationship. My mum had and still has low self-esteem, but nobody would believe it after meeting her!

Of course it is painful to know that she didn't have the strength and courage to act sooner. I have an idea of her in my head and being powerless or a coward is not part of that idea. She was brave even if she took a while to pull the breaks! My mum's situation was very dramatic and I think it's very hard to judge her.

I never thought of the drama from my perspective, so I never allowed myself to feel the situation from my point of view. When people told me to confront the situation, I didn't understand what the issue was with being the "child" of domestic violence and becoming a "normal" person.

I wished my family was "normal." I wish I had a present father that wasn't toxic, a father that loved me, that would give importance to my life events, that truly knew me as a person, but that never happened. My dad never knew for sure how old I was, my school year, if I preferred blue or pink, meat or fish.

At 26 years of age, I decided to give him another chance to prove that the memories I had were not made up but that I was available to make new memories. Everybody said I was making a mistake but I kept pushing forward the idea. I welcomed him to my house, but it was all a reason for him to manipulate me again. The thought that if he managed to convince me that I would talk to his dad to "help him change his life." And, even though I told him it was the last chance I would give him, he used me to get money. There, it's a fact. This is the dad I have: I only exist so he can gain something and he doesn't care if he loses me forever.

If her mother wasn't alive any more, I don't think I'd ever see him again, but I still go to her place to visit. At the moment, she's there alone. I mean, she lives with my uncle and my dad, which means that she lives through hell every day (that I know very well) and I can't feel well with that idea. Deep down I don't want to feel guilty, so I might visit her for selfish reasons. I know that sooner or later she will pass away and I don't want to feel a heavy conscience. I don't want to think that I abandoned her and didn't go there often enough or that I didn't do all I could. I am an only child, only grandchild, and I feel that I carry a lot of responsibilities. Still I think I'm in a more stable and accomplished period of my life where most of my wishes and dreams are becoming a reality.

One of my biggest, if not the biggest dream that I have, is being a mother. It is a dream that I have since I can remember, so it goes much beyond the biological clock. It is a wish that comes from inside, really. I will feel accomplished the day that I find out I'm pregnant. That dream is a life dream because it will be a life that I will love, protect, and dedicate my time. I give a lot of value to family and tranquility. If I can have both, even better!

## CASE 5

I don't want to say my name, but I also don't want a fake name. I simply want to share my story and hope other women can escape from their suffering that I still feel today.

I grew [up] in an environment of domestic violence. My dad would frequently beat my mum and he would then beat us when we tried to protect her. We were young but we would try to separate them. I kicked him sometimes and he would have his legs all bruised up. Me and my brothers grew up and the beatings were becoming less frequent. I was young but I still remember like if it was today: my mum would come back home from work, buy food, and would take a very long time. My dad would ask her all the time, "Bitch, where have you been?"

I remember one time she had the table set up for a meal. It's another situation I will never forget. We were supposed to eat roasted snapper. He holds on to the table and flips it. No dinner for us.

When I was 9 years old, I found out he had a lover right in front of our house. I remember she had a little girl who she took care of and told me we could play on the backyard. So I went since I wanted to play and then when I came back home he went to work and she came back home. I made my parents' bed and found 10 escudos. I thought it was weird, but I grabbed the money and went out to buy peanuts, lupin beans…it was a fortune! Afterward I sat in front of the lady's house. When she left the house, she saw me with all those things and asked me, "Where did you get all that money?" I said that I found the money on my parents' bed and she said that money was hers and that she was going to use it for shopping. I started thinking why was her money on the bed. When my mum got home, I told her about it. My mum then saw my dad through the window jumping over the fence. That relationship lasted 10 years.

Personally, I was never a person who enjoys flirting. I always said that I didn't want to marry so I wouldn't go through what my mum did. Meanwhile, I grew up and one day when I was 19, my aunt says, "Let's go outside to a friend's house." My future husband was there. Unfortunately, it was love at first sight. I never dated before but I think he was dating at the time and he met up with his girlfriend the day we met.

Two weeks later, my aunt calls me, "Do you know who's here?" she asks. I asked who. "It's Tó Manel, he says he wants to talk to you." I was so surprised. We met up and asked me if I wanted to date him. I said I would think about it, but he was always calling me and he would always come over on Sundays at lunchtime until the day we started dating. We dated sometimes for six years. He never truly showed himself, he was always very sweet.

We then married and he went to Africa, coming back a few months later. At the time, he would slap me occasionally. We had a trailer in a camping spot. I took my mum there once and he slapped me. My mum saw and asked, "What was that for?" But he simply said that it was nothing. What about me? I remained silent once again like I've always done before.

We would live 24 hours together because we worked at the same place. One day, our boss got replaced and he got promoted to that position. We worked at a warehouse and the first thing he told me to do when he became my boss was to sweep the floors. I never did that before, not even with the old boss because that was the janitor's job. I told him I wouldn't do it, but he insisted, "Yes you will!" He picked up the broom and he put it in my hands. I told him again I wouldn't do it and he beat me with the broomstick. If at the time I would have call[ed] the administration, he would have been fired. But I once again shut myself down and sweeped the floor.

I always received punches and slaps. The neighbors suspected that I did get beat. One of them was a close friend and would say that I wasn't okay because I was usually covered in bruises. I would simply answer that I hurt myself in the warehouse.

Years later, he was operated on his back and retired. I kept his position. He was furious that I kept his job and would say that I wanted to receive the same salary as him. He would be pissed all the time and wouldn't let me go to the company's Christmas or New Year's party. All would go but me. I was ashamed that I would always have to find an excuse. One day the company closed and it became total chaos. I lost my job and ended up staying at home for long periods of time. He would constantly blame me for not getting a job because I was the one telling him he should retire, but in fact he was the one that asked to retire earlier and only after he did that did they give me his job. I was so tired of him telling me I wanted money more than I wanted him!

After I had to stay home, things became unbearable. He would always find an excuse to hit me constantly until he one day tried to kill me.

After so many years of violence, my son only saw us fighting once. I don't forget what happened. I like to do crosswords. I always buy those little books and I do them. The living room was really warm and with little light because the blinds were shut. I asked him if it was okay to open the windows and that I would lean on it doing my crosswords. If he didn't want me to, I'd go somewhere else. Since he didn't approve, I went to my room and opened the window, finishing my crosswords. After a while I left the room and noticed a lot of brightness coming from the living room. He ended up opening the blinds. I told him, "Honestly Tó, I asked to open the window so I would keep you company but you didn't want to so I went to my room. Come on!"

He suddenly stood up, grabbed me, and took me to my son's room because nobody could see or hear anything from that part of the house. He grabbed my hair and knocked me down. He hit my head on the floor again, and again, and again. I can't tell how many times they were. He punched me and I would twitch and move in hopes that he would free me. I pulled the furniture where the TV was on and the cables popped because they stretched too much. Since I was screaming for help because he wouldn't let me go, he took me to the kitchen. During all that time, my poor dog would howl and bark, pulling on my clothes. Today, I think that he was trying to separate us. It [the dog] tried to help me getting him off me.

In the kitchen, everything that was glass was smacked against my head. I ended up with a lot of hematomas. There was blood everywhere. When I was powerless on the floor, he opened a shelf and took a knife. He jumped on me with hatred on his eyes and tried to cut my throat with the knife. I was lucky because I was wearing a turtleneck that would fold three times. I held on to the knife and tried to keep it away from me even though I was so weak. It seemed like God helped me twist the knife and I ended up with the knife on my hands.

I never managed to get him off me. I pushed everything in an attempt to get him off me. I only managed to move from under him because there is a space between the fridge and the wall and I held on to it. As soon as he grabbed my arm, I managed to run from him slipping under him. He kept my sweater, which was completely covered in blood. He pushed a stick into my mouth so I wouldn't scream and I bit his finger. I ran out the door and everyone was there ringing the bell. They even called my son. After all that happened, he had the nerve to say he didn't remember anything. When he came outside, all the neighbors were there and he said, "Is this the shit that you wanted? There you go." Afterwards, two ambulances arrived, one for each of us.

During all that aggression he would call me a bitch which would also hurt me a lot. What happened hurt my soul and I can't stop crying about what happened in the past and today because everyone respects me. I never met another man. He was the one that would come home with his zipper open. People would tell me but I wouldn't believe. My biggest mistake was never calling the police. Enough was enough, but I didn't do it.

We went to the same hospital and [were] taken care of at different times. Of course, I was the first to receive care because I was much worse than him.

After leaving the hospital, I went to my son's house for a week. My son would say, "Why dad? Why? You had such a good woman at home." My dad would barely answer him, saying, "She provoked me."

A few days after, I went to the police to remove my report but they said if the public ministry would find the case as a very serious matter, they would not close the case. And so it happened. They didn't close the case and he was under house arrest for eight months.

A few months later, I was in another house doing my crosswords. He got up and went to the other room to watch TV. I went up to him and asked him why he went to the bedroom to watch TV if there was no need to have two TVs turned on. I asked him why he didn't want to be next to me or if he wanted I could go to the bedroom so he would stay in the living room where we had a flat screen and he could be more comfortable. In the next instant as soon as I was leaving the kitchen, he comes over to me and punches me. It was like a horse kicking me. I mean, I think a horse kick wouldn't be that strong. I fell and hit my back on the floor. I started to swell up and my face looked like a cake.

I managed to call my son. When he got over he wanted to beat his dad, but I told him not to do anything. He grabbed him still but he didn't do anything as he saw his dad pushing me against the door and contacted the firemen and the police.

Meanwhile, when I went to the hospital, my husband tried to kill himself with ammonia acid. He took a sip and went to the hospital. In my opinion, he tried to simulate suicide but that didn't turn out well. He was the one who asked for help to the firemen. He had his schedule and his phone on top of the table and he disappeared with the documents. He did that because I went to my son's house.

He specified at the hospital that he didn't want any visitors. Would a person that is in a critical state that drank and drank still worry about paperwork? I don't believe that. Maybe he thought of everything. However, due to him not wanting any visitors, I went on vacations with my son. At the beginning it was hard for me, but my son helped me relax and insisted that I went with him. Dad already said he didn't want any visitors so nobody would see him.

When he got out of the hospital I felt sorry for him, so I went back home. It's been two or three months so far. I'm ready now though. I put a stone bust next to my nightstand. I'm ready in case he attacks. It might be hard for me because I like him a lot, but it's kill or be killed.

Honestly I don't think that's the solution because I've never been that kind of person, but the truth is the only thing that keeps me here is my son and my grandson. If not for them, I would have killed him already. At least this martyr would be over.

I know that I still like him while I'm writing this, but I don't know what I like about my husband. I never met another man, never liked another man. Liking someone is sharing, loving, fondness, a kiss, but I feel nothing like that for a long time. When we lived together without children, we would hold hands while watching TV, but then everything changed.

At that moment, regarding the case in court, I don't know what's going to happen or if he's going to jail. I'm confident that he's going to jail but I'm not completely sure yet. Let's wait to see if he really is going and then I'll take care of myself.

I find it curious while reading this testimony, I would have told this person to leave her husband already. But I don't exist, I believe that there is no other person like me. I don't know where to stand, I end up sitting behind.

For example, he wanted me to stop talking to a friend of mine who had breast cancer. Every day we would go to the coffee shop, we would go on walks and come back home. But he started complaining. He would get home and start calling us "lesbos." So I stopped being with her. It was very hard for me because we talked a lot and I helped her. I made her lose the shame of wearing a wig because in summer it would be very hot. I stopped going to the coffee shop just to stop hearing him. I even stopped painting my nails because I didn't want to hear anything.

I feel that the assaults I suffered and the insults I heard were very rough on me. I'm sick in the head, my body would get numb and I would have to go to the hospital. I get there and they give me medicine, something bitter and tell me I have a big depression. I have insomnia, vomits…

What's amazing is that even after all these things, I still sleep with him even though we don't have anything together. Sometimes he gets close to me but I push him back. I can't do it and I don't need it at all.

Although all this happened, I was never afraid of him and I am still not afraid.

I remember many times what my son told me when I came back to him after the second big beating. He told me annoyingly, "Well mum? Is this what you want for your life?" I would answer him with another question, "Who is going to take care of your father?" He simply told me to think about it and do whatever, but he didn't think it was a good thing. The conversation stopped there … I told my husband I would go back home if the idea pleased him, but I wasn't going to be a sandbag that he could beat up because it would be the last time and I wouldn't answer by myself either.

Although I talk to my son every day, I feel that he judges me in some way. However, I think that every person deserves to be in their home at ease. It's not that I was mistreated at his house. I just want my own place and I don't want to be an embarrassment for his marriage.

I never looked for a safe house although the doctors suggested me to. They are afraid that one day it won't turn out so great for me and I understand. This time I decided to rent a small house, but I don't have the money. I could collect half my earnings, but I don't want to do that.

I was never happy. I don't have any dreams, I would just like to live a few more years to see my grandson marry, but I won't see that. I'm 52 years old and I don't know why I say that, but it's just a hint.

I hope that anyone that reads my suffering and feels my tears can wish me luck. When I accepted to share my life story, I knew I wasn't going to write everything without shedding a tear. I spent a life crying alone. I hope many people read this book and [it] helps them in the future.

## CASE 6

My name is Paula and I'm 39 years old, but that doesn't matter as much. What matters the most is that I'm a woman hurt by life.

I've always been a good student. I went to elementary school and prep school with my future husband, but until fifth/sixth grade he wasn't the type of person I would deal with or play with him. We only started to socialize in seventh grade at the city's school and afterwards we started dating.

The dating period was normal. We had a few bothers, but nothing special. After ninth grade, I went back to my old high school, but my husband failed to pass due to not showing up to class to work at a construction site.

I was very young when we started dating. I was 16 years old and I wanted to leave school to start working. He was my only boyfriend, I never dated anyone else.

Three years later we got married, got a house and he managed to get a job at the GNR (Portuguese National Guard). He came to Lisbon to study a course and we ended up living in the suburbs. At this time, my oldest daughter was three years old because she was born right after marriage.

After some time in the GNR, he thought it was too much work and chaos. I wanted to stay where we were, but he decided to go back to our town. But before that happened, we spent a year in Porto and another year in Braga. Only afterwards did we find a place back home. After many years in the force, he switched stations often, but always close by.

Meanwhile I became pregnant with Filipa. We didn't plan this, we only wanted the oldest child. My marriage was never good because there were many complications up from the beginning of the relationship. I would see, hear, and keep quiet. I knew he would do drugs, drink a lot, and stay up many nights. He would come home when he wanted and wouldn't say a thing.

Five years ago I found out he was meeting with another woman. From there it was chaos, things went very bad. He would ask for forgiveness and I would leave the house. He would then beg me to come back to him. I will never forget 11 September. I knew through the phone that my husband was with someone else. It was my older daughter that showed up. I had all the proof in front of him and she asked me, "Mum, do you think it's weird dad gets more messages than me?"

Facing the truth hurts a lot. I was in a big depressive state. I lost 20 kilos in two months. I wouldn't eat, I would only drink coffee. He would come home at any hour and I would scream at him. He would tell me he would never repeat those behaviors and I ended up going back to him on 31 December at 7 pm. It was a festive season and I wanted my daughters to be in their house, in their rooms. But after a while he was already trading messages with the other woman. He asked for forgiveness but he would keep breaking his promises.

A few days after, he fell asleep on the couch. I saw his messages and one of them was from a bar. It said Caty or Fany wished his best customer a happy new year. When dinner time came, he asked me why I didn't eat. I said I didn't want to eat. I lost my hunger. He also asked me what was going on and I told him that we would talk after dinner so he could eat first.

We were still in the kitchen when I was about to pick up his phone but he anticipated himself and picked it first, knowing what I was going to talk about. He threatened to throw it at me. "You're stupid, a sack of shit, this is a playful trick by a friend of mine." I answered that I didn't know who he was and I never saw anything like that. It was hard for me to believe what he was saying.

He went to the living room and we kept arguing. He got up from the sofa and he hit me again with many punches to the head. In the middle of all of this, he would scream to my youngest daughter to keep eating her food. I wasn't capable of looking at the scared child. She would cry and wanted to go to her room.

In the past, the assaults would happen multiple times. My daughters and I were very afraid. He was in a horrible state and would react very aggressively. Even today, I can't stop getting emotional.

I came to the building stairs asking for help. My screams would echo throughout the building and the neighbors called the police. He grabbed my head and smacked it against the door. Until the police got here, he kept hitting me and my 11-year-old daughter tried to stop him. When the police got here, he confirmed what he did and I said I was afraid to go back home with my daughter. As soon as they knew what his job was, I knew nothing would happen. They said they would come back so I would file a report and maybe he would be calmer. After a while, the police came and said that they talked to him and I could calm down and not be afraid. "He has a gun," I said in panic. The policemen insisted that I could calm down and not be afraid.

The next day I went to the hospital because of the beating I took and when I came back home my daughter was afraid to come inside. She would say, "Dad will hurt us." But I saw that he wasn't inside, his car wasn't outside. We stayed home that day.

The morning after, I got up to take my daughter to school and he turned to me saying that I could only leave the house if I left behind my money, credit card, and other documents. When I gave him the stuff, he grabbed them with one hand and hit me in the hand with the other. He left me with no money. After leaving my daughter at school, I went to the police station to file a complaint.

When I came back home, I called my oldest daughter that was studying away from us and she told me, "Mum, you're insane in staying there. Grab my sister and come here. After the complaint you did, he's going to wreck you! Go to your friend's house and spend the night there. Come over to my house first thing in the morning."

These words are still engraved in my mind. It was all so intense that it marked me a lot.

I did as my daughter said so. The social worker paid my bus rides and when I got over to my daughter's house I already had lots of phone calls and messages insulting me, asking for rent money and threatening to stop paying the bills. The threats were chilling. A few hours later, he started spamming messages again and trying to call me, but this time he was begging me to come home. Since I didn't answer, he called my daughters threatening us again.

A few days later, I went to APAV (Portuguese victim support association). I was afraid because I didn't know what could happen after I left with a minor. When I went to my daughter's house I had to tell the police where I was going.

In one of the attempts of contacting my oldest daughter, he tried to tell us he was going to kill himself. He asked to talk to Filipa and to me, thanking us "for the good times." I refused to talk. Before turning off the call, he said, "Thank you for everything and goodbye forever." I started crying thinking he would do something, but my daughter calmed me down, "He's not going to do anything. He's just trying to manipulate you." It was just as he said. I didn't pay any more attention to him and since then he started to threaten me and my daughters' lives.

I called APAV to talk to the same assistant that helped me before and they told me I should go with my girls to a safe house. I told them I didn't want to. Actually, I didn't even know what is a safe house.

Since my daughter wouldn't answer her dad, she also started getting death threats. Moreover, he stopped paying car insurance and her college tuition, so she had to cancel her registration. He told her if she wanted anything that she should go work to get her own money. He was the one who was doing drugs and didn't know his daughter was already working.

He started with hashish and weed, but he ended up trying other drugs. I knew he did drugs since he was 11, even when we were dating.

Things got worse in the last four years because I stopped staying silent. I was quiet ever since we started dating. For example, at my daughter's wedding we were arguing at a coffee shop because he was paying everyone's coffee. I didn't like that and he would only say, "The money is mine, I worked for it and it's none of your business…" and I would stay quiet. After getting married, the first time I had to shut myself up was when João, my oldest daughter ,was still a baby. The discussion started because he would go for the coffee shop every night and he got all angry, beat me and he didn't want to give me my daughter. We were married for one or two months. He kicked me out of the house, locked the door, and kept the little girl inside. Afterwards I met up with my mum and my brother who was on vacations. My brother and mother-in-law went back to my house and knocked on the door but he didn't answer. He only opened the door to his mum but he wouldn't give me my girl.

My brother and mum didn't say anything because at the time we were dating, they told me he had a rough attitude, he would drink a lot, get pissed off with everything and spend days where he would not speak to anyone. After I chose to get married to him, my mum never talked about him ever again because she knew I messed up.

The pain that I feel is immense. I still think about the reasons that made me stick to this mistake for so many years and I don't even know the answer. I would say it was because of my daughters. Actually, I started living solely for my daughters. I erased myself completely, taking care of the house and my daughters. I knew I was the mother he never had. I knew his mother only existed to wash his clothes … she never gave him any love.

My daughters never had a kiss or sat on dad's lap. Today, my daughter sees her cousins sitting on my brother's lap and receiving kisses and sometimes comments that situation or just looks at them sweetly. All this makes me feel rage inside me, I just want to kill him. He never met any of my daughters' teachers or went with them to the doctor once. He would limit himself to driving them somewhere and paying the bills. I feel like my daughters never had a father, the same way I feel I never had a husband. The most I had was a person, a friend … more like a person I knew many years ago, but the truth is that a friend doesn't beat another friend, doesn't mistreat or insult.

When my daughter enrolled for college that's where I noticed something was wrong. I noticed my husband was different. He would stay up all night and drink with his friends and do drugs, but I never thought he was with someone else. It's so hard to hear, but my daughter still tells me today, "Mum, how is it possible that he wasn't cheating on you with the lifestyle he had, day after day?" Truth be told even the backseats of the car were all dirty. I didn't want to believe it.

Before I found out he cheated on me, he bought a gun because the ex-partner of that person he was seeing (who was a prostitute) started threatening him because he knew my husband was involved with her. Every time he would meet up with her he would take his gun. He would leave the gun carelessly. For example, my daughter got a cat with her friends in Braga and one time she took the cat home. The cat went under the bed and when she pulled it from under the bed, it was holding on to the gun.

Things were getting hard, so I called my husband's best friend who was also from GNR asking if something was wrong with Paulo. He calmed me down saying he would talk to him. A day later he called me saying that my husband told him he was having some issues at work. I did know he was having issues at work because one time they scolded him and his partners for being drunk during working house and people filed up reports against them. At first I believed he was changing because of that, but then I noticed something else was up. Since all cellphones were registered in my name and I asked for detailed bills, I would see all the dialed numbers for text messages and I would see that woman's number all the time. There were even times where we were both sitting on the couch together and he was texting her. I talked to him, told him about the situation, but he didn't do a thing about it. I left the house, I implored him, tried everything.

He is still working. He has always been an authority up until today. His superiors knew of his alcohol abuse. The GNR psychologist advised him to undergo a treatment four or five years ago because he had suicidal-homicidal tendencies and wanted to hospitalize him, but he didn't want to. His boss warned him about the situation and nothing happened because they always try to cover each other's backs.

Last year he didn't go through a night shift without being drugged or drunk. I say that convincingly because during the afternoon he would go out drinking with his friends and he wouldn't come home for dinner sometimes. He would head out from the bar to work. Since it was a night shift, they would go to some alley, fall asleep, and in the morning go back to the police station.

One time he came home with a partner and they spent the night there. They were exhausted during their shift, so his partner slept on my daughter's bed. When it was time, they went back to the station. He told me if someone was looking for them not to say a thing, and so I kept shut. He didn't even tell me where they went or anything. Still today, I don't know where they went. I spent many night without knowing if he was okay.

The saddest thing for me is that the GNR superiors gave and still give protection for these behaviors. If they didn't, him and his partners wouldn't be there anymore. That makes me lose some respect for the authorities. They all know each other and they go out drinking.

I made a filed complaint at the PSP (another Portuguese police entity) near my house and the first man that heard me seemed nice. When I told him my ex-husband was a GNR, he seemed surprised and was critical of his behaviors. The second man that talked to me was protecting my husband. He told me to talk to my ex-husband's superiors because if I filed a complaint there at the PSP, it would go to court and things would become bothersome. He discouraged me to keep on going with the complaint.

He already broke many of my cars. We had six cars and he broke all of them at night. One time it was 6 am and he called me completely drunk saying he hit a car and he completely wrecked our car. It was 6 am and he was going to work at 8 am, it was impossible for his boss not to know.

They know of the assaults against me because I reported it, but they don't know of all the others. I said I was going to file a report, but I never did not because he was part of the police but because of personal reasons.

As hard as it is for me to admit it, my life was being at home and at work, going to Filipa's appointments, and nothing else. He never wanted to go out with me. When I would tell him we could go out on Fridays or on the weekends, he would start shouting, "You know very well that I don't have weekends."

His life was only about the booze, he never helped me in anything. For that reason in these last years I understood that we had to go out together. I went to the coffee shop with him and Filipa, but his partners and friends didn't see me as "Paulo's wife." He would usually go alone.

Meanwhile in one of those nights out that I forced on him, he told me to go to a bar in another village because of the gun he bought. When we arrived, there was a man that asked me if everything was okay with me and Paulo. I said [yes] and asked why. I was perplexed with his explanation. The man told me, "The bar owner say he saw Paulo with a short woman who he introduced as 'his girl.' Since you're not short and you don't come here with him often I found it weird." I couldn't stand it and ended up venting with him. I told him what was going on and this man said I was crazy because you don't forgive betrayals. Although I heard very harsh truths that night, that night I felt like someone truly listened to me.

He would still carry that gun in the bar and he would show it to everyone who crossed him. When we came back home I was so afraid because he wouldn't let go of his gun and I thought he was going to shoot me. I thought he was going to kill me. When he was at the bar he wouldn't stop messaging the other woman. We were alone and I felt very awkward. I prayed to all the saints that I would arrive home safely because he wouldn't stop touching the gun. I didn't know if I would rest easy in my bed that night, I didn't open my mouth and he started blasting music on the car. He was so drunk! After that big scare that made me fear for my life, we still lived together for another two years.

Technically I'm still married, but I'm completely decided in not having that title. When I saw him at court, I was afraid to feel something for him again or having an urge to go back to him. If that happened it would be a problem because it was a sign that I wasn't okay. Today I like myself and my daughters much more than him and that gives me the strength to not go back to him.

I was exhausted and fed up with all this because I tried everything, but he would tell me the other woman wouldn't let him [go] because she threatened him to tell GNR that he was doing drugs. She is a 44-year-old woman who also does drugs, has three kids, has been in many relationships, and I think social services took her kids away and now she lives with her mum. She's the type of person that drinks a glass of wine in the morning and does drugs right after. I believed in his story, but I reached a point I couldn't take it anymore.

He swore he would talk to her so she could leave him and I told him I would go with him. We picked her up at her house and she spoke in front of me. He said that he wanted to stay with me and that he liked me a lot. After this conversation I was shocked; he asked me to leave the car so he would stay with her alone. Everything fell on me, I felt my body heavy and my heart beating very fast. It was such a backstab that it still hurts today. I asked him, "Do you realize what you're asking me?" He merely insisted that I got out of the car. I only had the strength to ask him, "But Paulo, you text this woman every day and you still have something to tell her that I can't hear?" Still, I left the car. It was such a hard time for me, I still question how could I humiliate myself like that. I have no answers. Maybe I just can't handle the truth … A few minutes later (which seemed an eternity), I opened the car door and said, "I'm sorry, but I think that's enough! You talked everything you had to, I want to go back home." During the trip home we started arguing and everything stayed the same. This means he kept texting her.

I found all of this in September. A couple of months later in November, I went to the doctor and he noticed something was wrong. He asked me what was going on. "You look so skinny," he said. I had already lost 20 kilos. I told him that I was being a victim of domestic violence and he directed me to a psychiatrist to take some pills. The psychiatrist wanted to hospitalize me, but I wouldn't let her because of my daughter. They gave me some pills and I went back home.

That same night he dropped me at my mum's house and went out to a biker reunion. I spent every day sleeping, I didn't want to be like that all the time without being able to move and constantly sleepy. I ended up not taking the pills anymore.

The deep pain that I suffered made me stand on the edge of the abyss. I tried killing myself because everything stayed the same. Even after failing, nothing changed.

The night before, he asked me to go deliver something to him at the coffee shop that was on top of my drawer. I knew what he was talking about, but I never saw such a big hashish rock. By its side was an earring. I showed everything to my oldest daughter. I asked if the earring belonged to her or a friend. She guaranteed me that it wasn't hers or a friend's. I wrapped the earring on a sheet of paper to hide it and went to the coffee shop to give it to him. He opened up the paper in front of everyone including my younger daughter and said nothing about the earring. We stayed there with a couple who were friends and he and the other guy went outside. Meanwhile, as they are rolling up a joint, the police arrived. The guy told him to be careful but my husband didn't care for the police. That same day my husband wanted to go out again and I told him that he should go home because of the state he was in before he wrecked another car.

When he took me home, he had the nerve to ask for 20 euros. I told him that if he was still going out, I would go too because it was late and he wasn't well. However, I didn't have the courage to do so. Since he was very drunk and Filipa was scared, I let him go. He only came back at almost 5 am.

The next day, I confronted him because of the earring and he said, "I don't know anything about it, must be Filipa's or one of her friend's." So I told him, "Yes of course, you find an earring in the car that belongs to Filipa or her friends and you keep it to yourself instead of putting it on the table to give it back." So we started arguing loudly.

I wouldn't sleep with him. I would only sleep with Filipa. Sexually, things worked very poorly, especially in the later years. He barely wanted me and I didn't find that normal. One time he tried to assault me and my grown-up daughter, and she said that if he wanted to beat me he would have to hit her first.

The night after the mess with the earring, I took a shower, put on clothes, and took my pills. I took them all at once. I sent a goodbye message to my daughter. She started calling her dad but he wouldn't pick up. I had already taken a lot of pills but I took even more. Afterwards, I don't remember anything. My older daughter told me she was the one calling an ambulance and my younger daughter woke her dad up that was sleeping on the couch. I was hospitalized for a week.

I didn't have to tell anyone what happened because the doctor already knew. Still, nobody filed a report. The doctor knew since our first schedule together and spoke with my husband. She asked him if he knew what he was doing and if he didn't have a head to think properly.

If I could go back in time and give me the liberty to undo my mistake, the thing I would do would be to never marry and never stop studying. I stopped studying because of him and I was a good student. After that, everything went wrong. I also blame my parents because if my daughter walked up to me and said she wanted to stop studying to go work at 16 years of age a[nd] date a person, I would never let her do that. My parents knew how he was and my mum warned me about his attitude.

We would live off his paycheck and had animals and veggies that his parents would give us. However, now I think that there might have been another source of income. The few times I went out with him I met people he would talk to and I met the chief of the gypsies there in the village. I know my husband has driven their van full of drugs from Spain. He would help the drugs to cross the border and he would get the bribe money and some of the drugs.

I ran from home and went to a friend's house before staying with my daughter. I thought that I couldn't run away with a minor, so I talked to a social worker about what was going on. I didn't have any money because during the last two years he would strip me of any money. My mum and my brother would often help me pay the bills and my daughter's tuition.

Sometimes I think that he has another woman living with him now. It worries me because they could be using my stuff and my daughter's things. I don't think he would do it though because it would seem bad for him in court. The judge told me that there should be an attempt to bond him and my daughter, but I would not like that and neither does my daughter. A father that threatened to death both his daughters does not deserve any contact with them. He would only pay the bills. If I could, I would erase my marriage from history and ended our relationship.

Today, I don't believe in love nor in men. I don't think I trust myself nor my daughters sometimes. I don't think I believe in anyone, I have no friends.

Today, I only have one dream: to be happy and at peace with my daughters. I want peace and quiet, have this whole situation completely resolved, have my daughters with me, and never see that thing in front of me ever again. I want to see my daughters happy. That would be enough for me because I left my life at 16 years of age for a life of self-neglect.

When I write these lines I get emotional remembering the saddest chapters of my life. I am currently in a safe house. It's not easy to live in a house like this for many reasons, but mostly because of my daughters. It's very, very complicated. I didn't even have money to buy my daughter some ice cream when we arrived. It hurts me to know that my daughters are suffering because of me. I feel worried and very frustrated because of it. I feel uneasy all the time. For example, last week I was more nervous because my daughter called me saying that dad was telling her he would kill her. My daughter is the one who has to run from an animal like him. At least we're at peace here and I don't have to wait for him to show up drunk. This peace is the only thing that makes everything much better for me.

## CASE 7

I'm 44 years old. I was born in a village in the inner regions of Portugal in a medium-class family. We were eight siblings, but later one died because of a disease. My dad owns some land, cows, and donkeys, and we would live off that. We had everything, all our needs were covered but we had a lot of work.

I only studied up to sixth grade because my parents couldn't provide for me and we lived away from the city. We lived in a village and we had no transportation. What we had was very limited because of our finances. It was very hard to have eight kids studying. My dad would always say, "If one goes, all have to go."

I am the third oldest daughter of the group. The youngest is 24 now. Meanwhile, my brothers left to work in Lisbon at a construction site. I stayed home farming the lands and helping my mum. Later, when I was 17 years old, I met up with my brothers to work at an apartment as a housekeeper. I stayed there until I got married.

I met him in the building I worked at as a mason. In the afternoon I went out to get my boss's daughters that arrived in a school bus and he would show up.

We started talking. He lived at my boss's building and he would be waiting for me on Saturday, which was the day I rested. From then on out we started meeting some mutual friends and started dating after six months.

The dating period wasn't always bad and neither was the marriage. The first three years of marriage were good. I don't know why he was attracted to me. I was a girl tricked by passion. He's 5 years older than me and that would give me some safety. When we married I was 21 and he was 26. I created an image of him that wasn't real.

I only realized later that he was inaccessible, unpredictable, and irresponsible. I started to see that every day. He wouldn't have the decency to pay the bills or the rent. He would work independently and one day he accumulated a huge debt when we were still dating. I was very oppressed. I felt like I was living in a concentration camp because if there was no money to pay the bills, I would be obliged to pay it.

When I started realizing this, I started thinking that I would have to move on because if I depended on him, things would get complicated. So, after not doing anything for a year because of the birth of my son, I went back to work, picked a school for him, and kept working as a housekeeper. I've been working there for 13 years now.

I'm a person that finds affection as something very important in people's lives. During my childhood my mother would get up very early to light up the fireplace and heat up our clothes because in the winter it was very cold. With my marriage I realized I was lucky to be born in a poor but loving family. I understood that he was also a victim above all because I never saw my dad beat my mum or hear him insult my mum. I believe he went through all that. When I was pregnant with my baby, I had a placental abruption. I was hospitalized and he came to see me at the maternity hospital but he had to leave because his dad broke his mum's arm. I never looked past those situations. I always thought that he and his five brothers should have tell [told] their dad to stop, but they never did. Four of them follow their dad's steps and are involved in violence towards women. A woman with black eyes and a swollen face is not the only case of domestic violence. There is much more behind the scenes.

He would call me so many names, even saying I had lovers. Me, someone who has always lived for her kids. That would humiliate me. I reached a point where I wouldn't feel any pleasure by pampering myself. I was affected by the way he lived his life. That's how I lived 15 years of an relationship that lasted 18 years. If I noticed it earlier, I probably wouldn't be in the same situation. I was still very young and I learned the hardest way.

Now, my kids are the only hope he has of being close to me again. For me, that's not thinking about the kids or the good of the family. He thinks we still have a chance together, but we don't. It's very hard for me to explain some situations in our life, so I decided to write about them.

We didn't care if the kids went to school or if they had food. I always took care of everything and he would still criticize the way I did things. When I would say how much the kids' books would cost, he would just say, "Whatever, you know what you're doing." At first I thought he had a few limitations, but later I came to realize he was just irresponsible. He would always have an excuse. "Oh, I don't know. You were the one who took care of that."

I never understood what was going on in his head. There was a time when I said I wanted a divorce since he wouldn't pay the bills. I feared that they would take money off my bank account. We talked about it and he agreed. We got divorced, but when he understood the reason why I wanted a divorce, he refused to sign the papers.

He reached a point where if he had five euros to spent in beer and with his friends, he was okay. I tried to help him, but I couldn't do it because like he would say, "I know what's going on and I do things the way I want them to be done." The divorce process ended and he thought that he could stay home and do nothing while I provided for him.

The first assault happened five years after being married. We were passing by the village at night. We went to a coffee shop, and there women can't talk. Coffee shops are for men only. Also, at the village there's an idea that a man that doesn't get drunk or beat his wife isn't a man at all. I don't know why, but he punched me right in front of everyone. Nobody reacted. I was shocked and I left the coffee shop with my one-year-old son. I thought about leaving my house and living with my parents, but they are Catholic and wouldn't know how to react. I was insecure and living with fear of not being able to go through this alone or what other people might think. It's a fear that leaves us oppressed for years.

Even after everything that happened, he still had a second child. He wasn't planned, but he was still born. He's an amazing kid, very intelligent. He was accepted in a junior team associated with one of the big football clubs. He went to the trials and was accepted. My kids are my strength, my happiness.

The oldest child saw his dad assaulting me. He confronted him once. Not physically, but verbally. My son is 1.80 m tall and he's very strong. If he wanted he would beat his dad since his dad isn't very buff and is weak because of alcohol and tobacco. For the last six years, he would come home drunk. It was a torture. Every day I would feed my kids before he would come home because he could never eat anything in peace when he would get home. It was repulsive for me to sleep with him. We reached a moment where we stopped having sex. He would try but I would stop him. He was someone who wouldn't respect me in any way. Not as a mother or his wife.

One day during an argument my ex-husband said, "Go fuck your dad and your bitch mother." My oldest son said, "Dad, grandpa António helped you and you're being a coward because you're offending mum and my grandparents." From there, my kid started stepping up against his dad.

In another episode during a party at one of my brother's house with all the family, he was drunk and he talked to me aggressively. One of my brothers who has emigrated said in a strong tone in front of everyone, "You don't talk to my sister like that." I knew that if he beat me, my brothers would do something about it.

He would also hit his kids besides me. I remember one time when my oldest kid was still under the effect of the dentist anesthesia and he wanted to force him to go to his football training. He just wanted to take him so he would go out and drink beer. That day he grabbed my son's hair and dragged him outside. In another occasion, he took him to his bedroom and challenged him for a fight. I was in the kitchen making dinner and they started arguing. When I went to look, my son was under him and he was holding a screwdriver. I don't know where I grabbed him, but I got him off my son. My son desperately called my brother who confronted him at the party to come over and I didn't let him. If I did, things would sure turn into hell. My husband went immediately to bed, completely drunk.

One other time, [he] scratched himself and said it was me and my kids that did that to him.

After that I started growing strength and I don't know where it came from. Maybe I was completely revolted for not being loved and having no support or affection. There was a "click" in my life, an inner strength provided by my brothers and my son. When I signed the divorce, I felt free.

There was only one occasion where I called the police. It was when I finally reached my limit. There was always hope that he would treat himself and get rid of booze from his life and be a different person. He was at home and he asked for money. He said it was for work. "You don't pay for gas, water, electricity, nothing. How do you manage to completely burn out 800 euros in a week?" I asked. I would say he spent it on alcohol, tobacco, fuel, and I think he also caught himself in some trouble. Maybe women.

At the end of the month, we planned to go to my parents' 50th anniversary, but that day he said, "I'm not going to the village." He was waiting for me to ask him why and if he didn't go then I wouldn't go. But no ... I simply said, "You're not going? Too bad. My parents [would] like you to go, but it's your business. Tomorrow starts my vacations and I'm catching a bus with the kids." He then got very aggressive and provoked a situation. I was ironing in the living room and the kids were in the sofa watching television. I don't know if he pushed him or pulled him. I just noticed that my youngest son was on the floor. My oldest son said, "Did you really need to do that? You could have hurt him." My ex-husband went to the kitchen and put a knife on his back pocket. He thought we would obey him thought violence. I dropped the iron and grabbed my phone. I called the police without him realizing it.

Afterwards, the younger brother sat next to his big brother who was texting. His dad would only scream, "I'll break everything, I'll break everything," and the oldest brother said not to break his phone because he paid for it with his summer job money. Then I see him with the knife pointed at him and his younger brother pushed him. I told him I already called the police. When he realized that I had really called the police, he wanted to jump out the window from the first floor.

The police arrived and they surrounded the entrance. The person who answered the call said not to turn it off so they could hear what he was saying. When the police knocked on the door, he opened it, took off his shirt and shouted, "Well? Who's gonna hit me?" The police had a rough while with him. They even did a breath test on him for alcohol, which was used as evidence in court. It said there was not enough alcohol in his blood to justify his behavior.

The next day, I contacted APAV, got home, packed up, and went with my brother to the village. I will never forget what my father told me. I still get emotional today, I need to breathe. While holding my arms, he told me, "You need to end this, you can't keep going on like this." I never told my family about it. They understood what was going on. The villages are all every close to each other and when I was dating my ex-husband, people told my dad "he wasn't a good man." A few years ago my dad told me, "Your eyes don't shine anymore." I was always daddy's little girl. My mum would tell me many times on the phone that my dad was worried because I seemed sad. At the time, I would fake it. My family never said anything. They always helped me but they never intervened with my decisions.

There was a time when I got a black eye but I would tell people I hit a door. Even though they heard screams a lot, they only talked about the noise the day I called the police. They were tired of hearing screams.

After that came the period of time when we were divorced but still living together. My sister and one of my brothers still insisted on giving me a place to stay. I thanked them, but said no. I had my own house not very far away from work and school for my two kids. It didn't make sense that I would leave my house because I wasn't the one that screwed up. I had the right to keep my house after signing the divorce papers. I told my ex-husband that he had a month to leave my house and he would always try to switch subjects. It was like nothing happened for him. The lady at court told me not to wash his clothes or cook food for him. If I did, I would be giving him hopes of coming back. One time he called my youngest son saying that he was going to kill himself because I didn't want him there.

One of my ex-husband's sisters asked me to give him another chance. "I gave him chances for 15 years," I said. I asked her if she wanted to be responsible for her brother's actions if he stayed at my house. I was rough, which was against my ways.

Afterwards, he got a job abroad and he went, but he didn't say where he was going. Sometimes he would call me saying he wanted to go back. I have some conversations written down. It was like nothing happened for him. He thought I was going to go after him but I didn't. I never missed him since I never received any affection from him.

Nobody warned me he was coming for Christmas. Before he came he called my brother asking to talk to me. My brother told him that he should have thought about what he had done and not speak to me. It was 9 pm. We were in our house with a neighbor's little girl that enjoyed playing with my son. Then, somebody knocked on the door. I thought it was the child's mum, but it was actually my ex-husband. He had an arm strapped to his chest and was very hungry. I told him to [go to] my sister's house which was 100 m from there. However, he didn't want to and he insisted ... His strategy was to move forward bit by bit so he could show himself to the kids.

The kids were in the living room. Meanwhile, the little girl walked upstairs back home and when my younger kid saw his dad, he sat on the sofa. He would look at his dad and I could tell he was thinking, "Here we go again!" My oldest son walked up to his dad to greet him and they hugged. He asked me to let dad stay home that night. Against my will, I allowed it. But I left it very clear that he was staying not as my husband but as my kids' dad. He could stay there until he went back to his village. I gave him food. He was very hungry and ill. My youngest went up to him against his will and greeted him.

He stayed there three days and then he went back to his parents' house. To this day he still tries to find reasons to come back home. He got closer to my parents but they don't understand that their attitude is one of civilized people. My parents and my children never asked me to go back to him. My mum's words were, "You can't cry over spilt milk." My family has always supported me but they never told me clearly to leave the relationship. If they did, I might've left the relationship sooner.

He never apologized or admitted the things he did to me in court. He thinks he's a victim and was never rude with other people. Only with me and my kids without a doubt. He would get very drunk and if someone asked him to take it easy, he would get pissed off. One time in the car my oldest kid told him to drive slower and he started zigzagging. I thought we were all going to die. Nothing happened because it was late and there was no traffic. When I got out of the car my legs were shaking heavily and when I took my 8-year-old kid at the time off his seat, he was covered in urine. This situation could not go on much longer. Now I blame myself for not acting sooner.

To whoever is reading the words I write and might be going through the same situation, please don't leave this problem for tomorrow. The signs are all there. It's just a matter of paying attention, which I didn't. After that fear took a hold of me. Fear of everything, him, other people's reactions... In order to defend myself, I had to think like him to try and understand what he wanted and which attitudes he would take in order to defend my own interests. I think these people have a problem with themselves. If I could enter their thoughts I would know how to defend myself in order to avoid conflict.

The advice that I give to women is that before becoming wives, housewives, or mothers please always remember that you are people who deserve to be respected in everything and that respect must be implemented by ourselves. That fear makes us guilty of what happens. It imprisons us and we don't know how to free ourselves. There is nothing that is as good and comfortable as peace and quiet. Leaving your house isn't easy, but it is possible, What's really hard is dealing with the divorce and the regulation of parental duties. But that's normal. I had problems for 16 or 17 years, what did you expect? Now it might take another 16 to fix everything up. If I didn't postpone this as much as I did, things would be easier.

When I go to my village, people must ask themselves how I can sustain two kids, but to me that's indifferent. They don't ask, but they think. What gives me the strength to move forward is that they didn't go through what I did and they didn't help me when I needed them the most. I was there and I know the trouble I went through, but what doesn't kill you makes you stronger.

In these 18 years of marriage, 15 were suffering. What's worst is that what hurt the most wasn't physical. When he would say I was useless and would end alone, I would stop and think, "But who's alone is him!" We can't break down with this type of conversation.

I can't help but saying my kids' teachers were never worried and wouldn't ask what was going on at home. I know I always gave everything to my kids in terms of affection because as a mother I would give my best. I'd rather come home and eat soup, some toast, or an egg and actually feel glad at my house and share our day without worries.

Today, I live calmly. There are unsolved problems but I will solve them eventually no matter the consequences. It's worth not being a part of that life. We don't exist, we're their objects. Prepare yourselves because there will be an enormous mountain you must climb, but it's possible to climb it with determination and equilibrium. Doing so means you value yourself because deep down I destroyed myself. If I ended this situation sooner, things would be different.

My dream is to educate my kids and guide them to a healthy lifestyle. Everything else is just a day at a time. For myself, I am looking for happiness. I want to live the rest of my life happy and in peace while taking care of my parents during their twilight years.

I didn't stop believing in love, but for now I'm not looking for someone else. I can't say "never" or "always" because you need to be careful with those words. If one day I meet someone who respects me, I won't say "never." It's not easy, but it's also not impossible.

# Conclusion

In psychology no action is empty of meaning. None of our behaviors happens by chance and no meaning is opaque. You can understand what's behind every behavior despite the inherent difficulties. Based on this idea, we tried to bring to light the significance of scientific knowledge on one side of the same coin: the domestic violence victim. According to Ellemberg (1959, cited in Costa, 2004), victim and aggressor represent a couple in which one of the parts is measured by the other, as in one personality will define the other. Thus, we advocate a holistic intervention that goes beyond the social sphere and contemplate the psychological intervention of both parties such as promoting psychotherapy as a transforming element of the brain's functioning (Cozolino, 2010; Gabbard, 2000; Vygotsky, 1996), and therefore, the way you deal with life events.

Investigating domestic violence allows us to control the popular ideology, according to which the space we call "home" is designed as a cause (eg, family breakdown at the beginning of delinquencies) and cure of crime (eg, rehabilitation by the family), but never as an event point (Saraga, 1996, cited in Machado, 2004).

When the relationship ends, there is a mental representation of separation and conjugal rupture as a failure. However, when one focuses on a brief historical wedding review, as well as the forms of violence within a spousal relationship, we found that a true failure is to stay in a marriage with someone who does not mean anything (Aires and Bulha, 2012) and who assaults and abuses continuously. Divorce is an integral part of the new marriage models. It is not the result of any new situation of instability. Thus, divorce does not put marriage into question but it takes part in its evolution (Pais, 2010). If necessary, it happens when individual projects are not in tune and the psychophysical integrity is compromised. However, such a move requires professionals to be aware of camouflaged stalking (Grangeia and Matos, 2010).

After reflecting upon statistics, we continue believing the disturbing fact that several authors (Baccino, 2006; Esplugues, 2008; Gracia, 2009; Karmen, 2010; Matos, 2003) emphasize an abysmal difference between the estimates of the prevalence of domestic violence and the number of officially recognized victims. Therefore, there is the metaphor of the iceberg, meaning complaints represent only a small part of the true dimensions of the problem, in that most cases of violence are below the iceberg's waterline and are socially and officially invisible.

Machado and Dias (2010) state that most authors consider that the prevalence of violence is underestimated because of a range of cultural values and attitudes that deny or conceal spousal violence, which may culminate in cases of spousal homicide.

Aware of the influence of such cultural values and attitudes embodied in beliefs, we tried to compile contributions to clarify personality aspects and influences of these elements, as well as the victim's understanding of the level of violence and its surroundings, always emphasizing accountability and an active stance toward the problem. Aristotle (n.d., cited in Kuhn and Agra, 2010) stated that the proximity between the author and a potential victim, as well as the lack of prudence of the latter, promotes the criminal act.

We would not like to end without mentioning three topics of utmost importance.

The first is that the consequences of abuse can be severe for the victim (eg, injury, depression, posttraumatic stress, job loss, homelessness, even death by homicide or suicide), but also for the perpetrator (eg, prison), for the children (eg, emotional scars, parental responsibility), and for society (Burguess and Roberts, 2010; Chan and Cho, 2010; Karmen, 2010; Stampfel et al., 2010).

The second aspect is that there are a myriad of domains that are affected, such as the relational (eg, moving and/or forced separations, interpersonal difficulties), maternal (eg, how much the violence affected the motherhood role, how it affected the children and their future life goals), professional (eg, absence from work, reduced productivity, being fired), sociocultural (eg, compliance with benevolent beliefs toward certain abusive attitudes), and interpretations associated with victimization (eg, dominant feelings, fake claims of accidents, beliefs in traditional stereotypes of domestic violence and the woman's role, fear of stigmatization and changes that occurred) (Matos, 2011).

There is an issue that is important to reflect upon in this final stretch as promoting elements for change. How much do apathy, emotional dependence, and/or trivializing beliefs of domestic violence also make the victim an accomplice of spousal violence? We underline accomplice, which is different from being guilty. That burden will always and undoubtedly belong to the aggressor. Based on all the literature and the research that has been carried out, the answer to the question stated above is both. The victim is a victim as much as they are an accomplice. If the woman who is unequivocally assaulted by her partner or husband is considered a victim and deserves this status in legal terms, it is also true that the victim is also an accomplice, given the express definition in the *Dicionário da Academia das Ciências de Lisboa* (2001, p. 1042) (Portuguese scientific dictionary), stating: "... colluded with another person in a fault, crime ..." In this case, we refer to a complicity by tolerance that requires a paradigm shift toward accountability and neuropsychological development of the victim and, I repeat, never an accountability toward blaming the victim. We highlight an awareness campaign on domestic violence organized by the Commission for Citizenship and Gender Equality (CIG; Government of Portugal) under the slogan "*Dê um murro na mesa*" (Punch the table), prompting an active attitude toward the victim. Remember the words of the participant in the second case, "I was an accomplice of this relationship. I would allow him to do what he did and would always find excuses. Several people knew of what happened and would tell me 'how you can handle something like that, that guy is worthless.' But I never acted upon it because I knew what I wanted for my life" (sic).

This is also the time to reinforce that for children exposed to interparental violence, the family representation seems distant as a context for affection, sharing, protection, and security to the extent that this context, rather than promoting a holistic development seems to promote one of risk. More and more safe houses advocate in the global intervention project with each household, a socioeducational monitoring of children that intervenes with the minor to get them into an atmosphere of emotional and physical safety in order to contribute to their stability and global development. The court is another institution that should increasingly include the variable of a child in their equations, and can for example promote a guided tour, prior to the hearing, in order to prevent secondary victimization (the involuntary result of the behavior of the various professionals who can produce additional difficulties to the victim and exacerbate their consequences and suffering).

In the 17th century, Portuguese philosopher Father Antonio Vieira wrote:

*Princes, Kings, Emperors, Monarchs of the World: you see the ruin of your Kingdoms, you see the sufferings and miseries of your vassals, you see violence, you see the oppressions, see taxes, you see the poverty, you see famines, you see wars, you see the killings, you see the captivity, you see the destruction of all? You either see it or you don't. If you see them why don't you fix it? If you don't fix it, how do you see it? You are all blind.*

If we adapted this text to the social scourge of domestic violence, which, as we have seen, according to the Parliamentary Assembly of the Council of Europe in 2002, is the leading cause of death and disability among women aged 16 to 44, surpassing cancer, road accidents, and even war, the text could be something like the following:

*Politicians, doctors, psychologists, social workers, judges, lawyers, officials, educators: Do you see the number of women who die each year, you see the number of orphans resulting from those events, you see the costs in response to a serious public health problem (109,000 million per year to the European Union, of which only 3% are directed to prevention), you see the disregard given to the contributions of scientific research (risk assessment criteria of femicide, the need for psychological intervention, in addition to psychosocial intervention, exposure to interparental violence as a risk to the healthy development of children, the need for specific training for the different agents in this, the emergency of promoting primary intervention programs in schools at an early age), you see the victimization caused by the very system that should protect victims (imposing penalties of suspended imprisonment for offenders and access to these children, even though they are living with their mother in safe houses, even in the absence any emotional bond between parent who assaulted their mother repeatedly in front of the child)? You either see it or you don't. If you see them why don't you fix it? If you don't fix it, how do you see it? You are all blind.*

Are we blind not to realize that a paradigm and practices shift with a view to effective intervention is urgent?

Victims continue to report surreal episodes and not all cases are properly accompanied by a suitable risk assessment, for which several officers already stated they have not been trained and some of those who were trained said they did not receive sufficient training; the legal practitioners continue to ignore that, according to international statistics, 75% of the infringing cases of child care for domestic violence and that the perpetrators parents tend twice more than the others to ask for custody of the child as a form of retaliation against the former partner or ex-wife, which causes a marked distress in the child because there is the possibility of going to be with those who mistreated their mother while exposing them to episodes of domestic violence; all the afforded possibilities are not used at full potential by the forensic psychological assessment team within the regulatory processes of parental responsibilities or on the ability and duty to testify, which will undoubtedly favor a court decision that meets the child's best interests.

It is true that if we compare today's reality with a reality not far from 5 or 10 years ago, we have improved a lot, but the steps taken cannot (or should not, anyway) drop in conformism or prevent us from looking at the road ahead because, as we saw earlier, there are still more steps to be taken.

# Afterword

This book by Dr. Paulino about spousal violence is worth celebrating as it has an essential quality—it is written in rigorous and clear language, two attributes that are not always found in scientific works. Moreover, this contribution comes from south Europe and makes the research conducted beyond central Europe and Anglo-Saxon countries powerfully visible, which is absolutely necessary if we wish criminology to be accessible to the findings and developments made in the whole scientific community.

In this work, Dr. Paulino presents the mainstream knowledge on violence against partners and reviews the main theories and empirical studies. Yet despite the immense amount of bibliography on this subject that has appeared in the last 20 years, there are still too many shadows that need clearing up. There are several reasons for this. First of all, many of these crimes belong to a private domain, which means that we can only study the samples that the legal system has identified. This, in turn, in the case of offenders, implies that the studied subjects are either those who have been convicted for this crime or the participants in programs designed to treat them. If aggressors of women are still to be identified (and such a phenomenon certainly exists), we can state very little about this situation. My thoughts particularly lie in subclinical psychopaths, who form part of society, especially exercise emotional or psychological violence, and have the immense capacity to manipulate their victims and society by presenting a positive image that never reveals the coercive and threatening behavior that they display at home. In a similar way, our knowledge about the women who suffer that kind of violence is really limited.

Secondly, another serious difficulty that characterizes this field is the lack of suitable instruments to predict repeat actions of domestic violence. Although violence prediction scales have become available in recent years, and have demonstrated reasonable success in reliability, as well as converging and predictive validity (such as HCR-20, PCL-R, or SARA), the number of false positives that we have to make to include most of the actual repeat offenders is still a heavy burden for professionals and the police to efficiently make such predictions. This is still probably quite true in violence against women; since many of these cases are only known if women report them, the professionals in charge of assessing the risk of repeated violent actions have limited knowledge about the real behavior shown by subjects.

In line with this last point, being able to predict which subjects will be the murderers of their partners is even more complex. Although we understand that variables like antisocial narcissist pathology or borderline personality, alcohol or drug abuse, or having a history of violence with other people can be relevant in many cases, the truth is that these factors certainly do not allow us to make minimally accurate predictions of the future murderer of a wife or ex-partner. When faced with such lethal action, the most feasible strategy consists in providing those women at higher risk with rapid strategies to ensure their safety when they perceive that they or their children are at risk.

Thirdly (although this problem is certainly not specific to this field), we have the reality of prevention whose main lines are quite fuzzy. A given perspective, which is well related with feminism theorists, ensures that the only efficient way to prevent violence against women is to develop equality politics that release women from the tie of patriarchy. Unfortunately, the relation between such patriarchy and the violence women suffer is far from being operatively specified in advanced societies (in countries where women are second-class citizens this is obvious; where women cannot drive or go to school, or choose their husband, evidently the submission situation is a structural phenomenon of these societies; consequently, violence is legitimized in these countries). Most men do not abuse their partners and live in the same societies where aggressors live in Europe or America. It is evident to those who study criminology that influencing the most important risk factors of an individual, community, or cultural type is a necessary, but costly and long-term enterprise. For instance, child abuse should be reduced, as should the number of young people born of a generation with no life horizon to fight for.

What I am asserting is that not all subjects (especially men in relation to the serious physical violence) have successfully managed to develop the capacity to establish a mature affectionate bond with their partner. Few things damage someone's self-esteem more (here I do include women because they can be violent in a close relationship) than feeling rejected. With such rejection, violent, or potentially violent, subjects believe that their personal integrity, their whole "self," is threatened. So with the few resources they have to face this, they seek the option of standing by what they are, which settles for an abusive-type relationship. I am reasonably convinced that the basis for a loving relationship, one with respect and in which one loves the other partner, lies in suitably developed emotional maturity protected by a way of thinking where the attitude of dominating the other person as a relationship strategy is rejectable or unacceptable.

Women must learn to not fall in love with men whose values and actions reveal the need to dominate rather than their capacity for mature love. In the very interesting part of this book that the author has reserved for studying cases, we perfectly realize the inner torment that many women had to suffer in order to be freed from a loving bond. Psychologists have traditionally called this phenomenon loving dependence. However, this term only expresses the notion that people still love someone even though this person ill-treats them or does not make them happy at all. The professionals who work with abused women not only have to deal with emotional and logistic support during their recovery to live an autonomous life (particularly those cases where victims have no meaningful social or family support) but also with the interior process of their cognitive and emotional restructuring so they can reinterpret their past not in light of what they wished it was but according to how their past actually was. In other words, victims' recovery expects them to at last understand the real meaning of love (which does not entail submission due to coercion), and for them to accept that they have been victims of unmatched love and see their future as a life scenario that makes complete sense.

This book is a valuable contribution that summarizes leading research and also acts as a resource to help professionals become familiar with the most critical points and challenges that require suitable intervention with either aggressors or their victims. Dr. Mauro Paulino's experience shows clearly in the way he points out each question, and also in the way he guides us to keep advancing, despite much of this progress, and the need for the support of profound transformations in the conscience of society and new generations. In many ways, violence against women in the Western world could act as a sound criterion to measure the degree to which we are able to construct a society that is increasingly more intolerable to any form of violence. We all must think about it because what worse threat for the stability of an individual and society than violence that forms part of the routine at home, a home that should be the safest place in the world? When a home breaks under the weight of fear and threat, of violence and murder, the whole building might topple.

**Vicente Garrido**
Associate Professor in Criminology
University of Valencia

# References

Academia das Ciências de Lisboa e Fundação Calouste Gulbenkian, 2001. Dicionário de Língua Portuguesa Contemporânea da Academia das Ciências de Lisboa, vol. I, p. 1042.

Aguiar, W., Ozella, S., 2006. Núcleos de Significação Como Instrumento Para Apreensão da Constituição dos Sentidos. Psicologia: Ciência e Profissão 26 (2), 222–245.

Aires, J., Bulha, R., 2012. A hora do sexo. Editorial Presença, Lisboa.

Aires, J., 2007. O amor é uma carta fechada. Caderno, Lisboa.

Aires, J., 2009a. Vai valer a pena: verdades do casamento e do divórcio contadas na primeira pessoa. Caderno, Alfragide.

Aires, J., 2009b. O amor não se aprende na escola. Caderno, Alfragide.

Aires, J., 2011. 15 minutos com o seu filho. Lua de Papel, Alfragide.

Aires, J., 2012. Perspetiva da psicologia pós-clássica na investigação forense na criminalidade. In: Almeida, F., Paulino, M. (Coords.) (Eds.), Profiling, vitimologia e ciências forenses: Perspetivas atuais. Pactor, Lisboa, pp. 17–47.

Albornoz, E., 2009. Aspectos clínicos y médico-legales de la violencia de género. In: Fariña, F., Arce, R., Buela-Casal, G. (Coords.) (Eds.), Violencia de género: tratado psicológico y legal. Editorial Biblioteca Nueva, Madrid, pp. 169–190.

Almeida, I., Soeiro, C., 2010. Avaliação de risco de violência conjugal: versão para polícias (SARA: PV). Análise Psicológica 28 (1), 179–192.

Álvarez, M., 2007. Manual de medicina legal policial. Castelló de la Plana. Publicaciones de la Universitat Jaume I.

Álvarez-Buylla, F., Herrando, C., 2007. Un programa de tratamiento psicoterapeutico para mujeres con estrés postraumatico como secuela psíquica de violencia doméstica y de género. In: Sales, L. (Coord.) (Ed.), Psiquiatria da catástrofe. Almedina, Coimbra, pp. 341–360.

American Psychiatric Association, 2013. Manual de diagnóstico das perturbações mentais, fifth ed. Climepsi Editores, Lisboa.

Andrews, D., Bonta, J., Wormith, J., 2006. The recent past and near future of risk and/or need assessment. Crime & Delinquency 52 (1), 7–27.

Anjos, C., 2015. Violência doméstica: Os números da vergonha nacional. Retrieved June 12, 2015 from: http://www.cmjornal.xl.pt/domingo/detalhe/violencia_domestica_os_numeros_da_verg onha_nacional.html.

Antunes, M., 2003. Violência e vítimas em contexto doméstico. In: Gonçalves, R., Machado, C. (Coords.) (Eds.), Violência e vítimas de crimes, vol. 1. second ed. Quarteto, Coimbra, pp. 43–77. Adultos.

Arce, R., 2014. A credibilidade do testemunho e o dano psíquico em casos de violência cntra a mulher: o sistema de avaliação global (sag). In: Paulino, M., Almeida, F. (Coords.) (Eds.), Psicologia, Justiça e Ciências Forenses: Perspetivas Atuais. Pactor, Lisboa, pp. 99–115.

Arroyo, M., 2004. Violencia familiar. In: Cañadas, E. (Ed.), Gisbert Calabuig: medicinalegal y toxicologia, sixth ed. Masson, Barcelona, pp. 486–504.

Associação Médica Americana, 2002. Intimate Partner Violence: Roadmaps for Clinical Practice. Retrieved June 12, 2015 from: http://www.vdh.state.va.us/ofhs/Prevention/dsvp/projectradarva /documents/older/pdf/intpartvio_roadmap.pdf.

Associação Portuguesa de Apoio à Vítima, 2010. Manual ALCIPE para o atendimento de mulheres vítimas de violência, second ed. Autor, Lisboa.

Associação Portuguesa de Apoio à Vítima, 2011. Estatísticas APAV 2010. APAV, Lisboa. Retrieved April 19, 2011 from: http://www.apav.pt/portal/pdf/Estatisticas_APAV_2010_.pdf.

Associação Portuguesa de Apoio à Vítima, 2015. Estatísticas APAV 2014. APAV, Lisboa. Retrieved June 12, 2015 from: http://apav.pt/apav_v2/images/pdf/Estatisticas_APAV_Relatorio_Anual_2014.pdf.

Ávila, T., Machado, B., Suxberger, A., Távora, M., 2014. Modelos Europeus de enfrentamento à violência de gênero: Experiências e representações sociais. Escola Superior do Ministério Público da União, Brasil.

Azevedo, A., 2013. Esquizofrénicos em medida de internamento: Análise diferencial das características e do risco de violência de homicidas e não homicidas. Dissertação de Mestrado em Criminologia da Faculdade de Direito da Universidade do Porto, Porto.

Baccino, É., 2006. Violence conjugales. In: Baccino, É. (Ed.), Médecine de la violence: prise en charge des victims et des agresseurs. Masson, Paris, pp. 119–129.

Badenes-Ribera, L., Frias-Navarro, D., Bonilla-Campos, A., Pons-Salvador, G., Monterde-i-Bort, H., 2015. Intimate partner violence in self-identified lesbians: a systematic review of its prevalence and correlates. Sexuality Research and Social Policy 12 (1), 47–59. http://dx.doi. org/10.1007/s13178-014-0164-7.

Baker, N., Buick, J., Kim, S., Moniz, S., Nava, K., 2013. Lessons from examining same-sex intimate partner violence. Sex Roles 69 (3–4), 182–192. http://dx.doi.org/10.1007/s11199-012-0218-3.

Banman, V., 2015. Domestic Homicide Risk Factors: Rural and Urban Considerations. University of Western Ontario, Ontario, Canada.

Becerra-García, J., 2015. Neuropsychology of domestic violence: a comparative preliminary study of executive functioning. Medicine. Science and the Law 55 (1), 35–39.

Bermúdez, M., Matud, M., Mantas, L., 2009. Consecuencias del maltrato a la mujer por su pareja. In: Fariña, F., Arce, R., Buela-Casal, G. (Coords.) (Eds.), Violencia de género: tratado psicológico y legal. Editorial Biblioteca Nueva, Madrid, pp. 109–118.

Bernard, C., 1978. Introdução à medicina experimental. Guimarães & Cth, Lisboa (Editores).

Black, T., Trocmé, N., Fallon, B., Maclaurin, B., 2008. The Canadian child welfare system response to exposure to domestic violence investigations. Child Abuse & Neglect 32 (3), 393–404.

Bonta, J., Andrews, D., 2007. Risk-need-responsivity: Model for Offender Assessment and Rehabilitation. Public Safety Canada, Canada. ISBN: 978-0-662-05049-0.

Bowen, E., 2011. An overview of partner violence risk assessment and the potential contributions of victim appraisals. Aggression and Violent Behavior 16 (3), 214–226. http://dx.doi. org/10.1016/j.avb.2011.02.007.

Burgess, A., Roberts, A., 2010. Crime and victimology. In: Burgess, A., Regehr, C., Roberts, A. (Coords.) (Eds.), Victimology: Theories and Applications. Jones and Bartlett Publishers, Sudbury, pp. 1–30.

Burgess, A., Roberts, A., Regehr, C., 2010. Victim services, legislation, and treatment. In: Burgess, A., Regehr, C., Roberts, A. (Coords.) (Eds.), Victimology: Theories and Applications. Jones and Bartlett Publishers, Sudbury, pp. 67–100.

Cala, M., 2005. La educación y los modos de discurso que promueve. Analizando grupos de discusión de mujeres y hombres. In: Cubero, M., Garrido, J. (Coords.) (Eds.), Vygotsky en la psicología contemporánea: cultura, mente y contexto. Miño Y Dávlia, Buenos Aires, pp. 217–240.

Campbell, J., Glass, N., Sharps, P., Laughon, K., Bloom, T., 2007. Intimate partner homicide: review and implications of research and policy. Trauma, Violence, & Abuse 8 (3), 246–269. http://dx.doi.org/10.1177/1524838007303505.

Campbell, M., French, S., Gendreau, P., 2009. The prediction of violence in adult offenders: a meta-analytic comparison of instruments and methods of assessment. Criminal Justice and Behavior 36 (6), 567–590. http://dx.doi.org/10.1177/0093854809333610.

Canavarro, M., 2007. Inventário de Sintomas Psicopatológicos (BSI): uma revisão crítica dos estudos realizados em Portugal. In: Simões, M., Machado, C., Gonçalves, M., Almeida, L. (Coords.) (Eds.), Avaliação psicológica: instrumentos validados para a população portuguesa, vol. III. Quarteto, Coimbra, pp. 305–331.

Canavarro, M., Dias, P., Lima, V., 2006. A avaliação da vinculação do adulto: uma revisão crítica a propósito da aplicação da Adult Attachment Scale-R (AAS-R) na população portuguesa. Revista Semestral da Associação Portuguesa de Psicologia XX (1), 155–186.

Carbó, P., 2006. Psicología de la victimización criminal. In: Verde, M., Roca, D. (Coords.) (Eds.), Psicología Criminal. Pearson Educación, Madrid, pp. 245–274.

Chan, K., Cho, E., 2010. A review of cost measures for the economic impact of domestic violence. Trauma, Violence & Abuse 11 (3), 129–143.

Cho, H., Hong, J., Logan, T., 2012. An ecological understanding of the risk factors associated with stalking behavior: implications for social work practice. Affilia 27 (4), 381–390. http://dx.doi.org/10.1177/0886109912464474.

Código Penal Português, tenth ed., 2008. Almedina Editores, Coimbra.

Coelho, C., Machado, C., 2010. Competências culturais no atendimento a vítimas. In: Machado, C. (Coord.) (Ed.), Vitimologia: das novas abordagens teóricas às novas práticas de intervenção. Psiquilíbrios Edições, Braga, pp. 169–195.

Conselho da Europa, 2008. Combating Violence Against Women: Minimum Standards for Support Services. Retrieved June 12, 2015 from: http://www.coe.int/t/dg2/equality/domesticviolencec ampaign/Source/EG-VAW-CONF(2007)Study%20rev.en.pdf.

Convenção de Istambul, 2014. Convenção do Conselho da Europa para a prevenção e o combate à violência contra as mulheres e a violência doméstica. Retrieved May 28, 2015 from: http://cid. cig.gov.pt/Nyron/Library/Catalog/winlibsrch.aspx?skey=E51FECF9544F4B5E864D2852A1F 1E304&cap=2%2c13&pesq=3&opt0=or&ctd=off&c4=off&c3=off&c1=off&c2=on&c8=off& c13=on&c14=off&c15=off&c16=off&arqdigit=off&bo=0&var3=conven%u00e7%u00e3o%2 0do%20conselho&doc=95339.

Corsi, J., Bonino, L., 2003. Violencia y género: la construcción de la masculinidad como factor de riesgo. In: Corsi, J., Peyrú, G. (Coords.), Violencias Sociales. Editorial Ariel, Barcelona, pp. 117–138.

Costa, J., 2003. Sexo, nexo e crime: teoria e investigação da delinquência sexual. Edições Colibri, Lisboa.

Costa, J., 2004. Ao sabor do tempo: crónicas médico-legais. Vila Nova de Famalicão. Quasi Edições.

Costa, P., McCrae, R., 2000. Manual Profissional NEO PI-R Inventário de Personalidade NEO Revisto. Cegoc-TEA, Lisboa.

Cousineau, M., Gravel, S., Lavergne, C., Wemmers, J., 2008. Das vítimas e vitimizações: a investigação quebequense da última década em vitimologia. In: Blanc, M., Quimet, M., Szabo, D. (Coords.) (Eds.), Tratado de criminologia empírica. Climepsi Editores, Lisboa, pp. 167–203.

Coutinho, J., Sani, A., 2008. A experiência de vitimação de crianças acolhidas em casa de abrigo. Revista da Faculdades de Ciências Humanas e Sociais, Universidade Fernando Pessoa 5, 188–201.

Coutinho, J., Sani, A., 2010. Casas Abrigo: A Solução ou o Problema? Revista Psicologia: Teoria e Pesquisa 26 (4), 99–108.

Cozolino, L., 2010. The Neuroscience of Psychotherapy: Healing the Social Brain, second ed. W. W. Norton & Company, Nova Iorque.

Csikszentmihalyi, M., 2002. Fluir. Relógios D'Água Editores, Lisboa.

Cubero, M., Mata, M., 2005. Cultura y procesos cognitivos. In: Cubero, M., Garrido, J. (Coords.) (Eds.), Vygotsky en la psicología contemporáea: cultura, mente y contexto. Miño y Dávila, Buenos Aires, pp. 47–79.

Datner, E., Asher, J., Rubin, B., 2003. Domestic violence and partner rape. In: Giardino, A., Datner, E., Asher, J. (Eds.), Sexual assault victimization across the life span, vol. 1. Universidade de Michigan: G.W. Medical Pub, pp. 347–362.

Davis, R., 2008. Domestic Violence: Intervention, Prevention, Policies and Solutions. CRC Press, New York.

Decreto Regulamentar n. 1/2006, de 25 de Janeiro.

Diaz, J., Petherick, W., Turvey, B., 2009. Victim lifestyle exposure. In: Turvey, B., Petherick, W. (Coords.) (Eds.), Forensic Victimology: Examining Violent Crime Victims in Investigative and Legal Contexts. Elsevier, San Diego, pp. 165–203.

Dobash, E., Dobash, R., Cavanagh, K., 2009. Out of the blue: men who murder an intimate partner. Feminist Criminology 4 (3), 194–225. http://dx.doi.org/10.1177/1557085109332668.

Douglas, J., Burgess, A.W., Burgess, A.G., Ressler, R., 2006. Crime Classification Manual: A Standard System for Investigating and Classifying Violent Crimes, second ed. Jossey-Bass, San Francisco.

Douglas, K., Kropp, R., 2002. A prevention-based paradigm for violence risk assessment: clinical and research applications. Criminal Justice and Behavior 29 (5), 617–658. http://dx.doi.org/10.1177/009385402236735.

Doumas, D., Pearson, C., Elgin, J., McKinley, L., 2008. Adult attachment as a risk factor for intimate partner violence: the "mispairing" of partners attachment styles. Journal of Interpersonal Violence 23 (5), 616–634.

Doyle, M., Dolan, M., 2008. Understanding and managing risk. In: Soothill, K., Rogers, P., Dolan, M. (Eds.), Handbook of Forensic Mental Health, vol. 10. Willan Publishing, Devon, UK, pp. 244–266.

Duros, R., Ardern, H., McMillan, C., Tome, A., 2009. What is the battered woman syndrome. In: Walker, L. (Ed.), The Battered Woman Syndrome, third ed. Springer Publishing Company, Nova Iorque, pp. 41–68.

Ely, G., Flaherty, C., 2009. Intimate partner violence. In: Andrade, J. (Ed.), Handbook of Violence Risk Assessment and Treatment: New Approaches for Mental Health Professionals. Springer Publishing, New York, pp. 157–163.

Engels, F., 2002. A origem da família, da propriedade privada e do estado, second ed. Edições Avante, Lisboa.

Esplugues, J., 2008. El enemigo en casa: la violencia familiar. Nabla Ediciones, Barcelona.

European Institute for Gender Equality, 2014. Estimating the Costs of Gender-based Violence in the European Union – Report. Retrieved June 16, 2015 from: http://eige.europa.eu/sites/default/fi les/MH0414745EN2.pdf.

European Union Agency for Fundamental Rights [FRA], 2014. Violence against Women: An EU-wide Survey - Main Results. Publications Office of the European Union, Luxembourg.

Falcón, M., 2004. Familia. In: Sanmartín, J. (Coord.) (Ed.), El laberinto de la violencia: causas, tipos y efectos, second ed. Editorial Ariel, Barcelona, pp. 77–87.

Faria, C., Fonseca, M., Lima, V., Soares, I., Klein, J., 2009. Vinculação na idade adulta. In: Soares, I. (Coord.) (Ed.), Relações de vinculação ao longo do desenvolvimento: teoria e avaliação, second ed. Psiquilíbrios Edições, Braga, pp. 121–158.

Feiteira, L., 2011. Manual de Avaliação de Risco. Instituto Superior de Ciências da Saúde Egas Moniz e Departamento de Investigação/Ação Penal de Lisboa, Lisboa.

Ferguson, C., Turvey, B., 2009. Victimology: a brief history with an introduction to forensic victimology. In: Turvey, B., Petherick, W. (Coords.) (Eds.), Forensic Victimology: Examining Violent Crime Victims in Investigative and Legal Contexts. Elsevier, San Diego, pp. 1–32.

Follingstad, D., 2003. Battered woman syndrome in the courts. In: Goldstein, A. (Ed.), Handbook of Psychology – Volume XI Forensic Psychology. John Wiley & Sons, Inc., New Jersey, pp. 485–507.

Freixo, M., 2010. Metodologia científica: fundamentos, métodos e técnicas. Instituto Piaget, Lisboa.

Gabbard, G., 2000. A neurobiologically informed perspective on psychotherapy. The British Journal of Psychiatry 177, 117–122.

Garcia, P., 2010. A multidisciplinary network: perspective on the domain of psychological violence in conjugality – Part 1. In: Vieira, D., Busuttil, A., Cusack, D., Beth, P. (Eds.), Acta medicinae legalis et socialis. Imprensa da Universidade de Coimbra, Coimbra, pp. 225–230.

Garrido, V., Sobral, J., 2008. La investigación criminal: la psicología aplicada al descubrimiento, captura y condena de los criminales. Nabla Ediciones, Barcelona.

Garrido, V., 2002. Amores que matam: assédio e violência contra as mulheres. Principia, Cascais.

Ghiglione, R., Matalon, B., 2001. O inquérito: teoria e prática, fourth ed. Celta Editora, Oeiras.

Giddens, A., 2001. Sociologia. Fundação Calouste Gulbenkian, Lisboa.

Gil, A., 1994. Métodos e técnicas de pesquisa social, fourth ed. Editora Atlas, São Paulo.

Gironella, F., 2008. Asistencia psicológica a víctimas: psicología para bomberos y profesionales de las emergencias. Arán Ediciones, Madrid.

Goleman, D., 2010. Inteligência Emocional, fifteenth ed. Temas e Debates Círculo de Leitores, Lisboa.

Gonçalves, R., Cunha, O., Dias, A., 2011. Avaliação psicológica de agressores conjugais. In: Matos, M., Gonçalves, R., Machado, C. (Coords.) (Eds.), Manual de psicologia forense: contextos e desafios. Psiquilíbrios Edições, Braga, pp. 223–245.

González, E., 2006. La psicología criminal en la práctica pericial forense. In: Verde, M., Roca, D. (Coords.) (Eds.), Psicología Criminal. Pearson Educación, Madrid, pp. 59–121.

González, M., 2010. Manual práctico de psiquiatría forense. Elsevier Masson, Barcelona.

Gonzalez-Mendez, R., Santana-Hernandez, J., 2014. Perceived risk and safety-related behaviors after leaving a violent relationship. The European Journal of Psychology Applied to Legal Context 6 (1), 1–7. http://dx.doi.org/10.5093/ejpalc2014a1.

Gracia, E., 2009. Violencia doméstica contra la Mujer: el entorno social como parte del problema y de su solución. In: Fariña, F., Arce, R., Buela-Casal, G. (Coords.) (Eds.), Violencia de género: tratado psicológico y legal. Editorial Biblioteca Nueva, Madrid, pp. 75–85.

Grams, A., Magalhães, T., 2011. Violência nas relações de intimidade: Avaliação do risco. Revista Portuguesa do Dano Corporal 22, 75–98.

Grangeia, H., Matos, M., 2010. Stalking: Consensos e controvérsias. In: Machado, C. (Coord.) (Ed.), Novas formas de vitimação em criminal. Psiquilíbrios edições, Braga.

Grove, W., Zald, D., Lebow, B., Snitz, B., Nelson, C., 2000. Clinical versus mechanical prediction: a meta-analysis. American Psychological Association: Psychological Assessment 12 (1), 19–30. http://dx.doi.org/10.1037/1040-3590.12.1.19.

Hadley, S., 2009. How to Screen for Intimate Partner Violence. Retrieved December 23, 2009 from: http://www.minnesotamedicine.com/PastIssues/August2009/Clinical HadleyAugust2009/tabid /3023/Default.aspx.

Hall, C., Lindzey, G., Campbell, J., 2000. Teorias da personalidade, fourth ed. Artmed Editora, Porto Alegre.

Hansenne, M., 2004. Psicologia da personalidade. Climepsi Editores, Lisboa.

Harris, G., Rice, M., 2007. Adjusting actuarial violence risk assessments based on aging and the passage of time. Criminal Justice and Behavior 34 (3), 297–313. http://dx.doi.org/10.1177/0093854806293486.

Herrero, C., 2007. Criminología (parte general y especial), third ed. Editorial Dykinson, Madrid.

Hill, M., Hill, A., 2009. Investigação por questionário, second ed. Edições Sílabo, Lisboa.

Hirigoyen, M., 2006. Mujeres maltratadas: los mecanismos de la violencia en la pareja. Ediciones Paidós Ibérica, Barcelona.

Holt, S., Buckley, H., Whelan, S., 2008. The impact of exposure to domestic violence on children and young people: a review of the literature. Child Abuse & Neglect 32, 797–810.

Houry, D., Rhodes, K., Kemball, R., Click, L., Cerrulli, C., McNutt, L., Kaslow, N., 2008. Differences in female and male victims and perpetrators of partner violence with respect to WEB scores. Journal Interpersonal Violence 23 (8), 1041–1055.

Howitt, D., 2006. Introduction to Forensic and Criminal Psychology, second ed. Pearson Prentice Hall, London.

Husmann, G., Chiale, G., 2010. Vidas subjugadas. Sinais de Fogo, Lisboa.

Karmen, A., 2010. Crime Victims: An Introduction to Victimology, seventh ed. Wadsworth Cengage Learning, Belmont.

Kaser-Boyd, N., 2004. Battered woman syndrome: clinical features, evaluation and expert testimony. In: Cling, B. (Ed.), Sexual Sexualized Violence against Women and Children: A Psychology and Law Perspective. The Guilford Press, New York, pp. 41–70.

Kaser-Boyd, N., 2008. Battered woman syndrome: assessment-based expert testimony. In: Gacono, C., Evans, F., Kaser-Boyd, N., Gacono, L. (Eds.), The Handbook of Forensic Assessment. Routledge, Nova Iorque, pp. 467–487.

Klein, A., 2009. Practical Implication of Current Domestic Violence Research: For Law Enforcement, Prosecutors and Judges. Department of Justice/National Institute of Justice, US - Washington DC.

Knight, R., 2015. Validation of a typology for rapists. Journal Interpersonal Violence 14 (3), 303–330. http://dx.doi.org/10.1177/088626099014003006.

Kohlrieser, G., 2006. Hostage at the Table. Jossey Bass, San Francisco.

Kroner, D., Mills, J., Reitzel, L., Dow, E., Aufderheide, D., Railey, M., 2007. Directions for violence and sexual risk assessment in correctional psychology. Criminal Justice and Behavior 34 (7), 906–918. http://dx.doi.org/10.1177/0093854807301559.

Kropp, R., Hart, D., 2000. The spousal assault risk assessment (SARA) guide: reliability and validity in adult male offenders. Law and Human Behavior 24 (1), 101–118. http://dx.doi.org/10.1023/A:1005430904495.

Kropp, R., Hart, D., 2004. The Development of the Brief Spousal Assault Form for the Evaluation of Risk (B-safer): A Tool for Criminal Justice Professionals. Research and Statistics Division of Department of Justice, Canada.

Kropp, R., 2004. Some questions regarding spousal assault risk assessment. Violence Against Women 10 (6), 676–697. http://dx.doi.org/10.1177/1077801204265019.

Kropp, R., 2007. Spousal assaulters. In: Webster, C.D., Hucker, S.J. (Eds.), Violence Risk Assessment and Management. Wiley, Chichester, pp. 123–132.

Kropp, R., Hart, D., Lyon, D., 2002. Risk assessment of stalkers: some problems and possible solutions. Criminal Justice and Behavior 29 (5), 590–616. http://dx.doi.org/10.1177/009385402236734.

Kuhn, A., Agra, C., 2010. Somos todos criminosos? Pequena introdução à criminologia e ao direito das sanções. Casa das Letras, Alfragide.

Leal, M., 2007. O investigador numa caminhada: a pesquisa rigorosa. IPAF, Lisboa.

Lei n. 45/2004 de 19 de Agosto. (2004). Diário da República – I série-A.

Leontiev, A., 1978. O desenvolvimento do psiquismo. Livros Horizonte, Lisboa.

Leontiev, D., 2005. Aproximación a la teoría de la actividad: Vigotsky en el presente. Eclecta Revista de Psicología General III (9 y 10), 29–39.

Lewis, G., Doyle, M., 2009. Risk formulation: what are we doing and why? International Journal of Forensic Mental Health 8 (4), 286–292. http://dx.doi.org/10.1080/14999011003635696.

Liem, M., Roberts, D., 2009. Intimate partner homicide by presence or absence of a self-destructive act. Homicide Studies 13 (4), 339–354.

Logan, C., 2014. Special issue: historical clinical risk management-20, version 3 (HCR-20V3). International Journal of Forensic Mental Health 13 (2), 172–180. http://dx.doi.org/10.1080/14 999013.2014.906516.

Luong, D., 2007. Risk Assessment and Community Management: The Relationship between Implementation Quality and Recidivism. University of Saskatchewan, Canada.

Luria, A., 1977. Las funciones corticales superiores del hombre. Editorial Orbe, La Habana.

Luria, A., 1976. Desenvolvimento cognitivo. Ícone, São Paulo.

Machado, C., Dias, A., 2010. Abordagens culturais à vitimação: o caso da violência conjugal. In: Machado, C. (Coord.) (Ed.), Vitimologia: das novas abordagens teóricas às novas práticas de intervenção. Psiquilíbrios Edições, Braga, pp. 13–44.

Machado, C., 2004. Crime e insegurança: discursos do medo, imagens do outro. Editorial Notícias, Lisboa.

Machado, C., Gonçalves, M., Matos, M., 2008b. Manual da Escala de Crenças Sobre Violência Conjugal (E.C.V.C.) e do Inventário de Violência Conjugal (I.V.C.), second ed. Psiquilíbrios Edições, Braga.

Machado, C., Matos, M., Gonçalves, M., 2001. Cultural beliefs and attitudes about violence against women and children. In: Gonçalves, R. (Ed.), Victims and Offender: Chapter on Psychology and Law. Politeia, Bruxelas, pp. 137–154.

Machado, C., Matos, M., Gonçalves, M., 2008a. Escala de crenças sobre violência conjugal. In: Almeida, L., Simões, M., Machado, C., Gonçalves, M. (Coords.) (Eds.), Avaliação psicológica: instrumentos validados para a população portuguesa, vol. II. second ed. Quarteto, Coimbra, pp. 135–149.

Magalhães, T., 2010. Violência e abuso: respostas simples para questões complexas. Imprensa da Universidade de Coimbra, Coimbra.

Markowitz, J., Prulhiere, V., 2006. Grupo de pacientes especiales. In: Polsky, S., Markowitz, J. (Coords.) (Eds.), Atlas en color de violencia doméstica. Masson, Barcelona, pp. 173–182.

Markowitz, J., Polsky, S., Effron, D., 2006a. Patrones de lesión y lesiones con forma figurada. In: Polsky, S., Markowitz, J. (Coords.) (Eds.), Atlas en color de violencia doméstica. Masson, Barcelona, pp. 21–58.

Markowitz, J., Polsky, S., Renker, P., 2006b. Aproximación clínica a la violencia doméstica. In: Polsky, S., Markowitz, J. (Coords.) (Eds.), Atlas en color de violencia doméstica. Masson, Barcelona, pp. 1–19.

Marx, K., 1990. O capital: crítica da economia política Vol. I Tomo I. Edições Avante, Lisboa.

Matos, M., Gonçalves, M., 2001. Narratives on marital violence: the construction of change through re-authoring. In: Gonçalves, R. (Ed.), Victims and Offender: Chapter on Psychology and Law. Politeia, Bruxelas, pp. 161–170.

Matos, M., 2003. Violência conjugal. In: Gonçalves, R., Machado, C. (Coords.) (Eds.), Violência e vítimas de crimes, vol. 1. second ed. Quarteto, Coimbra, pp. 81–130. Adultos.

Matos, M., 2005. Avaliação psicológica de vítimas de maus tratos conjugais. In: Gonçalves, R., Machado, C. (Coords.) (Eds.), Psicologia Forense. Quarteto, Coimbra, pp. 159–186.

Matos, M., 2006. Violência nas relações de intimidade: estudo sobre a mudança psicoterapêutica na mulher. Tese de Doutoramento não publicada, Universidade do Minho: Instituto de Educação e Psicologia.

Matos, M., 2011. Avaliação psicológica de vítimas de violência doméstica. In: Matos, M., Gonçalves, R., Machado, C. (Coords.) (Eds.), Manual de psicologia forense: contextos e desafios. Psiquilíbrios Edições, Braga, pp. 175–197.

Matos, M., 2012. Vítimas de violência doméstica: avaliação psicológica. In: Almeida, F., Paulino, M. (Coords.) (Eds.), Profiling, vitimologia e ciências forenses: Perspetivas atuais. Pactor, Lisboa, pp. 167–174.

Matud, M., Bermúdez, M., Padilla, V., 2009. Intervención psicológica con mujeres maltratadas por su pareja. In: Fariña, F., Arce, R., Buela-Casal, G. (Coords.) (Eds.), Violencia de género: tratado psicológico y legal. Editorial Biblioteca Nueva, Madrid, pp. 193–207.

McGrath, M., 2009. Psychological aspects of victimology. In: Turvey, B., Petherick, W. (Coords.) (Eds.), Forensic victimology: examining violent crime victims in investigative and legal contexts. Elsevier, San Diego, pp. 229–264.

McPhail, A., 2015. Feminist framework plus: knitting feminist theories of rape etiology into a comprehensive model. Trauma Violence Abuse 1–16. http://dx.doi.org/10.1177/1524838015584367.

Meloy, J., 2003. Pathologies of attachment, violence, and criminality. In: Goldstein, A. (Ed.), Handbook of Psychology – Volume XI Forensic Psychology. John Wiley & Sons, Inc., New Jersey, pp. 509–526.

Ménard, K., Pincus, A., 2012. Predicting overt and cyber stalking perpetration by male and female college students. Journal of Interpersonal Violence 27 (11), 2183–2207. http://dx.doi.org/10.1177/0886260511432144.

Messing, J., Thaller, J., 2014. Intimate partner violence risk assessment: a primer for social workers. British Journal of Social Work 23, 1–17. http://dx.doi.org/10.1093/bjsw/bcu012.

Messing, J., Campbell, J., Wilson, J., Brown, S., Patchell, B., 2015. The lethality screen: the predictive validity of an intimate partner violence risk assessment for use by first responders. Journal of Interpersonal Violence 1–22. http://dx.doi.org/10.1177/0886260515585540.

Ministério da Administração Interna, 2015. Relatório Anual de Segurança Interna 2014. Retrieved June 12, 2015 from: http://apav.pt/apav_v2/images/pdf/RASI_2014.pdf.

Mintz, A., 2004. Vinculação, casal e família. In: Guedeney, N., Guedeney, A. (Coords.) (Eds.), Vinculação: conceitos e aplicações. Climepsi Editores, Lisboa, pp. 183–191.

Mota, J., Vasconcelos, A., Assis, S., 2007. Análise de correspondência como estratégia para a descrição do perfil da mulher vítima do parceiro atendida em serviço especializado. Ciência & Saúde Colectiva 12 (3), 799–809.

National Coalition Against Domestic Violence, 2013. Pets and Domestic Violence Facts. Retrieved June 12, 2015 from: http://nationallinkcoalition.org/wp-content/uploads/2013/01/DV-Fact-SheetNCADV-AHA.pdf.

Norwood, R., 2002. Mulheres que amam demais. Sinais de Fogo, Lisboa.

Organização Mundial de Saúde, 2014. Violence Against Women: Intimate Partner and Sexual Violence against Women. Retrieved June 12, 2015 from: http://www.who.int/mediacentre/factsheets/fs239/en/.

Pais, E., 2010. Homicídio conjugal em Portugal, second ed. Imprensa Nacional-Casa da Moeda, Lisboa.

Pakes, F., Pakes, S., 2009. Criminal Psychology. Willan Publishing, Devon.

Paulino, M., Matias, M., 2014. O inimigo em casa: dar voz aos silêncios da violência doméstica, 2nd Edição. Prime Books, Lisboa.

Paulino, M., 2009. Abusadores sexuais de crianças: a verdade escondida. Prime Books, Lisboa.

Pérez, M., Martínez, D., 2009. Aproximación psicosocial a la violencia de género: aspectos introductorios. In: Fariña, F., Arce, R., Buela-Casal, G. (Coords.) (Eds.), Violencia de género: tratado psicológico y legal. Editorial Biblioteca Nueva, Madrid, pp. 63–74.

Pimentel, A., Quintas, J., Fonseca, E., Serra, A., 2015. Estudo normativo da versão Portuguesa do YLS/CMI: Inventário de avaliação do risco de reincidência e de gestão de caso para jovens. Análise Psicológica 33 (1), 55–71. http://dx.doi.org/10.14417/ap.883.

Plana, J., 1999. Manual de actuación sanitaria, policial, legal y social frente a la violencia doméstica: guión de actuación y formularios. Masson, Barcelona.

Poirier, J., 1999. Violence in the family. In: Hall, H. (Ed.), Lethal Violence: A Sourcebook on Fatal Domestic, Acquaintance and Stranger Violence. CRC Press, New York, pp. 259–292.

Polsky, S., Markowitz, J., Effron, D., 2006. Aproximación al paciente con traumatismo grave o múltiple. In: Polsky, S., Markowitz, J. (Coords.) (Eds.), Atlas en color de violencia doméstica. Masson, Barcelona, pp. 59–64.

Pritchard, A., Blanchard, A., Douglas, K., 2014. Risk Assessment. Oxford University Press in Criminology, Oxford. http://dx.doi.org/10.1093/obo/9780195396607-0095.

Pueyo, A., Echeburúa, E., 2010. Valoración del riesgo de violencia: Instrumentos disponibles e indicaciones de aplicación. Psicothema 22 (3), 403–409, ISSN: 0214-9915.

Quivy, R., Campenhoudt, L., 1998. Manual de investigação em ciências sociais, second ed. Gradiva, Lisboa.

Rebocho, M., 2007. Caraterização do violador português: um estudo exploratório. Almedina, Coimbra.

Redondo, J., 2010. A multidisciplinary network: perspective on the domain of psychological violence in conjugality – Part 2. In: Vieira, D., Busuttil, A., Cusack, D., Beth, P. (Eds.), Acta medicinae legalis et socialis. Imprensa da Universidade de Coimbra, Coimbra, pp. 231–239.

Regehr, C., Roberts, A., 2010. Intimate partner violence. In: Burgess, A., Regehr, C., Roberts, A. (Coords.) (Eds.), Victimology: Theories and Applications. Jones and Bartlett Publishers, Sudbury, pp. 197–223.

Renner, L., 2009. Intimate partner violence victimization and parenting stress: assessing the mediating role of depressive symptoms. Violence Against Women 15 (11), 1380–1401.

Roberts, A., Roberts, B., 2005. A comprehensive, model for crisis intervention with battered women and their children. In: Roberts, A. (Ed.), Crisis Intervention Handbook: Assessment, Treatment and Research, third ed. Oxford University Press, Nova Iorque, pp. 441–482.

Robinson, A., 2006. Reducing repeat victimization among high-risk victims of domestic violence: the benefits of a coordinated community response in Cardiff, Wales. Violence Against Women 12 (8), 761–788.

Rocañin, J., Forneiro, J., Iglesias, C., 2007. Manual de ciencias forenses. Arán Ediciones, Madrid.

Rojas, J., Lima, A., Morejón, E., Sánchez, M., Diañez, R., Rodriguez, D., 2002. Violencia intrafamiliar: enfoque de género. Revista Cubana de Medicina General Integral 18 (4). Retrieved December 23, 2009 from: http://bvs.sld.cu/revistas/mgi/vol18_4_02/mgi0242002.htm.

Saavedra, R., Fonseca, M., 2013. Avaliação do risco e gestão da segurança nos serviços de apoio à vítima: mulheres vítimas de violência nos relacionamentos íntimos. In: Sani, A., Caridade, S. (Coords.) (Eds.), Violência, Agressão e Vitimação: Práticas para a Intervenção. Almedina, Coimbra, pp. 273–295.

Saavedra, R., Machado, C., 2010. Prevenção universal da violência em contexto escolar. In: Machado, C. (Coord.) (Ed.), Vitimologia: das novas abordagens teóricas às novas práticas de intervenção. Psiquilíbrios Edições, Braga, pp. 137–167.

Samson, A., 2010. A violência doméstica: aprenda a identificar situações de abuso e a ser feliz. Livros de Seda, Lisboa.

Sánchez, A., Sierra, J., 2006. Evaluación psicológica en víctimas de maltrato doméstico. In: Sierra, J., Jiménez, E., Buela-Casal, G. (Coords.) (Eds.), Psicología forense: manual de técnicas y aplicaciones. Editorial Biblioteca Nueva, Madrid, pp. 295–314.

Sánchez, P., 2008. La relación de pareja. Eclecta Revista de Psicología General VI (13), 17–21.

Sani, A., 2006. Vitimação indirecta de crianças em contexto familiar. Análise social 180, 849–864.

Santos, J.C., 1997. Prova médica: que Prova? Reflexões sobre os exames periciais em matérias de abusos sexuais de crianças e adolescentes. In: Abusos sexuais em crianças e adolescentes I Seminário Nacional. Associação para o Planeamento da Família, Lisboa, pp. 50–55.

Santos, J.C., 2008. Violência doméstica: para uma intervenção pericial integrada. Comunicação Pessoal no Instituto de Medicina Legal da Delegação do Sul. Portugal, Lisboa.

Savater, F., 2004. A coragem de escolher. Dom Quixote, Lisboa.

Schraiber, L., 2010. Violência, gênero e saúde. In: Neves, S., Fávero, M. (Coords.) (Eds.), Vitimologia: ciência e activismo. Almedina, Coimbra, pp. 147–165.

Secretaria de Políticas para as Mulheres, 2011. Diretrizes Nacionais Para o Abrigamento de Mulheres Em situação de Risco e Violência. Autor, Brasília.

Selosse, J., 2001. Culpabilidade. In: Doron, R., Parot, F. (Coords.) (Eds.), Dicionário de psicologia. Climepsi Editores, Lisboa, p. 199.

Serafim, A., Marques, N., 2015. Transtornos da personalidade. In: Serafim, A., Saffi, F. (Orgs.) (Eds.), Neuropsicologia Forense. Artmed, Porto Alegre, pp. 241–248.

Serra, A., 1992. O interesse clínico das escalas de avaliação de auto-conceito e de coping. Revista de Psicologia Militar, número especial 1–17.

Shotter, J., 2006. Vygotsky and consciousness as con-scientia, as witnessable knowing along with other. Theory & Psychology 16 (1), 13–36.

Sierra, J., Buela-Casal, G., 2009. Evaluación psicológica de la violencia dentro de la pareja. In: Fariña, F., Arce, R., Buela-Casal, G. (Coords.) (Eds.), Violencia de género: tratado psicológico y legal. Editorial Biblioteca Nueva, Madrid, pp. 135–146.

Sojourner Center, 2015. Passion for Pets, Pet Parents and Protection. Retrieved June 12, 2015 from: http://www.sojournercenter.org/wp-content/uploads/2015/04/Sojourner-Pet-Companion-Shelter.pdf.

Sottomayor, C., 2014. Temas de Direito das Crianças. Edições Almedina, Coimbra.

Stampfel, C., Chapman, D., Alvarez, A., 2010. Intimate partner violence and posttraumatic stress disorder among high-risk women: does pregnancy matter? Violence Against Women 16 (4), 426–443.

Tap, P., Hipólito, J., Nunes, O., n.d. Escala de estima de si S.E.R.T.H.U.A.L.: Manual. Documento não publicado, Universidade Autónoma de Lisboa.

Thapar-Björkert, S., Morgan, K., 2010. But sometimes I think…they put themselves in the situation: exploring blame and responsibility in interpersonal violence. Violence Against Women 16, 32–59.

Triviños, A., 1995. Introdução à pesquisa em ciências sociais. Editora Atlas, São Paulo.

Turvey, B., 2002. Victimology. In: Turvey, B. (Coord.) (Ed.), Criminal Profiling: An Introduction to Behavioral Evidence Analysis, second ed. Elsevier Academic Press, London, pp. 137–155.

Turvey, B., 2009a. Intimate partner violence. In: Turvey, B., Petherick, W. (Coords.) (Eds.), Forensic Victimology: Examining Violent Crime Victims in Investigative and Legal Contexts. Elsevier, San Diego, pp. 299–327.

Turvey, B., 2009b. An argument for forensic victimology. In: Turvey, B., Petherick, W. (Coords.) (Eds.), Forensic Victimology: Examining Violent Crime Victims in Investigative and Legal Contexts. Elsevier, San Diego, pp. XIII–XXXIV.

Turvey, B., 2009c. Victim situational exposure. In: Turvey, B., Petherick, W. (Coords.) (Eds.), Forensic Victimology: Examining Violent Crime Victims in Investigative and Legal Contexts. Elsevier, San Diego, pp. 205–228.

Turvey, B., 2009d. Constructing a victim profile. In: Turvey, B., Petherick, W. (Coords.) (Eds.), Forensic Victimology: Examining Violent Crime Victims in Investigative and Legal Contexts. Elsevier, San Diego, pp. 73–95.

União de Mulheres Alternativa e Resposta, 2011. Observatório das mulheres assassinadas – dados 2010. União das Mulheres Alternativa e Reposta, Lisboa. Retrieved April 19, 2011 from: http://www.umar feminismos.org/index.php?option=com_content&view=article&id=326&Itemid=126.

Verde, M., 2005. Psicología de la victimización criminal. In: Verde, M. (Coord.) (Ed.), Manual de psicología jurídica e investigación criminal. Ediciones Pirámide, Madrid, pp. 149–165.

Vilanova, M., 2011. Cúmplices: liberte-se das relações de dependência. Sinais de Fogo, Lisboa.

Vilelas, J., 2009. Investigação: o processo de construção do conhecimento. Edições Sílabo, Lisboa.

Vygotsky, L., 1996. Teoria e método em psicologia. Martins Fontes, São Paulo.

Vygotsky, L., 2001. A construção do pensamento e da linguagem. Martins Fontes, São Paulo.

Walker, L., 1986. Psychological causes of family violence. In: Lystad, M. (Ed.), Violence in the Home: Interdisciplinary Perspectives. Mazel Publishers, New York, pp. 71–97.

Walker, L., 2004. El perfil de la mujer víctima de violencia. In: Sanmartín, J. (Coord.) (Ed.), El laberinto de la violencia: causas, tipos y efectos, second ed. Editorial Ariel, Barcelona, pp. 205–218.

Walker, L., 2009a. Descriptions of violence and the cycle of violence. In: Walker, L. (Ed.), The Battered Woman Syndrome, third ed. Springer Publishing Company, Nova Iorque, pp. 85–105.

Walker, L., 2009b. The battered women syndrome study overview. In: Walker, L. (Ed.), The Battered Woman Syndrome, third ed. Springer Publishing Company, Nova Iorque, pp. 1–19.

Walker, L., 2009c. Mental health needs of battered women. In: Walker, L. (Ed.), The Battered Woman Syndrome, third ed. Springer Publishing Company, Nova Iorque, pp. 359–388.

Walker, L., Needle, R., Duros, R., Nathan, A., 2009a. Sexuality issues. In: Walker, L. (Ed.), The Battered Woman Syndrome, third ed. Springer Publishing Company, Nova Iorque, pp. 167–198.

Walker, L., Richmond, K., House, T., Needle, R., 2009d. History. In: Walker, L. (Ed.), The Battered Woman Syndrome, third ed. Springer Publishing Company, Nova Iorque, pp. 21–39.

Walker, L., Shapiro, D., Gill, K., 2009b. Risk assessment and lethal potential. In: Walker, L. (Ed.), The Battered Woman Syndrome, third ed. Springer Publishing Company, Nova Iorque, pp. 107–144.

Walker, L., Tang, J., Nathan, A., 2009c. Substance abuse and domestic Violence. In: Walker, L. (Ed.), The Battered Woman Syndrome, third ed. Springer Publishing Company, Nova Iorque, pp. 213–239.

Wang, P., 2014. Assessing the danger: validation of Taiwan intimate partner violence danger assessment. Journal of Interpersonal Violence 13. http://dx.doi.org/10.1177/0886260514553114.

Women Against Violence Europe, 2011. Country Report 2011: Reality Check on European Services for Women and Children Survivors of Violence. Autor, Vienna, Austria.

Zayas, V., Shoda, Y., 2007. Predicting preferences for dating partners from past experiences of psychological abuse: identifying the psychological ingredients of situations. Personality and Social Psychology Bulletin 33 (1), 123–138.

Zeigarnik, B., 1981. Psicopatología. Akal Editor, Madrid.

# Index

*Note*: 'Page numbers followed by "f" indicate figures, "t" indicate tables, and "b" indicate boxes.'

Printed in the United States
By Bookmasters